NEW TAIWANESE CINEMA IN FOCUS

Traditions in World Cinema

General Editors
Linda Badley (Middle Tennessee State
    University)
R. Barton Palmer (Clemson University)

Founding Editor
Steven Jay Schneider (New York
    University)

Titles in the series include:
New Taiwanese Cinema in Focus
by Flannery Wilson

Post-Beur Cinema
by Will Higbee

American Smart Cinema
by Claire Perkins

The International Film Musical
by Corey Creekmur and Linda Mokdad
    (eds)

Spanish Horror Film
by Antonio Lázaro-Reboll

Italian Post-Neorealist Cinema
by Luca Barattoni

*Magic Realist Cinema in East Central
    Europe*
by Aga Skrodzka

The New Neapolitan Cinema
by Alex Marlow-Mann

Italian Neorealist Cinema
by Torunn Haaland

Czech and Slovak Cinema
by Peter Hames

Chinese Martial Arts Cinema
by Stephen Teo

Palestinian Cinema
by Nurith Gertz and George Khleifi

*African Filmmaking: North and South of
    the Sahara*
by Roy Armes

Traditions in World Cinema
by Linda Badley, R. Barton Palmer and
    Steven Jay Schneider (eds)

New Punk Cinema
by Nicholas Rombes (ed.)

Japanese Horror Cinema
by Jay McRoy (ed.)

www.euppublishing.com/series/tiwc

NEW TAIWANESE CINEMA IN FOCUS

Moving Within and Beyond the Frame

Flannery Wilson

EDINBURGH
University Press

© Flannery Wilson, 2014, 2015

Edinburgh University Press Ltd
The Tun – Holyrood Road
12 (2f) Jackson's Entry
Edinburgh EH8 8PJ
www.euppublishing.com

First published in hardback by Edinburgh University Press 2014

This paperback edition 2015

Typeset in 10/12.5 pt Sabon by
Servis Filmsetting Ltd, Stockport, Cheshire
and printed and bound in Great Britain by
CPI Group (UK) Ltd, Croydon CR0 4YY

A CIP record for this book is available from the British Library

ISBN 978 0 7486 8201 0 (hardback)
ISBN 978 1 4744 0557 7 (paperback)
ISBN 978 0 7486 8202 7 (webready PDF)
ISBN 978 1 4744 0814 1 (epub)

The right of Flannery Wilson to be identified as author of this work
has been asserted in accordance with the Copyright, Designs and
Patents Act 1988 and the Copyright and Related Rights Regulations
2003 (SI No. 2498).

CONTENTS

List of Illustrations   vi
Acknowledgements   vii
Traditions in World Cinema   xi

Introduction   1

1. Charting the Course: Defining the Taiwanese Cinematic 'Tradition'   14

2. Taiwanese–Italian Conjugations: The Fractured Storytelling of
   Edward Yang's *The Terrorizers* and Michelangelo Antonioni's
   Blow-Up   47

3. Mapping Hou Hsiao-hsien's Visuality: Setting, Silence and the
   Incongruence of Translation in *Flight of the Red Balloon*   76

4. Tsai Ming-liang's Disjointed Connectivity and Lonely Intertextuality   97

5. The Chinese/Hollywood Aesthetic of Ang Lee: 'Westernized',
   Capitalist . . . and Box Office Gold   126

6. Filming Disappearance or Renewal? The Ever-Changing
   Representations of Taipei in Contemporary Taiwanese Cinema   150
   Conclusion   165

Bibliography   170
Filmography   177
Index   179

LIST OF ILLUSTRATIONS

Figure 1.1 Wang Xiaoshuai's *Beijing Bicycle* (2001)   19
Figure 1.2 De Sica's *Bicycle Thieves* (1949)   26
Figure 2.1 An anonymous dead body, a victim of the shoot-out   65
Figure 2.2 White Chick, collapsed in the middle of the street   66
Figure 2.3 Zhou Yufen, awakened from sleep and worried about her
            novel   66
Figure 3.1 A cinematic recreation of Hou's childhood house (from *A
            Time to Live, A Time to Die*)   82
Figure 3.2 The puppeteer with Suzanne in the role of translator; Song
            observes   94
Figure 4.1 Lee Hsiao-kang and Tsai Ming-liang, in 2010, at the USC
            Cinema School   109
Figure 5.1 Simon, Wai-tung and Wei-Wei saying 'goodbye',
            Hollywood-style   137
Figure 5.2 Mr and Mrs Gao: 'I'm happy too'   137
Figure 5.3 Final shot, final humiliation   138

ACKNOWLEDGEMENTS

I grew up watching my father watch films. In our attic, I would stare in amazement at my father's stacks upon stacks of cinema books. The fact that my father was a philosophy professor who taught film courses did not seem in the least bit counterintuitive to my young mind. Why shouldn't a philosophy professor be interested in cinema?

These tastes, indeed, can, and often are, viewed as counterintuitive. Within humanities departments, we are often asked to choose between conflicting ontologies, frameworks, and methods. As a comparative literature graduate student with a natural interest in film theory, I took it upon myself to grapple my way through Deleuze's *Cinema* books. When I occasionally offered a report on my projects to my dad, he would often respond with something along the lines of: 'Good luck!' He was encouraging but I could sense that he may not have felt much fondness for Deleuze. I would take his general support for what it was worth, and continue with my writing.

One day, as I was browsing through a copy of my father's film book *Narration in Light: Studies in Cinematic Point of View* (1988) I noticed an interesting passage. The passage appeared in the final chapter, entitled, quite aptly I think: 'Morals for Method'. He was admonishing his readers and colleagues about a certain pernicious brand of broad-based scepticism, especially the remark: 'Most poststructuralist writing on film speculates on how it is that subjects are fixed in the position of dominant specularity and on the historical development and ideological consequences of this positioning . . .' (292). The passage continues, arguing that these theories tend to pigeonhole the classic

Hollywood narrative into a dominant ideological position. Certain classical film narratives are then deemed uninteresting and unworthy of serious study: '. . . what I do reject is any theory that makes these seductions a natural consequence of the forms of classical film and ignores the scattered but triumphant instances that show that this is not the case' (293). These words struck me as more than a plea to relinquish an unsatisfactory method of analysis – a method that allows us to throw up our hands and renounce our capacity to perceive – this was a moral imperative.

After reading the 'Morals for Method' chapter, I began to contemplate the pervasiveness of subjective approaches in contemporary film theory. I connected his plea to my own work on Deleuze. Though Deleuze has an obvious fondness for classical film narratives, the Hollywood films of the 1930s to 1950s exemplified (what he would define as) 'the movement-image'. Deleuze feels that the movement-image cannot separate itself from the subjectivity of the viewer because, in admittedly crude terms, the viewer knows what to expect. Classic conventions of narration – showing the bad guy die after he is shot, instead of leaving that insinuation up to the viewer – is more than just 'bad form'. Deleuze argues that the cinema of the movement-image actually fails on some sort of basic level (Trifonova 135). More generally, Deleuze defends a Bergsonian view of perception – that is, that the film camera eye is capable of perceiving images in the same way that human vision can (Turvey in Furstenau 44).[1] If one were to contemplate this notion for even a few moments, our intuitive sense might tell us that the Bergsonian notion of perception is suspect. We are able to investigate the myriad ways that narrative functions within film, not only because we can perceive but because we can reflect on what we have perceived. Inanimate objects cannot view the world as humans do, and I am certain that this is the case. Without subjectivity, we have little reason to work towards perfecting a method of explaining how human beings perceive film narrative.

As they relate to film studies, certain strains of cognitive theory are dedicated to describing the intricate ways in which narration functions in films. Cognitive theorists aim to make sense of events as they unfold in front of the eyes of the spectator. While watching a film, we as spectators may notice that narrators are unreliable or that editing is meant to confuse rather than illuminate. We may be taken off guard when diegetic peacefulness is broken by non-diegetic intrusions. And yet these phenomena, and our reactions to them, are all functions of the narrative. These are functions that the practiced film critic or cognitive theorist can interpret and describe. Chapters in *Narration in Light* are dedicated to 'classic' Hollywood films such as: *You Only Live Once, Letter from an Unknown Woman,* and *Rebel Without a Cause.* Though these are classic Hollywood films by most definitions, they do not hold some sort of dominant hierarchical position over other forms of film-making. These are the 'triumphant instances' of classic cinema that deserve as much critical attention as any other form of cinema.

Since I have always been uneasy about the practice of subscribing whole-heartedly to one school of theory at the expense of another, I could not help but wonder about these larger theoretical issues while planning this book. Clearly, most film scholars will attest to the need for a healthy dose of interdisciplinarity, and will recognise the importance of rigorous interpretive studies. And yet, the desire to study narrative often seems to clash with the postmodern suspicion of grand narratives. Could it be possible to 'retreat from theory' (Fursentau 5) without returning entirely to narratology? Is this sort of interdisciplinarity counterintuitive?

Noël Carroll, in his book *Engaging the Moving Image* (2003), aptly describes how things must continue if the field of film studies is to remain 'honest': 'Film theorists need to become interdisciplinary – not in the sense that they simply quote authorities from other fields – but in the sense that they become capable of thinking for themselves in terms of issues addressed by those other fields that are germane to film studies' (Carroll 189).[2] Interdisciplinarity should, of course, involve knowledge and thoughtfulness with regard to other fields but it should also include open-mindedness and curiosity. Those who have chosen to dedicate a large portion of their time to researching and engaging with cinema should be capable of thinking for themselves, as Carroll so rightly remarks. Curious scholars should be unafraid to delve into fields that may seem uncomfortable to them at first, to inform their work with a wider perspective.

I write about Taiwanese cinema, therefore, from the perspective of a comparatist who is interested in finding the balance between the national and the transnational in film studies. Writing about a 'tradition' in world cinema is not the equivalent of insisting upon the notion of 'national cinema'. In the introduction to their edited volume, *Traditions in World Cinema* (2006), series editors Linda Badley and R. Barton Palmer define 'cinematic traditions' as:

> . . . bodies of films whose commonalities . . . make them worthy of collective study. Most often, cinematic traditions are 'national' in the sense that they *constitute a form of difference* within a larger, more diffuse, and varied body of national films, and yet there are often *indispensable transnational connections* that foreclose any understanding of the tradition, solely within the terms of its 'native' culture. (my emphasis, 2)

In the spirit of Badley and Palmer's definition, then, this book defines 'cinematic tradition' in terms of both the national and the transnational. Though the book divides and defines films by virtue of their differences from other national traditions, it is not meant to imply that a film 'tradition' is one that can be discussed without referring to transnational connections.

This book was, of course, written with the 'Traditions' series in mind. Though it investigates themes similar to those in a recent addition to the 'Traditions' series, *New Taiwanese Cinema in Focus* is focused almost entirely on the New Wave and Second Wave movements, from the 1980s to the present. This book is aimed at an interdisciplinary-minded readership, including students and scholars in fields ranging from comparative literature, to film and media studies, to East Asian and cultural studies. My goal has been to provide an opening for others to begin and to continue making connections between the Taiwanese cinematic tradition and other world cinema traditions. In addition, my intention has been to write a book that will find its place in another context: the large body of excellent and influential work that has been carried out in recent years on Taiwanese, Chinese-language, and Sinophone cinemas. I have chosen to dialogue directly with issues raised by Chinese cinema scholars such as Shu-mei Shih, Rey Chow, and Yingjing Zhang, in particular. Overall, I attempt to place my 'theoretical dialoguing' with other scholars in the context of a book on film, centred, above all else, on close readings.

I am most grateful to my father, George M. Wilson, who taught philosophy (including the philosophy of film) at Johns Hopkins University in Baltimore, Maryland between 1972 and 2000; then at the University of California, Davis between 2000 and 2005, and finally at the University of Southern California in Los Angeles until his retirement in 2012. My father inspired my interest in film studies, aesthetics, music, and academic writing more generally.

I should also like to thank my dissertation adviser, Michelle E. Bloom, whose 2008 seminar on France and Asia at the University of California, Riverside inspired me to write on Taiwanese and Chinese-language cinemas in the first place. I should, furthermore, like to thank Fontaine Lien, Chenshu Zhou, Hongjian Wang, Xi Tian, and Kang Kai for helping me with my Mandarin. I would also like to thank Gillian Leslie, commissioning editor at Edinburgh University Press, as well as R. Barton Palmer and Linda Badley, series editors of *Traditions in World Cinema*, for encouraging this project in the first place. I am grateful to my husband Ryan and my brother Gareth for their support throughout the writing process.

Finally, I should like to offer a sincere thanks to all those with whom I have discussed the topic of Taiwanese cinema – and Taiwan more generally – both formally and informally throughout this difficult process. I am truly grateful to the people in my life who have given me the opportunity to write this book.

NOTES

1. See Furstenau, Marc (ed.) (2010), *The Film Theory Reader: Debates and Arguments*, Routledge.
2. See *Engaging the Moving Image,* Yale University Press, 2003.

TRADITIONS IN WORLD CINEMA

General editors: **Linda Badley and R. Barton Palmer**
Founding editor: **Steven Jay Schneider**

Traditions in World Cinema is a series of textbooks and monographs devoted to the analysis of currently popular and previously underexamined or undervalued film movements from around the globe. Also intended for general-interest readers, the textbooks in this series offer undergraduate- and graduate-level film students accessible and comprehensive introductions to diverse traditions in world cinema. The monographs open up for advanced academic study more specialised groups of films, including those that require theoretically oriented approaches. Both textbooks and monographs provide thorough examinations of the industrial, cultural, and sociohistorical conditions of production and reception.

The flagship textbook for the series includes chapters by noted scholars on traditions of acknowledged importance (the French New Wave, German expressionism), recent and emergent traditions (New Iranian, post-Cinema Novo), and those whose rightful claim to recognition has yet to be established (the Israeli persecution film, global found-footage cinema). Other volumes concentrate on individual national, regional or global cinema traditions. As the introductory chapter to each volume makes clear, the films under discussion form a coherent group on the basis of substantive and relatively transparent, if not always obvious, commonalities. These commonalities may be formal, stylistic or thematic, and the groupings may, though they need not, be popularly identified as genres, cycles or movements (Japanese horror, Chinese martial arts cinema, Italian neo-realism). Indeed, in cases in which a group of films is not already commonly identified as a tradition, one purpose of the volume is to establish its claim to importance and make it visible (east central European magical realist cinema, Palestinian cinema).

Textbooks and monographs include:

- An introduction that clarifies the rationale for the grouping of films under examination
- A concise history of the regional, national, or transnational cinema in question
- A summary of previous published work on the tradition
- Contextual analysis of industrial, cultural and sociohistorical conditions of production and reception
- Textual analysis of specific and notable films, with clear and judicious application of relevant film theoretical approaches
- Bibliograph(ies)/filmograph(ies).

Monographs may additionally include:

- Discussion of the dynamics of cross-cultural exchange in the light of current research and thinking about cultural imperialism and globalisation, as well as issues of regional/national cinema or political/aesthetic movements (such as new waves, postmodernism, or identity politics)
- Interview(s) with key film-makers working within the tradition.

INTRODUCTION

To this day, Taiwan remains a post-colonial region with an identity crisis. Like Hong Kong, Taiwan was a formally colonised region (an island nation) that is now independent. But, unlike Hong Kong which was a colony of the British – a distant nation – Taiwan was a colony of neighbouring Japan. The Chinese Civil War, a fight between loyalists to the Republic of China (the Kuomintang or KMT) and the Communist Party of China (the CPC), began in 1927 and did not end fully until 1950. At the conclusion of the war, China divided into the Republic of China (the ROC) in Taiwan and the People's Republic of China (the PRC) on the mainland. When the KMT Nationalists, led by Chiang Kai-shek, were ultimately defeated, Chiang and his army retreated to Taiwan. As a result, and especially since the end of World War II and the Chinese Civil War, Taiwan is engaged in a continual struggle to define itself in relation to both the Chinese Mainland and to Japan. In reaction, scholars and observers have commented that Taiwan remains torn between China, the so-called 'motherland', and Japan, the so-called 'fatherland'. In some respects, this metaphor is apt: like other regions that have gone through the decolonisation process, Taiwan struggles fully to reconcile its independent status.

Darrel William Davis expands on the notion of Taiwan as an identity-seeking nation in the introduction to his and Robert Chen's edited volume *Cinema Taiwan: Politics, Popularity and the State of the Arts*: 'Internationally, Taiwan works like a lab experiment in national self-definition. Domestically, though Taiwan politics and media often is [*sic*] a free-for-all, it is still emphatically free' (2007, 3). Davis continues by describing the island of Taiwan as an ambiguous geopolitical state, a foe to the PRC that nevertheless remains divided between the old-world, right-wing autocrats of Asian socialism and the new, diversely democratic population. Most importantly, Davis's point is that, despite Taiwan's struggle to define itself politically on the international stage, Taiwan's media remain 'free'. Unlike on the mainland, government owner-ship of media assets has been disbursed in Taiwan. The relative freedom of the media in Taiwan is the result of the Democratic Progressive Party's (DPP) sustained pressure on the opposition party (the Kuomintang).[1]

Despite the freedoms that film-makers in Taiwan enjoy, the financial sol-vency of the film industry itself remains in a constant state of precariousness. Further compounding the problem, many of the most successful Taiwanese film-makers have found more success abroad than at home. Internationally, Taiwanese cinema is associated with an 'art-house' aesthetic. Domestically, industry insiders bemoan that reputation. Art-house cinema can be thought-provoking but slow moving, depressing even, and it can reek of the intellectual elite. Partly as a result of Taiwan's ambivalent political landscape and partly as a result of the art house genre more generally, Taiwanese cinema is plagued with a 'feel-bad' reputation. The cinema of Taiwan, Darrell William Davis observes, contains overwhelming amounts of sadness (Davis 4). But, he is quick to add, sadness does not equal 'passive resignation' (5) within Taiwanese cinema. On the contrary, what he calls Taiwan's 'cultural narratives' have only become more interesting as a result of the divisiveness and tension within modern-day Taiwanese society (Davis, 5).

James Tweedie, in his essay: 'Morning in the New Metropolis: Taipei and the Globalization of the City Film' (2007), comments similarly to Davis, noting that sadness, as it relates to Taiwanese film, is not necessarily equivalent to passivity. Nostalgia for the past, in other words, is not incompatible with the need to move forward. One of the film-makers for whom nostalgia is not necessarily expressed as 'passive', is Taiwanese Second Wave (1990s to early 2000s) film-maker Tsai Ming-liang. Tweedie describes Tsai's aesthetic project as an active need to collect bits of the past before it has disappeared; to capture the cycle of development and destruction in Taipei and to 'collect traces left behind by its decay' (121). The act of collecting traces on film can be a nega-tive, neutral, or positive activity, depending on the context. In Tsai's 2001 film *What Time is it There?/Ni nabian jidian* (2001), for example, protagonists Shiang-chyi and Hsiao-kang meet on the Taipei Skywalk which was then torn down in 2002. Tsai's camera documents the destruction of the building though the skywalk itself is not essential to the plot. Though the film is shot in both Taipei and Paris, the lack of establishing and exterior shots suggests a certain arbitrary aspect of the setting. Because *What Time* is predominantly 'a film about film' (Bloom 2005, 20), its geographical settings, Taipei and Paris, are significant but not essential to the plot.

Though the film would not necessarily need to have been filmed in Paris, the fact that Tsai was invited to film in Paris is significant. For the past fifteen years or so, there has been a considerable increase in cross-cultural currents moving between French and contemporary Taiwanese cinema. Tsai, in particular, is intrigued by Paris and, more specifically, Paris of the 1950s and '60s, when the French New Wave movement was in its initial stages. In her article 'The European Undead: Tsai Ming-liang's Temporal Dysphoria' (2003), Fran Martin argues that, despite Tsai's intertextual citation of François Truffaut's *The 400 Blows* throughout *What Time?*, the director is not simply lamenting a bygone time era. Not only does Tsai cite European film-makers; he also cites popular Taiwanese and Hong Kong cinema. This self-reflexivity, or 'double citation' as Martin calls it, leads me to describe Tsai's films as local yet universal Taiwanese cinema.

The terms 'universal' and 'to local tastes' are obviously complex and, in many ways, subjective. In the context of this book, however, the term 'universal' simply means something that carries currency or meaning for an international array of viewers. It would be safe to say that a well-known film, such as Ang Lee's *Crouching Tiger, Hidden Dragon/Wo hu cang long* (2000), contains 'universal' appeal in the sense that the film grossed $213.5 million worldwide when it was released in 2000. On the other hand, it might make sense to say that a film such as Edward Yang's *Terrorizers* has 'universal' appeal in the sense that fans of Italian director Michelangelo Antonioni would appreciate Yang's slow-moving camera and objective distance from his characters. 'Universal', in other words, can be defined and measured in terms of money or in terms of the apparent 'sophistication' of the film text itself. The films which are discussed in this volume are 'universal' according to the latter definition. Clearly, the ability of the industry to sustain itself precedes all other concerns. The 'local/universal' dichotomy, observed within the 'text' of the film itself, rests on a more abstract plane altogether. Nevertheless, this book is propelled by textual readings of this more abstract dichotomy within Taiwanese cinema.

Though New Taiwan cinema functions as a special case study in intertextual, national yet transnational cinema, the idea of an intertextually rich, 'hybrid' film is not exclusive to Taiwanese cinema. Quentin Tarantino's *Kill Bill* (vol. 1, 2003), for example, functions as an elegant example of intertextual, hybrid film-making. *Kill Bill* – an American film that consciously integrates Japanese visual language into its plot – is emblematic of the sort of East–West hybridity that I discuss throughout this volume in the context of Taiwanese cinema. Tarantino's film moves effortlessly between genres such that the viewer must pay attention in order to follow its narrative leaps. In an interview about his film, Tarantino states that, if one were to attempt to find *Kill Bill* in a video store, it would be labelled as part of the 'revenge' genre.[2] Yet, even within the revenge genre, *Kill Bill* contains countless layers of subgenres: the kung fu movie, the Japanese samurai movie, the spaghetti western, manga, anime, and the Italian giallo, to name a few. In the film, Lucy Liu (a Chinese-American actress) plays O-Ren Ishii, the Chinese-Japanese-American leader of the Tokyo yakuza gang. In one particularly noteworthy scene, one of the gang members ridicules her mixed-race heritage and she quickly decapitates him as a warning to the others. She speaks both Japanese and English – she uses Japanese when she is being polite and when she is on the verge of death and English when she is warning her fellow Japanese gang members never to speak negatively of her heritage. Thus, in this sense, the viewer must actively engage in Tarantino's use of intertext – the cinephiles in the audience will probably notice it more – and, furthermore, the viewer must be aware of the linguistic and cultural exchanges as they play out within the film.

Similarly, this volume is devoted to Taiwanese films that play with and problematise this East/West dichotomy; films such as *Kill Bill*, which do not fall into predefined categories or genres, but rather contain elements that help to form and inspire the creation of new genres. All the films that are highlighted in this volume exhibit 'hybridity'[3] and, in some cases, 'adaptation'. The word 'adaptation', however, is not meant to imply regression or repetition in any way. The definition of 'adaptation', in the context of this volume, rests on the notion of intertextuality, citation, and translation rather than on homage or pure nostalgia. Adaptation, in Taiwanese cinema, leads to hybridisation in the sense that 'the old' is fashioned into 'the new'. New genres are created through the combination of innovative cinematic language (Tsai Ming-liang relies mostly on interior shots while filming in Paris, slowing the action down with exaggeratedly long takes, for example) with recognisable visual, aural or diegetic elements. These genres are 'recognisable' in the sense that most audiences will be familiar with love stories, police dramas, historical fiction, and so on. I do not sense any hint of imitation in the films of Edward Yang, Hou Hsiao-hsien, Tsai Ming-liang, Ang Lee, or any of the New Taiwanese filmmakers. On the contrary, these films 'reincarnate' the cinema of film-makers from other cinematic 'traditions' by, somewhat paradoxically, carving out a new niche for themselves altogether.

Overall, I do not argue that this body of cinematic texts can be accounted for in terms of a 'the national' but, rather, that these films represent a variety of styles, reflect different concerns, and can even, in some cases, be read in light of the auteur model. Though the volume offers a concise history of Taiwanese national cinema, the analysis focuses on close textual readings of specific films by Hou Hsiao-hsien, Ang Lee, Tsai Ming-liang, Edward Yang, and others[4] as stylistic differences, variations in content, and the political concerns of each film-maker are revealed. Each film in this volume demonstrates a differing level of engagement with international audiences. Because my aim is to emphasise the dialogue, either implied or direct, between Taiwanese and French and

Italian cinema, one might well ask: how and why is this a book about Taiwan in particular? I feel strongly that the book can be both 'about Taiwanese cinema' and also 'about Taiwan cinema's connection with other cinemas' at the same time. In fact, this is the very premise that fuelled my research.

Fitting broadly within the imperfect subheadings: 'Taiwanese New Wave and Second Wave cinema', the films that I discuss in this volume reflect the collective and social imaginative of Taiwan since the mid-1980s, as well as the complex nature of Chinese-language cinema more generally. The terms 'New Wave' and 'Second Wave' are imperfect subheadings in the sense that they can be vague, misleading, and even exclusionary. Douglas Kellner,[5] in a 1998 *Jump Cut* article entitled: 'New Taiwan Cinema in the 80s' argues that the 'wave' metaphor is ambiguous and inaccurate in the context of cinema production patterns. He writes: 'rather than seeing the 1980s Taiwanese films simply as a "new wave", as an artefact in film history, we should understand them as cultural and political interventions, as probings of Taiwanese society and history, and as self-consciously creating a distinctly national cinema.' (n.p.) Kellner argues that we should be wary of the label 'Taiwanese New Wave' because the term 'New Wave' is little more than a marketing term 'used to promote fresh entries into the international global market' (Kellner n.p.). As Kellner suggests, categorical terms such as 'Taiwanese New Wave' and 'Taiwanese Second Wave' are imperfect and can be misleading. Nevertheless, these terms do serve a useful purpose, in that they can be used to separate various movements chronologically. As long as films are not defined *only* in terms of the time period in which they were released, or for a marketing purpose only, then I see no harm in using them. The New Wave movement took place (roughly) between 1982 and 1990, and was supported by Taiwan's Central Motion Picture Corporation (CMPC). The first New Wave film, *In Our Time* (1982), was a collection of four different short films by four different Taiwanese directors, including Edward Yang. New Wave Cinema, like Italian neo-realism, focuses on the lives of working-class people struggling to survive on a day-to-day basis. Melodrama and exaggeration are shunned in favour of realism and an anticlimactic plot. Edward Yang's New Wave cinema tends to focus, in particular, on the alienating effect of modern-day city life. Hou Hsiao-hsien's early films tend to focus more on rural life and the Taiwanese colonial experience. Despite the quality of New Wave cinema, the Taiwanese population views the movement as a financial and artistic disaster. The Taiwanese government website reports that New Wave films were never a mainstream draw, and accounted for only a fraction of box office sales, even at the peak of the movement. The movement was criticised, the website continues, because it was seen as irrelevant to most of the population: 'Appealing only to a cultural elite, New Wave directors rarely sought local popular audiences and rejected commercialism, even while winning praise and fame internationally.'[6]

The Second New Wave, meanwhile, is a much broader term, comprising films that were made throughout the entire 1990s and 2000s. Film-makers as diverse as Chen Guofu, Ang Lee, and Tsai Ming-liang are all considered part of the Second New Wave. The definition of the movement is so vague, in fact, that the government website distinguishes it from the first New Wave in terms of its appeal to audiences. Though this group of film-makers was still interested in exploring the 'pain' of modern society, the government website explains, the films themselves were 'less serious and more appealing to general audiences'. The definition of the Second Wave is so abstract that it is close to being meaningless. I cannot imagine film-makers who are more different from each other than Ang Lee and Tsai Ming-liang. Lee's films have been wildly successful but he no longer lives in Taiwan. Is he then, a Taiwanese film-maker? Tsai's films, on the other hand, are extremely alienating to audiences and are often extremely racy but extraordinarily slow moving. Tsai has been called 'a poison' to Taiwanese cinema. I therefore use the term 'Second New Wave' very loosely as a means of referring to the twenty-year time period between 1990 and the recent past.

Over the course of the last decade, there has been a large number of articles and books written on the issue of time and space in Chinese cinema.[7] Jean Ma's recent book, *Melancholy Drift: Marking Time in Chinese Cinema* (2010), a study on Tsai, Hou, and Wong Kar-wai, is a milestone in its own right. Ma's book, unlike my own, focuses predominantly on representations of time in both Hong Kong and Taiwanese cinema. Other volumes, which focus more exclusively on Taiwanese cinema, include: Guo-juin Hong's *Taiwan Cinema: A Contested Nation* (Palgrave MacMillan, 2011) and Darrell William Davis and Ru-Shou Robert Chen's *Cinema Taiwan: Politics, Popularity and State of the Arts* (2007). Hong's book offers a broad discussion of Taiwanese cinema in relation to Chinese cultural practices, covering the entire history of Taiwanese cinema from the early twentieth century to the present. Davis and Chen's book is an edited collection of essays, and covers the span of the twentieth century as well. Other recent volumes include: *Island on the Edge: Taiwan New Cinema and After*, edited by Chris Berry and Feiyi Lu (2005), and *Taiwan Film Directors: A Treasure Island* by Emilie Yueh-yu Yeh and Darrell William Davis (2005). Berry and Lu's book is premised on the notion of cinema as 'cultural text', an assumption that is not completely unproblematic. Yeh and Davis's approach, meanwhile, is more similar to my own in that it assumes a more fundamental link between author and text. As Yeh and Davis attest, there are compelling reasons for organising Taiwanese cinema with some emphasis on the notion of the auteur. I do not argue that films should be discussed or categorised according to an old-fashioned notion of auteurism. Rather, in the Taiwanese context specifically, beyond the external factors that have created an environment in which locating outside funding has become necessary, there are thematic commonalities that bind the *oeuvres* of certain directors together.

This volume, therefore, is dedicated to careful textual analysis in the context of a precise movement and time period: contemporary Taiwanese cinema, from the mid-1980s to the present. I have written this book from the perspective of a comparatist who is familiar with a variety of cinematic traditions. Though I delve into relevant theoretical issues and in-depth textual readings of scenes, I do not attempt to present this body of films through the lens of any one political viewpoint. This introduction outlines the theoretical apparatus, baseline criteria, and philosophical modus operandi that continue to guide my study of national cinemas.

Chapter 1, entitled: 'Charting the Course: Defining the Taiwanese Cinematic "Tradition"', situates the Taiwanese film industry both historically and in the present day. I discuss the Japanese-controlled media output in Taiwan until around 1945 (Neri 33), noting that the censorship continued long after World War II. Most notably and horrifically, on 29 February 1947, protesters against the Kuomintang were killed and a period of extreme censorship began in the Taiwanese media industry (33). Between 1955 and 1974, Taiwanese-language films regained popularity which, in many ways, was an early indication of the burgeoning nativist movement. But there was a backlash against Taiwanese-language films. Between about 1964 and the early 1980s, the government made an effort to promote Mandarin-language films (Wu in Lu and Yeh, 77) which have become the standard ever since.

The 'New Wave' movement began in Taiwan with Yang's *In Our Time/ Guang yin de gu shi* (1982) and *Sandwich Man/Erzi de da wan'ou* (1983). A few years later, in 1986, the Democratic Progressive Party was officially founded in Taiwan. The founding of the DPP was an important milestone. This was the first party in Taiwanese history to oppose officially the Kuomintang and censorship more generally. Finally, in 1987, when martial law was abolished, the law banning the freedom of the press was abolished as well. Unfortunately, however, by 1987, the 'New Wave' was already being pronounced dead even as film-makers were signing a manifesto (Neri 35). But, by the early 1990s, though the 'New Wave' had ended, the 'Second Wave' was in full swing as a new generation of film-makers appeared on the scene. Second Wave film-makers, such as Tsai Ming-liang, had already worked in television and theatre before moving to cinema. This chapter ends, therefore, with a discussion of the current climate for film-makers in Taiwan, for both newcomers and for more established directors. The question that remains, and that will continue to do so throughout the course of this book, will be: what is at stake when attempting to create a film that will be successful with domestic audiences?

Chapter 2, entitled: 'Taiwanese–Italian Conjugations: The Fractured Storytelling of Edward Yang's *The Terrorizers* and Michelangelo Antonioni's *Blow-Up*', contains a discussion of the films of Edward Yang. At the beginning of Yang's *The Terrorizers/Kongbu fenzi* (1986), one of the female protagonists (played by Cora Miao) comments in a voiceover:

> I don't know what to do anymore . . . you know, at one time you counted on writing skills, real life experiences, whether they happened to me or to my friends . . . characters, plots, they actually existed. I took them down in my notebook. But it's become so meaningless to write in this way.

The voiceover characterises the themes that are inherent to Yang's style. As noted by Frederic Jameson,[8] Yang's films can be described as showcases of alienation in the modern city of Taipei, a space in which conventional plots and characters no longer exist and the notion of the 'grand narrative' is called into question. Unlike some of the other Taiwanese film-makers that are discussed in this volume, Yang uses voiceovers and dialogue to express the 'heaviness' of life in modern-day Taipei. His films are not taciturn or uncommunicative. My analysis of Yang's films therefore relies not only on camera movement but also, to a large extent, on what the characters say and think. Towards the middle of the chapter, I trace plot and thematic similarities between Yang's *Terrorizers* and Italian director Michelangelo Antonioni's *Blow-Up* (1967), concluding overall that both films function as analogies for modernism.

Chapter 3, entitled 'Mapping Hou Hsiao-hsien's Visuality: Setting, Silence, and the Incongruence of Translation', is a study of silence, miscommunication, and untranslatability within Hou's cinematic world. Unlike Yang's films, many of which are still difficult to purchase in the United States or Britain and Europe, Hou's films are, in general, much easier to find (in restored quality, at least). Hou holds an international reputation for his cinematic portrayals of Taiwan in a historical, colonial context, and this reputation is well earned. Hou's earliest films, *The Sandwich Man* (1983), *Dust in the Wind/Lian lian feng chen* (1986), and *A City of Sadness/Beiqing chengshi* (1989), depict the Japanese occupation of Taiwan during World War II, which was a taboo subject in Taiwan when the films were released in the 1980s. The films stirred controversy and led the Taiwanese industry in a new, long-lasting direction.

In addition to his penchant for controversial subject matter, Hou is known among film scholars for his disinterest in plot and character development in favour of objects and settings (1). James Udden, in his book *No Man an Island: The Cinema of Hou Hsiao-hsien* (2009), argues that Hou is 'at his best' when attempting to focus on a bygone era in Taiwanese history (170). Udden argues, furthermore, that Hou's post-2000 films are 'challenging' and interesting, but that: 'they do not seem to break as much strikingly new ground' (170).

In fact, many of Hou's post-millennium films – *Millennium Mambo/Qianxi manbo* (2000), *Three Times/Zuihao de shiguang* (2005), and *Flight of the Red Balloon/Le voyage du ballon rouge* (2007)[9] in particular – contain more 'challenges' than Udden suggests.

Hou's *Red Balloon,* for example, was shot in Paris, and consists of two women protagonists: Suzanne (Juliette Binoche), the eccentric French woman who performs in puppet shows, and Song (Fang Song), a Taiwanese film student, hired by Suzanne to babysit her son Simon. Hou's film oscillates between French and Chinese, revealing and celebrating instances of non-translatable, imperfect correspondence between cultures. Though Jean Ma describes Hou's *Red Balloon* as a 'remake' of Albert Lamorrise's *The Red Balloon/Le ballon rouge* (1956) (83), the film is best described as a 'tribute' layered in cross-cultural hybridity. Like Tsai, Hou prefers the long take, a still camera, and a noticeable absence of wordy dialogue. The lack of speech in Hou's films contributes to an overall feeling of non-ironic 'sweetness' and the hidden (often strong) emotions of his characters. Many of Hou's films (*Dust in the Wind, Millennium Mambo, Three Times*) are simple love stories. The emotions of the characters are expressed through subtle gestures (holding hands, sidelong glances and so forth). Often, as Hou's camera seems to suggest, these small gestures are demonstrative of the untranslatable nature of love, fondness, and nostalgia for the past.

If Hou's films are nostalgic, then Tsai Ming-liang's films are haunted. Like Hou, Tsai prefers to use extremely limited dialogue but there is no underlying 'sweet' quality to Tsai's films. Chapter 4, entitled: 'Tsai Ming-liang's Disjointed Connectivity and Lonely Intertextuality', defines 'disjointed connectivity' and reflects on this pervasive sense of loneliness. Tsai's earlier films: *The River/He liu* (1994), *Vive L'Amour/Aiqing wansui* (1994), *The Hole/Dong* (1995), and *Goodbye Dragon Inn/Bu san* (2003), though less obviously transnational, express the theme of loneliness in similar ways. Faced with little support from the Taiwanese government, film-makers such as Tsai (as well as Hou and Yang, as we have seen) were forced to seek funding from international sources. In a certain way, this allowed these film-makers stylistic flexibility, especially Tsai, who was able to 'find his voice' by experimenting with a variety of cinematic techniques.[10] But Tsai's 'voice' is not appealing to everyone. The characters who appear and reappear in different forms throughout Tsai *oeuvre* are isolated from themselves and from others and, for this reason, his films have been almost unanimously described as sad and depressing. Tsai himself characterises his own work best, I think, when he comments: 'My films have no climax and they are not dramatic, and not very complex. I replace narrative pleasure with the detail of life. But it is hard to get close to reality. I try to provide ridiculous elements, which are part of reality itself.'[11] Tsai's most recent film *Lian/Visage/Face* (2009) is the director's ultimate experiment in intertextuality. The film itself is composed of an infinitely complex web of cinematic and literary references, from Salome to Pasolini to Truffaut. The film functions as a vehicle for Tsai to incorporate the figures of the French New Wave (Jean Pierre Léaud, Fanny Ardant) into his own cinematic vision – a mixing and matching made in Tsai's personal 'cinematic heaven'.

Tsai's first three films: *Rebels of the Neon God/Qing shaonian nuozha* (1992), *Vive l'Amour* (1994), and *The River* (1997) were funded by Taiwan's Central Motion Picture Corporation (the CMPC) while his fourth film, *The Hole* (1998), was commissioned by French distributors and a French–German television network, and funded only in part by the CMPC. *The Hole,* therefore, represents a shift for Tsai from a national to a transnational production model, the model that continues to characterise his work. Tsai's subsequent films represent varying degrees of 'transnational influence', and were shot in Taiwan, France, Malaysia and various combinations therein. Specifically, *What Time is it There?* (2001) and *Visage* (2009) were both shot in Taiwan and in France, and *Goodbye Dragon Inn* (2003) and *The Wayward Cloud/Tianbian yi duo yun* (2005) were shot in Taiwan. *I Don't Want to Sleep Alone/Hei yan quan* (2006), commissioned as part of an international series for the New Crowned Hope Festival in Vienna in 2006, was shot in Malaysia (Ma 83).

Tsai's *What Time* is the director's best-known film internationally. It is a film about alienation, set in two distinct cities: Paris and Taipei. *What Time* is also a 'film about a film' (Bloom 2005, 319) in the sense that the protagonist (Hsiao-kang) becomes obsessed with François Truffaut's *The 400 Blows/Les 400 coups* (1959). In this way, the film reaches beyond the local to a global, cinematically sophisticated audience. Though it undeniably deals with alienated subjects who are lost in postmodern urban space, the film is more interestingly read in terms of Tsai's directorial relationship with his characters. That is, one can read the film more largely as a comment on the dying status of the auteur in cinema. Furthermore, the ghosts that haunt this film can be 'brought to light' by interpreting many of the cinematic elements that appear fantastic or supernatural in terms of intertextual and intratextual citation. Tsai as a film-maker demonstrates 'disjointed connectivity', a technique that endows the spectator with a unique perspective. Through the use of parallel cuts, viewers can see the interrelations between characters, both in space and in time, which creates a feeling of 'omniscience' in the spectator. Tsai's use of 'disjointed connectivity' allows the viewer to move into alternative space. The film's protagonists, Shiang-chyi and Hsiao-kang, are like 'amnesiacs' who fail to see the apparatus that connects them to each other and to themselves.

Chapter 5 moves away from hauntings, ghostly characters and depressed auteurs and into a discussion of the wildly successful Ang Lee. The chapter, entitled: 'The Chinese/Hollywood Aesthetic of Ang Lee: "Westernized", Capitalist . . . and Box Office Gold' traces Lee's career from its beginnings in

1979 when he moved from Taiwan to the United States. Since the early 1990s, Lee has been directing blockbusters, that is, films that are financially successful on an international scale. Though Lee still shoots in Taiwan, he is based, primarily, in Hollywood. Because he has produced many well-known films in English (*Sense and Sensibility*, 1995; *The Ice Storm*, 1997; and *Brokeback Mountain*, 2005) and has lived in the United States for many years, Lee is frequently referred to – often in the form of a critique – as an 'Asian-American' or 'Westernized' director (Mills, 67). Media outlets and scholars alike do not quite know what to make of him.

Chinese/feminist film scholar Rey Chow, for example, describes Lee's *Lust, Caution/Se, jie* (2007) as 'orientalist' because of its depiction of brutal, masochistic sexuality and 'detailed exoticism'. In a chapter from her new book, *Framing the Original: Toward a New Visibility of the Orient* (2012), Chow suggests that Lee's effort to recreate the intimate and intricate details of 1940s China is a masochistic act because the details of the portrait will always be inaccurate. She posits: '. . . are Ang Lee's fastidious efforts as director also masochistic, in that although he believes he is carrying out a mission to restore the bygone China of his parents' generation, the mission can never be accomplished no matter how hard he tries?' (562) Chow takes issue with Lee's insistence on detail, arguing that Lee takes liberties with Eileen Chang's original story and adds graphic sex scenes without justification. By attempting to re-enact the past so precisely, Chow concludes, Lee fails to do justice to the subtle metaphoric quality of Chang's story.

Though Lee's attention to detail in all his films is obsessive, almost to the point of insanity, it is not clear to me that this detail is necessarily 'harmful' in Chow's sense of the term. Though I would not necessarily 'defend' *Lust, Caution* (2007) against Chow's critique, I do feel that readers should be aware of the screenwriter James Schamus's perspective on the film.[12] My discussion of *Lust Caution/Se, jie* within the context of this chapter is prefaced by an analysis of Lee's earlier films, *The Wedding Banquet/Xi yan* (1993), in particular. Through a comprehensive discussion of Lee's career, this chapter provides readers with a broader view of Lee's *oeuvre* so that they may judge his body of work in the context of the New Taiwanese Cinema movement (as opposed to through the more narrow theoretical lenses of feminism, cultural imperialism or psychoanalysis). Overall, critics and scholars are too quick to discount Lee's cinema along artistic lines – either because his work has been deemed 'conventional' or because Lee has continued to attain box office success. The phenomenal successes of Lee's *Crouching Tiger, Hidden Dragon* (2000), *Brokeback Mountain* (2005) and, most recently, *The Life of Pi* (2012) should be reason enough to justify a discussion of Lee in the context of other Taiwanese film-makers.

Chapter 6, 'Filming Disappearance or Renewal? The Ever-Changing

Representations of Taipei in Contemporary Taiwanese Cinema', reflects on current and potential future trends in Taiwan's film industry. As noted in this chapter, one of the most significant questions that underlies the current state of the industry can be summarised by Lin Wenchi's question: '[are current Taiwanese films] still dominated by representations of Taipei as a city associated with illness, death, and ghosts' (Neri 227)? Wenchi's question leads back to the original question of this volume: why does contemporary cinema in Taiwan still tend to be perceived by mainstream Taiwanese audiences as depressing, slow moving and impenetrable? Art house film-makers with little regard for box office success, such as Tsai Ming-liang, arguably contribute to this stereotype. But the answers to these questions are complex and the stereotypes are not always consistent. In this final chapter, I argue that the ethos of sadness trope does not accurately account for an array of emerging film-makers who are questioning the 'aesthetics of death' that surround Taiwanese film-making. Arvin Chen, the Taiwanese-American director of the 2010 film *Au revoir Taipei/Yi ye Taibei*, exemplifies this trend. Though Chen is not a self-proclaimed 'Taiwanese filmmaker', his successful entry into the international film festival circuit raises important questions about the future of Taiwanese cinema.

Other recent box office successes in Taiwan, such as *Cape No. 7/Haijiao qi hao* (Wei Te-Sheng, 2009), *Monga/Bang-kah* (Doze Niu, 2010), and *Night Market Hero/Ji pai ying xiong* (Tien-Lun Yeh, 2011), are generally thought to have veered away from the aesthetic and thematic elements of both the New Wave and the Second Wave. Though many of these films are ignored by film scholars, dismissiveness may be counterproductive in this case. If audiences in Taiwan are willing to pay to see Taiwanese-funded films, the government is more likely to provide funding to up-and-coming film-makers. Films such as *Cape No. 7*, even if they cannot be categorised as 'New Cinema' in a strict sense, do meet an important need 'at home'. In fact, a domestic blockbuster, such as *Cape No. 7*, may not be as different from films such as Hou's *Three Times* as film scholars may want to believe. Both films are, after all, love stories that confront Japanese colonialism in a sweet, yet poignant, style. Though the elite audiences of art cinema may be hesitant to shower praise on such films, this prejudice may be unjustified. Many of these popular films, in fact, do share a variety of themes with films of the so-called New Wave.

NOTES

1. For more on the current state of the censorship debate in Taiwan, see 'In Face of Mainland Censorship, Taiwanese Revisit Reunification Question' *The Atlantic*, Feb 23, 2013.
2. See You Tube interview 'Quentin Tarantino: Kill Bill'.
3. The term 'hybrid' has many connotations, especially within the realm of postcolonial

studies. Homi Babha and Hamid Naficy have used the term to describe cultural fusion, heterogeneity, and rupture. For Babha and Naficy, the hyphen used in hybrid terms denotes 'horizontality' or the possibility for multiple identities. My usage of the term, as I will explain, is slightly different from that of Babha and Naficy.

4. In addition to these close textual readings, I also discuss the industry-specific differences between each of the film-makers. For example, Tsai is concerned with gaining funds from foreign producers but not with box office success in Taiwan. Ang Lee, on the other hand, is concerned with procuring funds and with box office success (he moved to Hollywood, after all), and his films often cater to a generalised, international audience.
5. See Kellner's *Jump Cut* article.
6. See 'Cinema', Taiwan Government Entry Point, 26 May 2010, from the Ministry of Foreign Affairs <http://www.taiwan.gov.tw/ct.asp?xItem=27553&ctNode=1924&mp=1001>
7. Michelle E. Bloom's 2005 article served as my introduction to Tsai, and to the idea of Sino-French cinema more generally. Since 2005, Bloom has published several other pieces on the concept of the Sino-French cinema (see Bloom, 2011).
8. See Jameson on *Terrorizers*.
9. Referred to hereafter as *The Red Balloon*.
10. For instance, mixing amateur actors with professionals, perfecting the long take, and integrating documentary-style camera work into a fictional narrative (Hughes).
11. From a question-and-answer session after the screening of *Rebel of a Neon God*, at the University of Southern California Cinema School in November 2009.
12. Schamus is a busy man who wears multiple hats. He is a long-time partner of Lee's, working not only as a screenwriter and the CEO of Focus Films but also as a film professor at Columbia University in New York.

I. CHARTING THE COURSE: DEFINING THE TAIWANESE CINEMATIC 'TRADITION'

What if we stopped asking whether cinema can be some sort of magic door opening onto absolute time, and instead asked about cinema's role in the construction of different temporalities in different societies, politics, cultures, classes and so forth. (Berry, in Khoo and Metzger, 113)

Historical Context, Cultural Background

Contemporary Taiwanese cinema (from the 1980s to the present) must be understood in relation to, and in reaction against, earlier forms of film-making on the island. Though I do not consider the large body of films that were produced between 1895 and the early 1980s to comprise the New Taiwanese cinematic 'tradition', one cannot understand the context out of which this tradition arose without looking back into history. One must look beyond the frame, so to speak, to see within it.

The earliest films which were produced on the island of Taiwan were Japanese products, examples of 'imperial Japanese film culture' (Gaskett 3).[1] Japan controlled the majority of media content in the earlier half of the century, a control that was tied directly to a rapid succession of Japanese military victories. This control extended in both ways: not only did Japanese filmmakers 'set up shop' in their extended empire, but non-Japanese filmmakers from within that empire were drawn away from their own countries and into Japan. Throughout the 1920s and 1930s, filmmakers from Taiwan, Korea, China, and Burma all travelled to Japan in order to train at the 'best' facilities:

Japanese film studios. On the flip side, Japanese cameramen travelled to China and Manchuria to shoot newsreels and fictional thrillers such as *The Village at Twilight* (*Yuhi no mura*, 1921). By the mid-1930s, the Japanese media had replaced Hollywood as the main source of information and entertainment for millions of East Asians living under Japanese control.

The Japanese presence in Taiwan began at the end of the first Sino-Japanese War in 1895 when Japan was given full control over the island.[2] China, whose army had not been sufficiently modernised, was quick to fall to the technologically superior Japanese army. A *New York Times* article from 1894, tellingly titled 'Japan Anxious for a Fight: The Chinese Are Slow and Not in Good Shape to Go to War', predicted the beginning to the end to the war. The *Times* journalist describes the Japanese military as: 'well-drilled and well-armed, enthusiastic, and homogenous [*sic*]' while, in comparison, 'so far as we know, China has comparatively little to show' ('Japan Anxious' n.p.). The journalist continues, noting that, though the Chinese army was thought to be large, it was not thought to be well equipped. This prediction turned out to be accurate; though China's army was, indeed, massive, Japan's military had been modernised and streamlined under a major restoration effort by Emperor Meiji.[3]

In simplified terms, Japan's major war victory forced China towards modernisation. As China moved away from Confucianism and toward nationalism, China's central authority made a large-scale effort to reunify the country. Though the Republic of China was founded in 1912, the central authority had quickly fragmented into regional warlord rule. In an effort to eliminate the warlords and reunify, the Chinese Nationalist Party (or Kuomintang/KMT) sent their National Revolutionary Army on a sweep through China. The Kuomintang fought to recapture power from the Japanese empire and the Communist Party of China (the CCP). Though the Nationalist leader, Chiang Kai-shek, controlled the Kuomintang on the mainland between 1927 and 1937, Chiang was driven to Taiwan after the end of the second Sino-Japanese war and during the Chinese Civil War in 1949. After the Japanese had left in 1945, Chiang quickly established Kuomintang rule in Taiwan, the beginning of an era that is known by the chilling name 'White Terror'. For the next thirty years, until his death in 1975, Chiang's Nationalist government reinforced martial law in Taiwan and punished dissenters.

Long before Chiang's presence on the island, the Japanese had functioned as ruler–colonisers of Taiwan. The Japanese era lasted for fifty years, beginning with the Treaty of Shimonoseki in 1895 and concluding with the Japanese defeat at the end of World War II in 1945. Because China had ceded Taiwan to the Japanese as part of the Treaty of Shimonoseki, Japan was in control of all Taiwanese media output throughout this entire period. For an entire half-century, then, Japan controlled industrialisation efforts, education, transport, and media output in Taiwan. As a part of the deal, Japan also controlled the production, distribution and exhibition of all early film shot in Taiwan.

Films from all over the world – especially American and European films – were imported and shown in Taiwan, even during the height of Japanese control. Records indicate that at least ten Edison films were imported on to the island of Taiwan as early as 1896.[4] Hollywood studios, such as Paramount and Universal, set up offices in Taiwan, or they placed Taiwan's management under the control of their Tokyo offices. Despite this influx of Western films, however, Japanese cinema dominated the earliest Taiwanese theatres. A Japanese circuit-run company was set up in 1915 so that films which were shown in Tokyo could be seen in Taipei one month later. There was no attempt to democratise this process. Imported by the Japanese, foreign films were not shown for the entertainment needs of the Taiwanese population. Because most of the native Taiwanese population did not speak Japanese, the language of the films themselves was a barrier. All imported films in Taiwan, regardless of national origin, were required to carry Japanese subtitles (Xiao and Zhang 47). Large theatres, such as the Fang-Nai Pavilion in Taipei, were intended for Japanese audiences only (Gou-Juin 20). In the early years of Japanese rule, films were projected outdoors because of a lack of bricks-and-mortar theatres. By 1941, a total of forty-nine theatres had been built in Taiwan. The theatres were divided into three classes in an ongoing effort to segregate Japanese and Taiwanese filmgoers: Class A theatres showed Japanese films and charged the highest ticket prices; Class B theatres, meanwhile, were not air-conditioned but they did show Chinese and Taiwanese films. The open-air projection areas were the Class C theatres. By almost every measure, the Japanese effort to shut out Taiwanese filmgoers was a success. Until the end of World War II, 70 per cent of film audiences were Japanese (49).

In 1901, the Japanese shot their first film in Taiwan, a propaganda documentary entitled *Introducing Taiwan Today* (1903), created in support of Japanese rule over the island (Zhang and Xiao 47).[5] Japanese cinematographers, like tourists, were eager to capture on film the rugged mountains and rolling plains of the Taiwanese landscape. Filtered through a coloniser's lens, however, Taiwan's aboriginal tribes were depicted as 'savages' and barbarians (Ghermanni).[6] Overall, early Japanese cinema in Taiwan comprised two types: *rengasi* (that is, 'chained drama') which was used to complement stage plays; and *benshi*. In this latter type of silent films, the *benshi* (renamed *benzi* by the Taiwanese) served as a commentator throughout the duration of the film. The role of the *benshi* was highly prized and well paid as evidenced by the fact that *benshis* were billed at a higher rate than film stars at the time (Xiao and Zhang 48). Though the colonial government did not aggressively interfere with Taiwanese indigenous culture during this period, Japanese officials closely monitored film theatre output and *benshi* commentary (Deslandes). Foreign imports were closely monitored as well, though Japanese control of media outlets was more underhanded than blatant. Control was retained through reward for compliance rather than through punishment for subversion. Den Kenjiro, the Japanese Governor General of Taiwan between 1919 and 1923, adopted the Doka policy – a policy of 'assimilation' whereby the spread of Japanese language and culture throughout Taiwan was encouraged and rewarded. Part of this 'assimilation' required that the colonised class cut ties with mainland Chinese culture and, more specifically, with Shanghai-produced films. The first mainland Chinese film in Taiwan, *The Revival of an Old Well* (directed by Dan Duyu), was imported from Shanghai in 1923. Though more than three hundred films from Shanghai were distributed in Taiwan between 1923 and 1945, many others were either censored or confiscated upon arrival on the island. Images of Chinese Nationalist leaders Sun Yat-sen and Chiang Kai-shek were frequently deleted. In the late 1930s, at the height of the second Sino-Japanese war, the Japanese banned entirely Chinese-made films from entering Taiwan.

In 1921, the Culture Bureau established a circuit film group in Taiwan. The group then produced a film entitled *Eyes of the Buddha/Da Fo De Tong Kong*, directed by Tanaka King (1922), the story of a young Taiwanese girl who is rescued from the clutches of a Chinese official by a heroic Japanese soldier. As he savagely attempts to force the girl to marry him, the Chinese official is scared away by the flashing eyes of a Buddha statue (47). The message of the film is unimaginative at best; *Eyes of the Buddha* is a typical 'coloniser' romance, a variation on the 'Pocahontas' theme that appears consistently in imperial film and fiction. In an unpublished piece entitled *The Return of the Vanishing Formosan* (2009), Darryl Sterk describes this recurring phenomenon in literature and in film as an allegorical relationship between the Taiwanese aboriginals and the colonisers:

> The fact of the aboriginal maiden introduces the idea of the nation's temporality, to the temporal ideologies of Progress and Preservation, to modernity. Filming or writing her aboriginal origin and her present predicament has been a way for filmmakers . . . to *emplot* the nation as a story with a beginning at the moment of love at first sight between a settler man and an aboriginal maiden . . . (my emphasis, Sterk 1–2)

Sterk is describing the 'white man's burden' theme that appears in contemporary films such as *Pocahontas* (1995) and *Avatar* (2009) in the context of early Taiwanese cinema. *Pocahontas*, like *Avatar*, has been critiqued for its clichéd storyline: the white man arrives, enlightens the aboriginals, teaching them how to follow a Western way of life, and obtains the love of a 'native' woman, all within a two-hour span.

When Sterk mentions the idea that film-makers tend to 'emplot the nation as a story', he is referencing historian Hayden White's concept of historiography. To 'emplot the nation as a story', though it sounds complicated, means: to create a beginning and ending point in a nation's history (either real or imagined) in order to show how that nation has changed as a result of the colonisation. Because Sterk is discussing a historically motivated work of cinema,[7] he is wise to refer to White here. When White first explains his notion of historiography, in his well-known essay 'The Question of Narrative in Contemporary Historical Theory' (1984), he posits that although history is composed of real events, those events are written down and constructed by narrators. He writes:

> The content of historical stories is real events, events that really happened, rather than imaginary events, events invented by the narrator. This implies that the form in which historical events present themselves to a prospective narrator is *found* rather than *constructed*. (27, emphasis added)

White argues that the narration of historical events can be presented in a nearly infinite number of ways, depending on how the narrator chooses to 'emplot'[8] them. The narration of history, aka historiography, is therefore a 'vehicle for the transmission of messages' (41). It is the 'content' of these messages alone that contain 'truth-value', according to White, not the manner in which they are encoded. In White's opinion, 'truth-value' is not innate to the manner in which a historian chooses to transmit 'content' and, therefore, history should be thought of as 'constructed' as opposed to 'discovered'. Though White does not explicitly define the terms 'content' or 'truth-value' in this essay, he would presumably agree that we can define historical events based, at least partially, according to *when* they happened (in other words, chronologically).

White does not attempt to deny that the content of history possesses a truth-value;[9] he argues only that the content of history can be recounted in a variety of ways. Interestingly, White employs the term *allegoresis* or 'allegory' to describe how one should view historical narratives, and his description of the term recalls the notion of *recusatio*: '. . . rather than regard every historical narrative as mythic or ideological in nature, we should regard it as allegorical, that is, saying one thing and meaning another' (45). Those who narrate history (that is, historiographers), in other words, shape and transform events into distinct 'patterns of meaning', says White (45). The truth of these events can arise *only* indirectly, through *allegoresis*, because everything else is merely chronicle.

Because White's overall thesis is not particularly controversial when stated in simple language, I leave any past or potential debate of this particular essay to historians.[10] White's thesis is central, however, insofar as it relates to Sterk's argument, namely that, in order to create a comprehensive image of a nation, it

Figure 1.1 Wang Xiaoshuai's *Beijing Bicycle* (2001).

is often necessary to create a narrative around that image. In this case, Japanese film-makers in colonial Taiwan imagined romance between the coloniser and the colonised. This is how the film-maker creates a pattern of meaning and leaves this unique carving behind. *Eyes of the Buddha* is one of the many possible 'narrating vehicles' through which the story of Japanese colonialism on Taiwan can be told. In Tanaka King's film, the intimidating Buddha eyes warn the Chinese man not to get in the way of the 'heroic' Japanese occupiers. The Japanese soldier is not a hero as much as he is a romantic figure who is deemed acceptable by the Buddha.

A passage from the similarly themed novel *Buddha's Eyes* by Donald Moore (2002) describes the glowing eyes as fiery red rubies that instil fear in Yang, the protagonist of the novel: 'at the far end of the rotunda, in an alcove, Buddha sat on a stone pedestal, his eyes glowing as he looked directly at Yang. Yang was frozen in place. At any moment, he expected to hear Buddha's voice damning him for violating a sacred place' (Moore 6). The powerful image of Buddha's eyes is a narrative ploy that is meant to instil fear in those who might be thinking of rebelling and, in turn, minimise the chances of an uprising. The Japanese occupiers, meanwhile, are portrayed as romantic heroes who do not ever seem to infuriate the Buddha.[11]

Overall, it should be emphasised that the Japanese regime exploited the native Taiwanese population for their own film-making purposes from the late 1920s until the early 1940s. The industry did not allow Taiwanese actors or crew members to participate in the film-making process until the late 1920s. In fact, the first successful film to feature Taiwanese actors and to employ a Taiwanese crew was *Bloodstain* (Zhang Yuhe, 1929). The film's plot was simple yet universally appealing: a young woman and her lover venture into the mountains to seek revenge on her father's killer (Zhang and Xiao 48). Though the film was produced by the Taiwan Motion Picture Study Society and employed native Taiwanese actors and make-up artists, the Japanese controlled everything else related to the making of the film.

The Taiwan Motion Picture Production Office produced two further notable films in the 1930s: *Wu Feng the Righteous Man* (Ando Talo, Jiba Hiroki, 1932), the story of a Qing Dynasty official who saves people from the island aborigines, and *Map of the Seven Star Cave* (Jiba Hiroki, 1932). Though both films were labelled Japanese–Taiwanese co-productions, the Japanese continued to control nearly every aspect of the production process. Finally, *Sayun's Bell* (Hiroshi Shimizu, 1943) tells the (supposedly true) story of a young Taiwanese aboriginal girl named Sayun Hayun who falls from a bridge and dies while helping a Japanese policeman with his luggage. In reality, the facts surrounding this 'true event' remain mysterious. But the 'Sayun myth', as it came to be called, was a valuable tool for the Japanese regime. The film capitalised on the myth which was, in turn, an attempt to rally the general public by painting the girl as a martyr for the Japanese cause.[12]

Because the film industry in Taiwan was so heavily controlled and monitored by the Japanese colonists, it would be odd to refer to Japanese-produced cinema as Taiwanese cinema at all. The industry itself was seen as temporary, the quality of the screenwriting was poor, the scripts were censored, and the Japanese were hired to fill any roles requiring specialised skills. The definitional complexities continue even in the period after the fall of the Japanese empire. Restrictions on media output did not improve after World War II; in fact, arguably, they became worse. On 29 February 1947 protesters against the Kuomintang were killed and a period of extreme censorship began in the media industry. After 1949, during the Kuomintang era, the Nationalist government promoted so-called Healthy and Social Realist films, a genre intended to promote 'healthy' ideals while, at the same time, obscuring negative aspects of society, such as poverty and class jealousy (Zhang 133). Like the earlier Japanese imperial films, Healthy Realism was the product of a government that was interested in communicating a particular message: in this case, the message that cinema must remain an uncurious, unquestioning, innocuous medium. Gong Hong, the newly appointed head of Taiwan's Central Motion Picture Corporation in the early 1960s, planned a decided move away from the Taiwan/Japan co-production model in order to promote 'healthy cinema'. Pessimism, instigation of class jealousy, romance, and 'erroneous ideology' were disallowed (133). Chiang Kai-shek's regime was quick to ensure that cinema would not be used to probe historical or social tensions (Kellner n.p.). Though Taiwanese-language cinema was popular between 1955 and 1974, film genres themselves were restricted either to musicals or to traditional operas. Once television became popular in Taiwan in the mid-1960s, the Nationalist government deemed Mandarin the official language for all media. Throughout the 1970s and into the early 1980s, the Taiwanese film industry was forced to compete with the action-packed, highly successful Hong Kong martial arts genre. For the most part, artistic resistance came in the form of literature, rather than through images.[13]

Because of Taiwan's colonial past, film scholars struggle to situate its film history within the national/transnational critical framework. Guo-juin Hong, for example, asks how we might rethink this critical framework in the light of transnationalism. Unfortunately, the question itself is a bit of an anachronism. That is, though it is clear that the history of film-making in Taiwan is directly and undeniably intertwined with Japanese colonialism and the Nationalist party, it is less clear why the acknowledgement of these historical circumstances should require film scholars to revise their own critical frameworks. The struggle to situate the Taiwanese cinematic 'tradition' between 'not quite national' and 'not quite transnational' is a balancing act that can get the film scholar only so far. This is where Raymond Williams's conception of culture comes in handy: just as the Japanese colonist could not create films that accurately reflected the lives of Taiwanese natives, the film scholar cannot engage in meaningful critical inquiry in the midst of cultural bias. Culture is the product of unrestrained creativity, not maintenance of the status quo. The New Cinema directors arrive at a moment in which creativity begins.

In the early 1980s, Taiwan New Cinema film-makers sought to distance themselves from these entertainment- and propaganda-oriented genres entirely. Free from direct intervention from the government, Taiwan New Cinema directors succeeded in creating an entirely new genre – or 'tradition'. The genre carried over themes from the Taiwanese nativist literature of the 1960s and 1970s.[14] Cinematically, the aesthetic echoed with that of both the Italian neo-realist and French New Wave movements. For reasons of space, clarity, and simplicity, therefore, I begin my discussion of New Taiwanese cinema at the beginning of the 1980s, with the films of Hou Hsiao-hsien and Edward Yang. In the context of this book, the 'tradition' begins when Taiwan democratises. The Taiwanese cinematic tradition encompasses the Mandarin-language films of Taiwan and of Taiwanese-born directors.[15] One might very well argue that the phrase 'Mandarin-language cinema from Taiwan' is unnecessarily limiting. Ang Lee, after all, employs cast, crew and production teams from Hong Kong, the mainland, the United States and Taiwan. Lee's *Crouching Tiger Hidden Dragon* (2000), in particular, represents the move towards the internationalisation in Chinese-language cinema in that the spoken dialogue of the film itself consists of myriad accents and dialects. Still, the Mandarin-language cinema of Taiwan – as a distinct 'tradition' of world cinema – differs significantly from the Mandarin-language cinema of the mainland and elsewhere.

The decision to focus on Taiwanese cinema of the past thirty years is based on both historical (or contextual) and aesthetic (or textual) rationales.[16] From a historical perspective, the 1980s in Taiwan was a politically turbulent, yet exciting, decade. Within the span of about three years (1986–9), the Democratic Progressive Party (DPP) was established (1986) and President Chiang Ching-kuo abolished martial law (1987). The ending of martial law allowed for opposition parties to form, legally, for the first time in thirty-eight years (Neri 35).[17] In the 1980s, the Taiwanese film industry was resurrected, to a large extent, by directors who came to be associated with the Taiwanese New Wave movement; film-makers such as Hou Hsiao-hsien, Edward Yang, and Ang Lee (Neri 34–5). In 1984, Song Chuyu, the head of the Government Information Office, and a self-proclaimed film buff, established the Golden Horse International Film Festival, a move that was probably precipitated by feelings of competition with the Hong Kong film industry. Song proclaimed that film-makers in Taiwan should aim to create 'professional, artistic, international' cinema, and that the finished products should be sent to compete in international film festivals (Zhang 56).[18]

Unfortunately, when Hou declared his disdain for commercial film-making, domestic interest in his films declined substantially. In terms of ticket sales, Hou's 1989 film, *City of Sadness*, turned out to be one of the director's final box office successes in Taiwan (Curtin 97). The success of the Taiwanese film industry in the 1980s, therefore, was ephemeral. In retrospect, the first New Wave was not, in itself, an indicator of lasting change. In some ways, the movement is best described as a blip in the history of Taiwanese cinema. Nevertheless, the success of Taiwanese cinema in the 1980s has not been forgotten and it has certainly set a precedent. The films that were produced in Taiwan in the 1980s were noteworthy, overall, from an aesthetic standpoint. Taiwanese New Wave cinema (and later Second Wave cinema)[19] features restrained camera movement, elliptical (versus linear) storytelling, narrative reliance on long takes, and deep-focus shots. The protagonists of Taiwanese New Wave cinema are 'ordinary' people, not 'bigger-than-life' heroes (Zhang 57).[20]

Scholars such as Darrell Davis Williams have argued that Taiwan's long history of ambivalent politics has fostered a cinema that contains overwhelming amounts of sadness.[21] But, Williams is quick to add, sadness does not equal 'passive resignation' (5) within this type of cinema. On the contrary, Taiwan's 'cultural narratives' (as he refers to them) have become more interesting only as a result of the divisiveness and tension within modern-day Taiwanese society (5). Along similar lines, Mei Ling Wu argues that New Taiwan Cinema is based on an 'ethos of sadness', and that the industry is currently in an era of 'post-sadness', an endless cycle of entrapment, displacement and fruitless attempts at renewal (Sheldon and Yeh 77). While many films by Hou, Yang and Tsai are certainly 'sad', it would be inaccurate to label all contemporary Taiwanese cinema as sad, elliptical, dense and obscure. By failing to investigate or 'poke at' claims, such as Sophie La Serre's, that '. . . migration and identity crisis are the leitmotifs of Taiwanese filmmakers . . . between 1982 and today' (Neri 200), we risk painting the movement in unnecessarily broad strokes. Not all Taiwanese cinema is sad, especially not in the post-1990s industry. Luckily, many films (such as Arvin Chen's *Au revoir Taipei* and Doze Niu's *Monga*) express hope for renewal and change – for both the fate of the industry itself and for the image of a modern Taipei more generally.

Any rigorous analysis of national cinema should reflect discursive and cultural practices, gender, class and the like, as Robert Stam argues in his discussion of 'filmic nationalism' (290).[22] I take for granted the idea that national cinema is an ever-changing, phantasmic 'image' that cannot be pinpointed precisely. Regardless, one of the distinguishing points of contemporary Taiwanese cinema is its inimitable intertextual, hybrid nature. Even more specifically, it is fruitful, from a film studies standpoint, to describe and analyse Taiwanese film-makers' cross-cultural relationship with French and Italian cinema. The intent is not to argue that film-makers, such as Tsai Ming-liang or Hou Hsiao-hsien, are somehow indebted to earlier European cinema movements or that, somehow, this cross-cultural relationship is built upon imitation or any lack of creativity. On the contrary, the supposition is that all national cinema is also, and somewhat paradoxically, already transnational. Since the 1980s, Taiwanese film-makers have been influenced by Hollywood and by European cinema but to greater and lesser extents. By discussing examples of transcultural influence within specific films, I shall show that the Taiwanese context can be used as a model for rethinking the concept of transnationalism more generally.

There are significant cross-cultural currents that move between French and contemporary Taiwanese cinema. Tsai Ming-liang, one of the most well known (and notorious) of the Taiwanese art house directors, for example, is intrigued by Paris and, more specifically, the Paris of the 1950s and 1960s. It would be difficult to discuss Tsai's work without reference to the French New Wave movement auteurs, particularly François Truffaut. But Tsai is not simply nostalgic for the French New Wave nor does he care to recreate the movement. Fran Martin has argued that, despite Tsai's intertextual citation of François Truffaut's *The 400 Blows* (1959) throughout *What Time is it There?* (2001), Tsai is not simply lamenting a bygone era. The sophistication of the intertextuality eschews such a reading. Tsai's breadth of influence extends far beyond his European cinematic predecessors, extending to Hong Kong popular cinema, such as the Grace Chang musicals of the 1950s. This self-reflexivity – or 'double citation' as Martin calls it – can also be described as international fluidity or East–West hybridity.[23]

Despite the hybrid nature of other forms, the Sinophone, the Mandarin-language cinema of Taiwan, as a 'tradition' differs significantly from the Mandarin-language cinema of the mainland and elsewhere. Mainland Chinese films (unlike Taiwanese films) are produced within the constraints of the socialist system. As a result, directors who do not wish to produce their films underground are salaried by the state. The State Administration of Radio, Film, and Television and the Publicity Department have controlled the production and distribution of films since 1949. Though the Government Information Office 行政院新聞局 provides funding to the Taiwanese film industry, only a small number of Taiwanese films are distributed on the mainland. Taiwanese films are typically considered 'foreign' (one major exception being *Cape No. 7)*.

The tensions flow in the other direction as well. In 2010, for example, the Shanghai Film Festival had plans to showcase a large number of Taiwanese films as part of a Taipei film week. These plans were abandoned, however, when the Taipei Film Commission found out that festival brochures described the films' country of origin as 'Taiwan, China', and quickly pulled the films from the festival (Frater).

To remain competitive with film-makers in Taiwan, mainland Chinese film-makers have become extraordinarily resourceful. With the import of Hollywood and Hong Kong films into China after 1994, domestic studios on the mainland have felt intense pressure to 'keep up' with the Taiwanese and Hong Kong industries (McGrath 5). By the late 1990s, mainland directors were seeking liaisons with private film production companies and sharing labels with domestic studios to remain both relevant and viable (McGrath 6). As New Wave film-makers in Taiwan were coming together in the early 1980s, Fifth Generation (3) film-makers came together on the mainland. Mainland films must be backed by a domestic studio and will be distributed domestically only under an official studio label (McGrath 3). Fifth Generation directors, such as Zhang Yimou, Dai Sijie and Stanley Kwan, sought to meet the demands of audiences, domestically and internationally, working with regional studios to create aesthetically lush, psychological films with well-known actors. Zhang Yimou, for instance, achieved critical success with his film adaptation of Mo Yan's novel *Red Sorghum* (1987). Yimou's success provided an opening for other Fifth Generation film-makers such as Chen Kaige whose 1984 film *Yellow Earth* depicts 1930s-era Communism in the Shaanxi province. Both graduates of the Beijing Film Academy, Yimou's and Chen's films reflect the influence of their experiences as labourers[24] in the Cultural Revolution. In his essay 'Futures of Chinese Cinema: Technologies and Temporalities' (2009), Chris Berry explains that Fifth Generation films were successful in the global market for mainstream art house films because they 'translated' the story of the Cultural Revolution:

In the same way that national epics – with the Cultural Revolution as their centerpiece – helped Zhang Yimou and Chen Kaige to insert their work in to the global market for mainstream art films, modernistic thematic and aesthetic devices helped to position Taiwan New Cinema in the early to mid-1990s. (Berry 23)[25]

After the Tiananmen Square incident in 1989, the so-called Sixth Generation of mainland film makers (4) – Wang Xiaoshuai, Lou Ye, Zhang Wang and Jia Zhangke – began to produce films without state funding. Wang Xiaoshuai's 2001 film *Beijing Bicycle/Shiqisui de danche*, for example, reflects the concerns and aesthetics of Sixth Generation film-makers and their complex intertextual relationships with Italian neo-realism. This form of the 'Sino-Italian' differs significantly from the loose Sino-Italian intertextuality that we find in Edward Yang's *Terrorizers*. In the first scene of Wang's film, a country boy named Guo Lian-Guei (played by Cui Lin) lands his 'dream job' as one of the FeiDa mail couriers. As a newcomer to the city, Guei is infatuated with the concrete skyscrapers and hordes of people who populate the streets of Beijing. He is also incredibly stubborn – a characteristic that remains consistent throughout the course of the movie. He is motivated, overall, by his desire to make enough deliveries to cover the cost of the bike. The bike is, for Guei, a ticket to wealth and success – the key to a new identity. As long as the bike is in his possession, he will not have to wake up from the capitalist dream that allows him access into these mysterious skyscrapers, into the secret, decadent lives of the privileged class.

For film-makers of the Sixth Generation, certain themes seem to stand out: the divide between rich and poor; the rural versus the urban; and the lure of capitalism. Because Sixth Generation film-makers are often required to produce their projects without the support of the Chinese government, the resulting films tend to be made quickly and without expensive equipment. This is, in part, why the cinematic style of the Sixth Generation – the preference for hand-held cameras, a non-linear narrative, and a documentary-like feel – has also been compared with Italian neo-realism and with the French New Wave. Mainland director Jia Zhangke, for instance, has cited French New Wave director Robert Bresson as one of his central influences.

But Wang is more reluctant than Jia to cite specific influences. Film buffs will already have noticed that the plot of *Beijing Bicycle* is highly reminiscent of Vittorio De Sica's Italian neo-realist film *Bicycle Thieves*: in both stories, a man from the country comes to the 'big city' (in De Sica's film it is Rome) to look for work. On the first day of the job, the man's bike is stolen by a thief, a fact that results in the man's loss of his livelihood and sense of self-worth. Both films highlight the unjust disparities that exist between socioeconomic classes in the context of modern urban life, and both are filmed in a social-realist style.

Figure 1.2   De Sica's *Bicycle Thieves* (1949).

Interestingly, Wang denies that there is a relationship between this film and De Sica's despite his acknowledgement that De Sica's film is 'very, very famous', and that some people, who were working for him at the time, were worried about 'stealing' from it.[26] While it is unclear why Wang did not wish to associate himself with Italian neo-realism in this particular interview, Sixth Generation film-makers such as Wang do not want to appear to be copying from others, and this worry is justified. To develop a unique cinematic style, he must seek independence from government funding. As an 'underground' direc- tor and a voice for the under-represented majority, Wang aims to create films that will resonate, first and foremost, with domestic audiences.

Wang's film contains the same sense of crisis, the same realism that perme- ated De Sica's film. Though the action of Wang's film is motivated specifically by the loss of Guei's bike, the bike itself functions as an emblem within the narrative, allowing specific aspects of Chinese modernity to peak through. The film begins in realist, documentary style, as potential mail couriers are being interviewed on-camera for a position in the FeiDa courier company. The disembodied voice of a woman interrogates a series of male candidates, none of whom is older than his late teens. The men appear both nervous and

unsure about their responses, worried that their young age and lack of experience might disqualify them from the job. One man claims that he was once
a farmer; another man claims that he was once a radio disc jockey. Luckily,
despite their nervousness, all the men are hired as couriers. The boss warns the
men that 'their image is our [the company's] image' and that they must now
think of themselves as 'the courier pigeons of today'.

The scene is reminiscent of Jean-Luc Godard's French New Wave film
Masculin Féminin: specifically, the interview scene with Miss 19, a beauty
queen and 'typical' young French woman of the 1960s. Miss 19 – and the scene
more generally – is introduced with the somewhat unflattering title: 'Dialogue
with a Consumer Product'. Miss 19 herself is an object of consumption, something to be ogled and devoured by the Marx and Coca-Cola generation. 'Once
I was chosen', she comments, 'everything changed.' The reporter continues:
'What is more important – a car or a diploma?' 'Well, I have both now,' she
replies.[27] Similarly, in the context of Wang's film, even though the bike couriers
are given the impression that they have been chosen, specially, for their roles
in the company, they have been co-opted by the FeiDa Company as consumer
products. Like Miss 19, they are the representatives of a carefully manipulated
corporate image. Though they have been given the opportunity to enter the
capitalist workforce, they have entered an increasingly exclusionary urban
space that does not welcome members of the lower class into its inner ranks. If
Godard's Miss 19 character critiques a certain brand of watered-down, mass-
market feminism, Wang's protagonists critique mass-market populism. That
is, though there is a real divide between rich and poor, this divide is often not
as easy to perceive as one might think. Often, the dichotomy between rich and
poor is exaggerated by those in the middle, and by those who are desperate to
project a false veneer of success.

As a representation of post-Mao era Beijing that reaches the level of parody
at times, it is no surprise that *Beijing Bicycle* was, upon its release, censored
by the Chinese government. In the film, the contrast between rich and poor
is expressed in stark terms, and the decadence of the elite is fully exposed.
Furthermore, Wang has been unafraid to express his own opinion about modern-day Beijing. In an interview about the film, Wang stated candidly: 'The
system in China right now has a lot of holes, and a lot of people seem to be
struggling to find their own way . . . stubbornness is what oftentimes gets them
through. It's certainly a common characteristic a lot of peasants have, and in
the big city, it helps them survive' (Tang, n.p.). Before 1 January 2008, Chinese
labourers had minimal protections from the corporations that employed them.
The passage of the law ushered in a new age of written contracts, severance
pay and, in general, less systematic abuse of low-paid labourers on the mainland. As *Daily Beast* writer Jonathan Adams reported just a month after the
passage of the law:

> They [the Chinese government] realized the sources of the discontent: the cleavage between urban and rural, employed and unemployed, the domestic versus the export sector. At the turn of the twenty-first century, then, Beijing was not a particularly pleasant place to work, especially as a rural-born labourer. The lack of written contracts (合同) meant a lack of accountability on the part of corporations; and, as we can see in the film, agreements between employees and employers were often verbal. (Adams, n.p.)

The films of both De Sica and Wang feature unflattering depictions of a variety of social institutions: churches, bordellos, the backs of stores, and cramped workplaces. Both films take place, predominantly, on the streets. The spaces that the characters inhabit are dingy and alienating, and the streets of the city are always filmed in a fragmented way so that, as viewers, we are in a constant state of disorientation. In Wang's film, the wealthy Beijing citizens are clearly cordoned off from the lower classes. Or at least, this is the image that they would like to project. In one particularly noteworthy scene, Guei and his friend are spying on a rich woman from behind the wall of the friend's food stall. The men are impressed, not only by the woman's beauty and elegance, but by her seemingly endless supply of dresses and wardrobe changes. This scene is interesting, in particular, because it functions as a sort of unrealistic, dream-like sequence in an otherwise very realistic film. The cuts within the scene highlight the fantastic aspects of the woman as well as the subjective nature of the men's perspective. To Guei and his friend, the woman behind the glass appears exotic and magical like a rare and beautiful bird at the zoo. She is not real but rather a symbol of the sort of lifestyle these men imagine the wealthy class to possess. And yet, despite their wonder and awe, this is *not* the sort of lifestyle that these men desire for themselves. Guei's friend, for instance, comments that he has heard a rumour that, in modern hotel bathrooms, classical music pipes through the speaker system. Though he is clearly impressed by the notion of a musical lavatory, he states, nevertheless, that, if he were ever to find himself in that situation, he would be too distracted to pee.

As it turns out, in fact, the woman behind the glass is only an image. She is not wealthy at all; rather, she was hired to work for a wealthy woman but is fired when the woman finds out that she was trying on all her fancy clothes. Wang's film reminds us, again and again, that first impressions are often mistaken; people are often not as they seem. Mirrors, glass and even the camera lens itself can play tricks on the eye. As in Yang's *Taipei Story* and *Terrorizers*, reflective surfaces become a motif that appears throughout Wang's film, signifying the beautiful yet alienating and empty world of the Beijing upper class. At one point in the film, Guei attempts to enter into a fancy hotel through a revolving glass door so that he can deliver a package. As he stares at the mechanisms of the door in awe, the door makes a full spin and pulls him back around to the outside of the hotel. Guei is so ingenuous, in other words, that he is unfamiliar with the common technology of modern-day urban space. He comes from another world and he is unprepared for the harsh, unforgiving and overexposed nature of life in twenty-first-century Beijing.

Wang's film is not so much a critique of post-Mao decadence in contemporary China as it is a critique of the illusion of decadence in post-Mao China. Though the distinctions between classes are often exaggerated (especially by those who have the capacity to flaunt their wealth), these distinctions often turn out to be little more than an illusion. At first, we are led to believe that the person who steals Guei's bike must be a low-life criminal. Then we are shocked to see that the thief is a clean-cut schoolboy. Finally, we come to realise that all our assumptions up to this point are mistaken because the schoolboy did not steal the bike himself – rather, he bought the stolen bike at a flea market and was ignorant of the fact that it had been stolen in the first place.

Though the schoolboy, Jian (Bin Li), is clean cut, wears a suit, and possesses an air of aristocracy, he has a less than ideal family life. Though he appears rich and well-to-do, we find that he is not as different from Guei as we were initially led to believe. His father is too poor to buy him a bike which is why he secretly obtained it in the first place. He is, furthermore, eager to impress a pretty girl named Xiao (Yuanyuan Gao). By constantly shifting our expectations and preconceptions throughout the course of the film, Wang encourages his viewers to look beyond superficialities and first impressions in order to seek out the motives behind a person's actions. For the characters in Wang's film, objects and other material forms of wealth cannot bring happiness. Though good relationships between family members, friends and loved ones are the key to a fulfilling life, these relationships are frequently overlooked in the struggle to survive on a day-to-day basis. Wang is unafraid to use the film as a rhetorical tool for this heavy-handed, moralistic message: 'if you are stubborn, you will have a greater chance of getting what you want. If you are willing to let people take advantage of you, you will remain oppressed.' This message is, in fact, common among Sixth Generation film-makers. In his book *Painting the City Red: Chinese Cinema and the Urban Contract* (2010), Yomi Braester describes the films of the Sixth Generation as platforms for politically charged messages and sites of rebellion. Many of these films, Braester comments: 'focus on marginalized subcultures and self-marginalizing counter-cultures, including juvenile delinquents . . . to present the city as the battleground between oppressive collectivity and rebellious individuals' (Braester 242). In many ways, Braester's description of Sixth Generation cinema echoes André Bazin's description of Italian neo-realism as a movement that 'reacted ideologically to the control and censorship of the pre-war cinema' (Bazin 19–20). Wang (as a so-called Sixth Generation film-maker) and De Sica (as a so-called neo-realist film-maker) do share similar qualities. Both directors endow their films with a sense of urgency which is presented in a joltingly real, yet meditative, style. Each director, moreover, uses film to expose the ugly underbelly of society, to uncover the shadows that are often hidden from view. There is joy as well as sadness in the lives of everyday urban citizens, and those in the wealthy class are not as isolated from all of this ugliness as they might have us believe.

Stylistically, Sixth Generation films tend to be political – edgy' even – with a focus on the divide between rich and poor. The controversial nature of these films has meant that film-makers such as Zhang and Wang are banned from screening their films domestically, even to this day (Zhen 265). Luckily, as they have continued to gain exposure internationally (5) many Sixth Generation film-makers have been able to secure joint ventures, procure funding from outside sources, and distribute their films worldwide. Unlike Fifth Generation film-makers, who found success in the global market because of their skill with lavish storytelling, Taiwan New Cinema film-makers found success because they captured and 'translated' the modernist aesthetic of 1980s Taiwan. New Wave film-makers, such as Edward Yang, Te-Chen Tao, Chen Kunhuo and Hou Hsiao-hsien, were provided with government capital to compete with the Hong Kong industry. Hou's *City of Sadness* (1989), which depicted the 228 Incident (a massacre of thousands of native Taiwanese after the takeover by the Kuomintang in 1947), was the first film in the history of Taiwanese cinema to take on such a sensitive subject. The government-funded revival of the industry was a success, though short-lived. By the early 1990s, the First New Wave was already declared 'over' as Second New Wave directors, such as Tsai Ming-liang and Ang Lee, gained both national and international recognition.

Since the end of the 1990s, joint ventures and cross-cultural exchanges have been occurring with increasing regularity between Taiwanese cinema on the one hand and French and Italian cinema on the other. Bloom's term 'Sino-French cinema' describes films in which 'France' and 'China'[28] can be said to 'interact', where the term 'interact' can refer to citation, setting, financial collaboration or thematic resonance more generally. We may quickly run into a definitional problem, however, when using the term 'Sino-French' to describe interactions that may be either text based (within the text) or paratextual (outside of the text). We should be careful not to conflate external political constraints with directorial choices. To distinguish the textual from the paratextual, we must first answer some basic questions: what makes a film 'hybrid' or transnational in the first place? After all, films that appear transnational at first glance often carry nationalist agendas, and vice versa.

The definitional problems arise again when we consider the fact that 'Sino' in this context can refer either to Taiwan or to the mainland. Though we might not have an issue with defining 'Sinophone' as Mandarin-language cinema, we still need a way to differentiate between Sinophone cinema from Taiwan and

Sinophone cinema from the mainland. Shu-mei Shih's definition does not work here either because, according to Shih, Sinophone includes other regions of the Chinese diaspora outside the mainland. The textual and contextual distinctions between Sixth Generation and New Wave Taiwanese film-makers are pronounced. It would therefore seem that we need more – not less – precise ways to define transnational, hybrid and diaspora cinemas. As my research continues, therefore, my own definition of the terms 'Sino-French' and 'Sino-Italian' cinema – as subgenres of hybrid cinema – are in a constant state of transformation and renovation.

Though not as constrained politically, art house film-makers in Taiwan must also turn to international sources to fund their projects. Like Sixth Generation directors, therefore, Taiwanese art house directors create films that possess a certain level of international appeal. This is no accident, of course. Unlike film-makers on the mainland, such as Wang, who have flatly denied the influence of European cinema on their work, Taiwanese film-makers, such as Tsai Ming-liang and Hou Hsiao-hsien, openly acknowledge their allegiance to earlier national cinema movements such as the French New Wave and Italian neo-realism (McGrath 7). Besides export potential, there is also import potential. The Taipei Film Commission is actively inviting foreign film-makers to visit Taipei to shoot their movies (9). Arvin Chen's *Au revoir Taipei* is, again, one instance of this type of import. Chen travelled to Taipei from California to film an 'authentic' film about Taiwan that would also be seen by international audiences. When the film became a modest success, the arrangement turned out to be beneficial for the Taiwanese industry, for Chen and for the film itself.[29]

Overall, since the democratisation of the political landscape in Taiwan, Taiwanese cinema has become internationally fluid. In Taiwan, film-makers have realised that to make money, or at least, to strike even, they must make films to suit the tastes of domestic audiences (Su 109). Despite and, perhaps, because of the enthusiasm of international audiences, domestic audiences have begun to feel alienated. Su Chui-hong, a reporter for the contemporary periodical *Panorama Taiwan* recently observed: 'Ever since *A City of Sadness* won a Golden Lion award at the Venice Film Festival in 1989, top Taiwanese filmmakers turned increasingly to art house cinema that alienated mainstream tastes . . . hardly any genre films or mainstream commercial films were made during this time [between 1989 and 2008]' (Su 102–3). Film-makers who do not wish to be cursed with the 'art house' label must secure funding from domestic sources to produce mainstream commercial films (Ma 83). A negative audience response can be measured in terms of poor box office revenue. It is possible to calculate the formula for box office success. Film-makers and producers in Taiwan have, in fact, studied the Hollywood model to see how to sell films and reached an agreement on a formula that will predict success (dubbed the 'Midas formula') (Su 103).

When *Cape No. 7* was released in Taiwan in 2008, mainstream audiences responded with enthusiasm. The film was a surprise hit, encouraging once-alienated audiences to return to the cinema. Chu Wen-ching, director of the Government Information Office in Taiwan, has proudly declared that *Cape No. 7* was successful precisely because of the film's appeal to local viewers. The success of the film, proclaimed Chu, was a rare example of localisation winning out over globalisation. *Cape No. 7* had the requisite 'Midas formula': grass-roots appeal, a contemporary setting, and a link to Taiwanese colonial history. Part of the formula involves creating hype about upcoming releases with the help of new media: posting 'making-of' footage on Internet sites and blogs or holding limited advanced screenings (Su 109). For the popular media, the success of Te's film has served as proof that film-makers must appeal to local tastes to do well domestically.

Yet none of these facts or formulas seems to answer the key question: *why* does auteur cinema fare so poorly with audiences in Taiwan? The answer to this question can, of course, be related to an image problem. Even the French New Wave movement waned in popularity by as early as 1965 when French audiences began to desire commercial, bigger-budget films (Lanzoni 239). Auteurs tend to serve an important reactionary function within the broader media landscape. With mainstream audiences, on the other hand, dense and obscure film-making tends to be viewed in a negative light. Auteurs are popularly (and often justifiably) viewed as paternalistic coddlers of their celluloid 'babies' – an image that can often work against them.

We do have a practical sense of *why* these films are struggling: the Taiwanese government is often unwilling to provide funding to film-makers and, just as often, French/European distributors are happy to pick up the production costs (Ma 83). Yet even explanations such as these do not explain why the Taiwanese youth would not support the efforts of Taiwanese film-makers or pay to see their films. We still do not know why, exactly, the movement is viewed so negatively 'at home' and, on the other hand, why these films are so readily accepted in the international art house scene.[30] Why are film-makers such as Tsai and Hou really viewed as 'box office poison' (Ma 9) as Jean Ma and others claim? Are young people in Taiwan simply looking for light-hearted Friday night entertainment and don't want to be bored or saddened? Is this an anti-intellectual reaction?

There is a small, concentrated group of auteurs in Taiwan, and their appeal does depend, to some extent, on their ability to secure international funding and to work within the frame of the 'transnational co-production' model. The very existence of these auteurs does depend largely on their international appeal. On the other hand, I would be hesitant to argue that any sort of 'anti-intellectual' sentiment among Taiwanese audiences is the sole cause for Tsai's and Hou's box office failures. At the very least, this explanation is too simplistic. A few of the directors themselves have stated, in clear terms, that they are not concerned with catering to mass audiences. These declarations of disdain certainly contribute to the poisonous cycle that appears to surround the industry. Yet such an explanation would still fail to account for directors such as Ang Lee who studied in the United States and has achieved enormous box office success in Taiwan and abroad. One might argue, of course, that this process 'naturally' occurs in most national cinema movements, not just in Taiwan. But, while the French New Wave movement is over fifty years old and Italian neo-realism is approaching seventy, the process is occurring in Taiwan right now, at this very moment. Certainly, to remain viable, Taiwanese cinema will need to continue to please domestic audiences. But the Taiwan example represents a new model for thinking about transnational cinema more generally. Film scholars will need to reconsider the notion of national cinema. These are changes that sprouted in the 1980s, shifted in the early 2000s, and continue to this day.

In his recent book, *Taiwan Cinema: A Contested Nation on Screen*, Gou-Juin Hong describes the Taiwanese film industry as both 'a film history without film' and 'a national cinema without nation' (18). These statements might sound puzzling – if not downright oxymoronic – to those who are unfamiliar with the contemporary discourse that currently surrounds Taiwan cinema studies. How can film history exist when there are no films to study? How can a national cinema exist where there is no nation? Hong's description of Taiwanese cinema as 'a film history without film' – a somewhat figurative expression – can actually be understood in a quite literal sense: early cinema imported from China into Taiwan was regularly censored and confiscated by the Japanese. Similarly, when the Nationalist party took over the Taiwanese commercial film industry, studios churned out close to 373 state-funded educational films and newsreels (Lim and Ward 97).

In his recent essay, 'National Cinema as Translocal Practice: Reflections on Chinese Film Historiography', Yinjing Zhang notes that the nearly two thousand Taiwanese dialect films (*Taiyu pian*) that were produced between 1955 and 1981 were suppressed by Taiwan's Nationalist government. It was not until 1990 that the Chinese Taipei film archive made a concerted effort to 'rescue' these lost dialect films (Lim and Ward 20).[31] In a very literal sense, therefore, the industry was 'without film' because so many of the archives were repressed and even erased from existence.

The setbacks that the Taiwanese industry faced were also related to its proximity to more successful film industries. Throughout the twentieth century, Japanese, Hong Kong, and mainland cinema were technologically sophisticated and attracted name-brand talent. For decades, the Taiwanese film industry was neglected and received little or no funding, while Hong Kong's film industry gained momentum and thrived (Udden 145). James Udden, in his chapter in Hjort and Petrie's edited volume *The Cinema of Small Nations* provides one possible reason for these setbacks: 'Taiwan may function, act, and in many ways thrive like a small 'nation' should, but most countries in the world do not recognize the island as an independent nation out of geopolitical obsequiousness toward its neighbouring behemoth, the People's Republic of China' (144).[32] In other words, despite Taiwan's antagonistic status toward the PRC, other countries do not dare to risk their own relationships with China. The international community does not, and will not, officially recognise Taiwan as an independent entity. Among a host of other problems that this lack of recognition may cause, one problem is that it becomes difficult to define Taiwanese cinema as the tradition of an independent nation. We can begin to see why Hong describes the industry in such oxymoronic terms. In many ways, Taiwan is still facing an identity crisis as Darrel William Davis points out in *Cinema Taiwan*. Hong's second statement, that Taiwanese cinema is a 'national cinema without nation', can therefore be understood in literal terms as well. For Hong, the ambiguity of Taiwan's geopolitical status means that the films which are produced on the island cannot ever be defined in terms of the national cinema model.

Despite the cogency of Hong's statements, there are ways around this definitional nightmare. We could still define the parameters of Taiwanese New Cinema, if we were so inclined. Where does it begin? The movement begins more or less with the anthology *In Our Time* in 1983 and ends with the dismantling of the film constitution only a few years later. The Second Wave movement begins soon after as both Hou and Yang tweak their style while Tsai Ming Liang and Ang Lee enter on to the Taiwanese stage, and subsequently, into the international psyche. Of course, we might not want to move in that direction either. The national cinema model is itself a hotly contested notion. Song Hwee Lim, in his essay 'Six Chinese Cinemas in Search of a Historiography', notes: '. . . the very model of national cinema has been vigorously challenged in the discipline of film studies in recent years, to the extent that any usage of the model almost invariably brings with it an apology' (Lim and Ward 35). This scepticism surrounding the national cinema model is present in all areas of film studies, not just in the small field of Taiwanese film studies.[33] And yet, even if we were to accept the 'hotly contested' national cinema model, we might still remain unable to define Taiwanese cinema in terms of one clear tradition. Because Taiwan is still considered a part of greater China by the Republic of China, the Taiwanese film industry is lost in a dark political limbo.

The questions that arise as a result of Taiwan's politically precarious situation do not have easy answers. How can a set of films even exist that: (a) belong to a national cinematic tradition, and (b) have no connection to any nation? Either, it would seem, we should define national cinematic tradition according to a designated set of rules – and stick with that definition – or we should refuse to do so. Further, how can we enter into the discussion if we are uncertain about whether or not national cinema can be discussed as a viable category in the first place? If Taiwan can be said to have a national cinematic tradition, then that cinema cannot be without 'nation'. On the other side, if we are inclined to deny that Taiwan should be defined as a nation, then shouldn't we conclude that there is no such thing as Taiwanese national cinema?[34]

As these questions show, there is a variety of problems that begin to arise when attempting to define Taiwanese cinema as a 'tradition'. The cinema of Taiwan has become a paradox unto itself – transnational yet national simultaneously – a hybrid of East Asian and Western cinematic traditions.

In the Taiwanese industry, the dichotomy between 'director-based' films and commercially viable films is emphasised to an exaggerated extent. Ostensibly, this exaggerated dichotomy stems from two separate desires on the part of film-makers. Art house film-makers in Taiwan are largely dependent on international distributors for funding, and the resulting films are aimed at international audiences. On the other hand, commercially viable films in Taiwan tend to be produced *without* the potential for international export in mind. But this dichotomy is not as clear-cut as this brief summary might make it appear. Through textual studies and close readings of particular films, I argue that, although this opposition between art house and commercial film may be very 'real' in financial terms, there is no clear boundary between the transnational and the national within the bounds of any particular cinematic text.

My discussion of Taiwanese cinema also resonates with Raymond Williams's definition of culture as both a 'whole way of life' (Williams xviii) and as a mode of interpreting and sharing a common human experience:

> The idea of culture describes our common inquiry, but our conclusions are diverse, as our starting points were diverse. The word, culture, cannot automatically be pressed into service as any kind of social or personal directive . . . The arguments which can be grouped under its heading do not point to any inevitable action or affiliation. They define, in a common field, approaches and conclusions. (Williams 295)

This definition of culture is relevant in two ways: first, Williams's definition emphasises the idea that culture cannot be forced on to a society; culture cannot be used as a tool for shaping society in one direction or another. Though critical inquiry can certainly be built around the notion of culture, we must be willing to revise and rework our modes of inquiry as historical conditions change. I am fond of Williams's definition for a second, more general reason: his notion of culture allows for variation in scholarly approach. Film scholars should not be required to identify with one culture over another in an effort to produce meaningful analysis. Critical inquiry, in other words, encompasses the 'cultural' but is not defined by it.

If, as Williams asserts, culture cannot be shaped, then it certainly cannot be forced. The problem of 'forced culture' arises when we attempt to define Taiwan's early cinematic period. Because Taiwan's mass media were controlled by the Japanese for the first half of the twentieth century, we may question the sense in which these early films can be described as 'Taiwanese' at all. At the same time, Japan's colonial presence shaped the Taiwanese film industry, and the influence extends into the twenty-first century. In this sense, it would be a mistake to ignore the effects of the Japanese empire on the national psyche and, most importantly, on the film-makers who reacted – and continue to react – to that experience.

CONTEMPORARY DEBATES, THEORETICAL CONSIDERATIONS

The tensions which exist in the current transnational/national cinema debate are not readily solvable. No longer eager to divide global cinema by hemisphere, continent or region, many film scholars embrace the language of postmodernity and the postcolonial to unite common themes within contemporary cinema. Analysis of postcolonial, diaspora and Third World cinema often goes hand in hand with themes such as alienation, displacement and temporal fracture. When beginning this volume, I was inspired by film scholar Gilberto Perez's definition of cinema in the most general of terms. In his 2002 book *The Material Ghost*, Perez eloquently describes all cinema as a 'space of representation' (17), a space in which the images that appear in front of us are neither reproductions nor illusions of reality. The images on the screen, rather, are constructions that are derived – and yet remain simultaneously distinct – from reality. For Perez, cinema can be thought of as 'a parallel realm that may look recognizably like reality but that nobody could mistake for it' (17). Perez's definition of cinema is appealing in that it rests neatly between the material and the illusory. Though 'cinematic reality' parallels so-called 'material reality', one is never muddled by the other.[35]

Realising the full implications of Perez's definition of cinema creates tension from the perspective of a comparatist and a 'transnationalist', for many reasons. If we are to think of cinema as a distinct reality that is separate from our own, we cannot argue that cinema flawlessly reflects history or national discourse. At the same time, we certainly cannot argue that cinema is not in any way constructed and derived from the reality of history or national discourse. This paradox often rears its head in contemporary film scholarship. In my own analysis of Taiwanese cinema, I seek to find the balance, so to speak, between fragmentation and unity. As Perez points out, the perceived unity of an object (that which we are studying) does not imply the unity of the perceiving subject (the person who is studying) (5). Of course, the reverse holds true as well: the perceived unity of one's own subjectivity does not imply the unity of an object. If we were to discuss 'displacement in contemporary Hong Kong cinema', for example, our analysis should not rest entirely on viewing Hong Kong as a 'fragmented object' but it also cannot assume that Hong Kong is not a 'fragmented space' in any sense of the term. Likewise, though it would be difficult comprehensively to analyse Wong Kar-wai's *In the Mood for Love* (2000) without knowing anything about 1950s Hong Kong, it would be a shame to assume that we would not be able to analyse the film unless we learned perfect Cantonese.

Though the question: 'what is the "transnational" in film studies?' may sound basic, the literature that has been written in response is anything but precise or definitive. 'Transnational cinema' is an imperfect term that requires constant retooling and reassessment, especially as it relates to Taiwanese cinema. 'National cinema', as the term stands in recent scholarship, tends to be viewed as a 'problematic' category, whereas 'transnational cinema' is viewed as more inclusive (mainly because the term is meant to take global and local factors into account) (Choi 310).[36] Because Taiwan is not fully independent, this categorisation process becomes even more problematic. More generally, there are at least four central problems that continue to arise, that continue to test the strength of the 'national cinema' studies frame, and that have yet to be resolved. One primary concern is the question of whether or not film narratives position viewers vis-à-vis any one national discourse.

For example, in their introduction to *Theorising National Cinema* (2007), Vitali and Willeman pose the question: '[do film narratives] position viewers in the historical force-field that is "the nation?"' (7). For Vitali and Willeman, this question goes hand in hand with three further worries: (1) do films 'reflect' or 'stage' national discourse? (2) must we assume that these films reflect/stage the dominant ideologies within nations at given times in history? (7), and (3) despite compelling reasons to think otherwise, why do we tend to assume that the term 'national cinema' implies coherence, especially coherence as it relates to reception and production within 'legal borders' (Vitali and Willemen 17). Here Vitali and Willemen accurately describe the basic worries associated with the 'national cinema' model. But both they, and we, have yet to clarify the simplest of all concerns: are 'national' and 'transnational' cinemas related, overlapping, or entirely separate? Because these highly problematic issues continue to arise again and again, the rejection of 'national cinemas' as self-contained categories might initially appear advisable, or even necessary – especially in relation to a 'non-separated' nation such as Taiwan. If, then, cinema scholars are no longer willing to accept 'national cinemas' as relatively coherent 'bodies of textuality' (Vitali and Willemen 18), it would appear obvious that we need an entirely new modus operandi. One plausible alternative would be to describe international cinemas (the case of Taiwan included) as 'situated but universal' (240), locally produced but globally consumed. Because cinema has the capacity to cross national borders in a cultural, psychological, collabora- tive and literal sense, we might assume that all cinemas (provided that a film is able to be viewed in a country other than the one in which it is produced) should be labelled 'trans-national'.

But I would warn against such a conclusion. I worry that an outright rejec- tion of 'the national' risks losing an important mode of analysis. As Chris Berry aptly states in his essay 'From National Cinema to Cinema and the National: Chinese-Language Cinema and Hou Hsiao Hsien's "Taiwan Trilogy"', 'to turn away from the national in the current era is to confuse deconstruction with destruction' (Vitali and Willemen 154). In an effort to move beyond black-and-white thinking and to avoid the 'national cinemas' paradigm alto- gether, film scholars invent alternative theoretical frameworks. While these alternative modes of analysis are often useful, they carry their own risks. At best, theories that reject 'the national' entirely lead towards an impractical approach and, at worst, they disrupt remaining possibilities for the grounded discussion of Taiwanese cinema specifically and world cinema more generally.

Will Higbee's article, 'Beyond the (Trans) national: Towards a Cinema of Transvergence in Postcolonial and Diasporic Francophone Cinema(s)' (2007), exemplifies this type of risky approach. Higbee argues for a move beyond 'the national' *and* 'the transnational' to a new mode that he calls a 'cinema of trans- vergence' (79). Adopting Marcus Novak's concept of 'transvergence'[37] and Deleuze and Guattari's concept of the 'rhizome', Higbee argues that (trans) national, postcolonial, and diasporic cinemas can be better described without reliance on 'binaries' or strict categories. But Higbee admits that he is not offering an alternative to the notion of the 'trans-national', only a new 'posi- tionality'. Someone who is uncommitted to the concept of transvergence might wonder: why *not* offer an alternative approach if the current modes of analysis are not particularly descriptive or helpful? Furthermore, one might see points of contradiction within this type of non-committal argument. The basic problem lies in the following question: are 'the national' and 'the transnational' two separate concepts? Either they are distinct concepts or they are not but they cannot be both. If, as Higbee initially argues, they are separate concepts, both on either side of an unhelpful binary, it makes little sense to make statements such as: 'it [my study] will also attempt to go "beyond" the (trans) national to evaluate current theorizing around the idea of "transnational" cinema and its potentially problematic relationship to contemporary notions of globalization . . .' (80) Higbee's statement appears to negate the overall point that the binary national/transnational exists. By placing the 'trans' in parentheses, Higbee implicitly suggests that either the 'trans' could be imagined to be in the state- ment or not, and that whether it is or not is of little importance.

This specific confusion seems to be a wide-scale problem that extends beyond the confines of Higbee's article. In their introduction to *Futures of Chinese Cinemas* (2009), Olivia Khoo and Sean Metzger refer to 'the transnational' as a 'cognate' of the national: '. . . this volume argues for an engagement with time and technology that is limited neither to the discourse of the nation nor its *cognates* (the transnational) and ostensible antecedents (empire)' (13, my emphasis). The use of the word 'cognate' in this particular context is unclear. Do Khoo and Metzger simply mean to say that the term 'transnational' contains the word 'national' within it, or that these two words carry the same meaning but come from different origins? I would argue that these two terms are not cognates at all, though they are also not opposites. Because so much is at stake when we analyse films in terms of national discourse and/ or global forces, we must be careful to avoid conflation or opaque terminology wherever possible. Because I am wary of rejecting one unsatisfactory paradigm in favour of another, I agree with Higbee when he points out that scholars such as Sheldon Lu[38] are too quick to elevate 'the transnational' in an effort to move away from the 'messy business'[39] of national cinema. But Higbee does not fully explain why national cinema became such a 'messy business' in the first place. Does the study of 'national cinemas' necessarily entail the study of dominant ideologies or hegemonies?

In the introduction to his comprehensive volume, *Taiwan Cinema: A Contested Nation On Screen*, Guo-hui Hong asks a similar question in the context of the Taiwanese cinematic tradition:

> With Taiwan's film history deeply imbricated with its multiple colonial histories and international politics, how can the critical framework of the national, suspended and sustained at the same time by the political, yield a productive revision of Taiwan's 'national' film history under transnational influences? (5)

Implicit in Hong's question is the idea that transnational 'influences' lead to revisions of the national cinema model. Earlier film critics, however, did not tend to insist that national cinemas, as bodies of textuality, must be temporally and geographically fixed. For instance, in his 1942 book on German cinema, *From Caligari to Hitler*, Siegfried Kracauer argues that national cinema does not reflect a 'fixed national character', only that films are prone to reflect: 'collective dispositions or tendencies as prevail with a nation at a certain stage of its development' (8). Kracauer thought only that dominant ideological discourse tends to become noticeable in the cinema of a nation when that nation is in crisis.[40] German expressionism, for instance, could be said to reflect a deep-seated psychological reaction against Nazi propaganda in the period leading up to World War II. But Kracauer never maintained that national cinema always reflects the collective mentality or disposition of a nation. Similarly, Taiwanese New Wave cinema emerged at a time of massive change (but not necessarily crisis) for Taiwan, a period in which productivity increased as restrictions on the media loosened. In this sense, the New Wave reflects a deep-seated reaction against the silence surrounding Japanese colonialism and the subsequent KMT-ruled government.

Rather than argue that 'national cinema' has always existed in some pure form, then, it might be simpler to toss the coin and argue that the notion of transnationalism and border-crossing have always been endemic to the cinema. After all, as Higbee points out, even the French pioneers of cinema, such as the Lumière brothers, knew that cross-national circulation of their films was important to their success.[41] When we concede that transnational cinema has always existed in some form or another, however, we must further concede that the term 'transnational' is close to meaningless (Higbee 80).[42] It would likewise seem difficult to ascertain that there was a distinct period of time in which national cinemas reigned. It seems like faulty reasoning to assert both that 'the transnational' has always existed and also that 'the transnational' is a relatively new paradigm for studying and thinking about film. For this reason, it may not be feasible to shift all of a sudden the discourse of cinema studies to hide all the 'messy business' of national cinema. Surely it is possible and helpful to shift around outdated discourse when the need arises but it seems to me far too quick a move to assume that everything is 'transnational' now because 'the national' has been deemed too messy.

Chris Berry argues that, although the idea of 'the nation' is a problematic concept, this idea does continue to 'produce meaning' in a powerful way. By creating the binary: national = bad and trans = good, we risk losing 'historical and cultural specificity' (Berry 2009, 81), and by using broad theoretical apparatuses to create a new, privileged positionality *du jour* (what Higbee calls 'the cinema of transvergence'), critics such as Higbee succeed only in creating a second purposeless binary that continues to lack specificity. We are, oftentimes, too willing to forget that there is a binary in 'binaries': we tend to privilege no fixity, loose ends and fuzziness over clear-cut, oppositional categories which are perceived as constraining and hegemonic. But we do not stop to point out the irony that is inherent in these methods. Certainly the goal of film studies is to analyse cinema in nuanced, sophisticated terms but to create another binary altogether is counterproductive. If binaries are 'bad' and we want to get away from them, we need not move to the opposite extreme, a land in which there are no fixed conclusions and only open-ended possibilities which we then call 'good'. Indeed, I worry that such an extreme analytical move creates more confusion than 'good'.

The 'transnational cinema studies' model is imperfect and yet so is the 'national' model, especially in reference to a non-nation such as Taiwan.

Beginning with the premise, therefore, that the study of national cinemas must not be abandoned entirely but rethought and retooled, I embrace Berry's notion of 'the national' as a loose concept. Like Berry, I do not reject the term outright in favour of 'the transnational' because I see the potential for complexity and nuance that it holds. As Berry eloquently states: 'the national is no longer confined to the form of the territorial nation-state but multiple, proliferating, contested, and overlapping' (149). Thus, according to Berry's model, 'the national' can still remain bound to 'the transnational' within the context of film studies. According to Berry's model, the discourse of 'the national', as a means of understanding world cinema, continues to grow insofar as these various cinemas are bound to the discourse of 'the transnational'. The increasing possibilities for global collaboration, distribution and reception do not negate the possibility for diverse national and cultural identities to differentiate themselves.

In the area of Sinophone cinema studies especially, film scholars are hesitant to label Chinese-language cinema as anything but transnational in nature. In her article, *Kung Fu Hustle: Transnational Production and the Global Chinese-Language Film* (2007), Christina Klein prefers the term 'global Chinese-language film' over 'Chinese blockbuster' (189), arguing that by adding the words 'global' and 'language' she accounts for cultural diversity. Though I agree with Klein's statement that 'Chinese cinema today is inescapably transnational' (189), it does not follow from this statement that the notion of national cinemas has always been 'something of a convenient fiction' (189). She accuses certain Chinese film scholars of clinging to the idea that Hollywood functions as a hegemonic threat in relation to the production and distribution of Chinese-language films. If these accusations are correct, however, they imply that these same film scholars believe that Chinese cinemas reflect some sort of idealised 'cultural purity' (191). In my view, it is perfectly sensible to accept that Hollywood plays a large role 'behind the curtain' in Chinese cinema production and is, in this sense, 'transnational'. But surely one can simultaneously believe that national identity still plays a role in the creation and reception of these films without insisting on cultural purity or homogeneity.

Though most contemporary film scholars – Sheldon Lu and Yingjin Zhang included – prefer the term 'transnational' cinema(s),[43] I have coined an alternate, or supplementary, term: 'East–West hybrid cinema'. In his introduction to the edited volume, *Chinese Transnational Cinemas* (1997), Sheldon Lu proposes that Chinese 'national cinema', as he calls it, can be seen only within 'transnational cinema' (3). He argues that all Chinese cinema[44] since its birth (cinema produced in the mainland, Taiwan and Hong Kong) must now be viewed as 'transnational' because recent globalisation, consumption and commercial patterns have all but abolished the notion of national cinema. If we were to draw a diagram of Lu's definition of 'transnational', we might imagine a number of small circles, all labelled 'national', being consumed by one large 'transnational' circle. The smaller circles disappear into the larger one and their whereabouts become unclear.

In his 2002 book, *Screening China*, Yingjin Zhang warns against Lu's transhistorical conception of Chinese cinema (73) and proposes, instead, that we must view the 'problem' of Chinese cinema studies as a negotiation and dialogue between the local and the global (4). Borrowing from Wilson and Dissanayake, Zhang uses the term 'glocal' (global + local) to describe the types of urban spaces that Chinese/transnational cinema scholars seek to analyse and to define (255). Instead of the 'national' being swallowed by the 'transnational', as in Lu's model, Zhang envisions a new method of 'screening' (that is, projecting, concealing and scrutinising) Chinese cinema. We might now imagine a large concept entitled 'Screening', enclosing three subproblems to be analysed: (1) what is 'Chineseness'? (2) how do we avoid Eurocentrism in our analyses of Chinese cinema? and, finally, (3) how do we negotiate between the local and the global?(4)[45]

While I find Zhang's thesis apt in that it manages to clarify issues with previous analytical models such as Lu's, I am uncomfortable with what his thesis entails; certainly, it is preferable for cinematic analysis to take both postcolonial discourse and visuality into account while simultaneously avoiding 'sweeping theorization' and Eurocentrism (Zhang 83). But do film scholars need to disregard the Western cinematic theory that they might otherwise use to avoid safely the pitfalls that Zhang warns against? Or, if I need not disregard Western theory but carefully cherry-pick through it, how do I know which theories to avoid so that I will not be labelled Eurocentric? 'Western film theory' in itself is not a uniform monolith containing one consistent point of view; in fact, quite the contrary.[46] The problem with Zhang's model is that, if I unreservedly grant it, I will already be pigeonholed into a Eurocentric position that I did not choose for myself.

One might imagine 'East–West hybrid cinema' as a space containing three categories: 'nationality', 'European cinematic influence' and 'global channels'. These categories are, in turn, interconnected within that space. One category does not gain hierarchy over the other, though I want to make it clear that the category 'global channels' is not equivalent to mimicry or pure, backward-looking nostalgia. The type of cinema that I am describing is never passive; on the contrary, hybrid cinema moves constantly forward and into territories that cannot be neatly defined by any sort of diagram or model. The purpose of the above description is, therefore, only to provide a generalised (admittedly imperfect) image of the term 'East–West hybrid cinema'. This generalised image serves only as a base metaphor upon which one might construct a more precise cinematic analysis.

My suggestion to incorporate this supplementary metaphor derives from my dissatisfaction with the term 'transnational' as a means of defining the problem of the 'glocal' in the context of late capitalism. The prefix 'trans-' is synonymous with lateral movement. It is a prefix of action that suggests crossing – over borders, boundaries and oceans. If so-called 'transnational' cinema knows no borders, then it makes little sense to use a term that implies the need for the very thing that it denies: national borders. As I noted in my introduction to the edited volume, *Intermingled Fascinations: Migration, Displacement and Translation in World Cinema* (2011), I resist the term 'Sinophone' as coined by Shu-mei Shih. I am uncomfortable with her usage of the term for the following reasons: Shih defines the Sinophone as: 'a network of places of cultural production *outside* China and on the *margins* of China and Chineseness . . .' (4, my emphasis). For Shih, the 'Sinophone' is always an inexact copy of 'Chineseness' as defined and predetermined by those on the Chinese mainland (that is, of Han decent, Mandarin-speaking, and so on). It is for this reason, among others, that Shih believes that the 'Sinophone' resists 'easy suturing' and encourages 'difficulty, difference, and heterogeneity' (5).

Yet, by wilfully excluding mainland China in her definition of the Sinophone,[47] Shih reaffirms the dichotomy of dominance/minority resistance that she seeks to break free from. Painting China as the dominant empire that must be destabilised by the outlying Chinese diaspora, she manages not only to separate outlying communities further from the mainland and also, paradoxically, to reinforce their connection to it. If we are to assume that the world is now 'borderless' (Shih 6), why create a needless border between China proper and the margins or diaspora communities? When I refer to 'Sinophone cinema', therefore, I am referring to a cinema that encompasses the cinematic traditions of the mainland.

To avoid all this confusion, therefore, it would be ideal to avoid the notion of the 'nation' altogether while emphasising notions such as fusion, hybridity and intertextuality. Though representations of nationhood and citizenship are central aspects of hybrid cinema, the term is not defined by its relationship to the national. Using the hybrid metaphor, one can furthermore avoid choosing sides in the global/local dichotomy. Though Zhang's new term 'polylocality' manages to avoid the 'crossing' imagery that I find misleading, it seems to choose the side of the local.

Complex cultural exchanges occur with such frequency between 'Eastern' and 'Western' cinematic traditions that the dichotomy is close to meaningless. The fact alone that, in recent years, the term 'Sino-French' cinema has been coined,[48] is a testament to the necessity for a term that describes the cultural fusions, conversations and citations that continue to occur between Chinese and French cinemas. Unfortunately, despite some notable exceptions,[49] real-life cinematic interactions and collaborations between Italy and China are less common than those between France and China. While I grant that the term

'East–West' might have the unintended consequence of suggesting polarisation or dichotomy, it does, nevertheless, describe a precise phenomenon that would be otherwise difficult to characterise.[50] A fundamental question remains: why should cinematic analysis preoccupy itself with defining and categorising ethnic identities to begin with? While Zhang is focused on how to avoid Eurocentrism when analysing Chinese cinema, Shih warns us that we must now be careful to avoid 'China-centrism' as well. Though both Shih and Zhang provide excellent models for the study of Chinese/Sinophone cinema studies, if I were to take their models literally, the result would be that it would be nearly impossible for me to avoid all possible 'centrisms' if I am to attempt to analyse particular Chinese cinema texts. For this reason, I have chosen to use the 'hybrid'[51] model – if for no other reason than to provide an alternate metaphor for the concept of 'transnational cinema'.

NOTES

1. See Gaskett, Michael. *The Attractive Empire: Transnational Film Culture in Imperial Japan*, Honolulu: University of Hawaii Press, 2008.
2. In 1894, Japan became a serious threat to China for the first time since the late sixteenth century by challenging China's right to control Korea. The first Sino-Japanese War lasted for less than a year and ended with the Treaty of Shimonoseki. Not only did the treaty require that China relinquish suzerainty over Korea but, moreover, China was required to cede Taiwan, the Pescadores (or Penghu) islands, and the Lioadong Peninsula in Manchuria to Japan.
3. See <http://sinojapanesewar.com>
4. See Gou-Juin (18). A Japanese merchant brought ten Edison films to Taipei in 1896, before the arrival of films in Kobe, Japan.
5. See also Gou-Juin (19).
6. Unfortunately, most of these early films are no longer in existence or are extremely difficult to find.
7. Fictional, but set in a historical time period, a type of docu-drama perhaps.
8. Meaning to interpret them or place them in a specific genre such as comedy or tragedy, etc.
9. Though, admittedly, his aforementioned essay does not attempt to deal with film analysis as it relates to the question of historical narrative.
10. Although White's writing style is lucid, it is still unclear to me how White suggests that historians should operate, if narration is merely a 'vehicle'. Although his thesis appears valid, it fails, in my opinion, to offer a reasonable alternative.
11. According to Venerable Master Hsing Yun, the Buddha becomes angry with you only if you mistreat others: 'the Buddha would get angry with those who were only concerned with their own welfare and had no regard for the hardships of others'. See <http://www.blia.org>
12. See <http://www.taiwanfirstnations.org/watan.html>
13. For more, please see the Brighton 'Amoeba' blog. He discusses the early days of cinema in Taiwan (and provides film stills).
14. Taiwan nativist literature, or *xiangtu wenxu*, was a genre of realism that depicted ordinary people dealing with the everyday struggles associated with modern Taiwan. The genre was originated under Japanese rule and enjoyed a resurgence of popularity in the 1970s.

15. One might very well argue that there are issues with the phrase 'Mandarin-language cinema from Taiwan' because Taiwanese-born directors, such as Ang Lee, employ cast, crew and production teams from Hong Kong, the mainland, Taiwan, and the United States. Lee's *Crouching Tiger Hidden Dragon* (2000), in particular, began a trend towards internationalisation in Chinese-language cinema, and the film itself consists of myriad accents and dialects. Regardless, I can state, with a reasonable degree of accuracy, that the predominant language of the films that I discuss in this book is Mandarin. The Mandarin-language cinema of Taiwan, as a 'tradition', differs significantly from the Mandarin-language cinema of the mainland and elsewhere.

16. Also, to limit the focus of the discussion. My dissertation, *Echoing Across the Mediterranean and the Pacific: Cinematic Resonance and Cross-Cultural Adaptation in Contemporary European and East Asian Cinema* (2011) was dedicated to a broader discussion of East–West hybridity, and included additional subgenres: Franco-Korean, Franco-Japanese, and Hong Kong pastiche.

17. See 'Taiwanese Society Under Martial Law Remembered', in China Town Connection, contributed by *The Taipei Times*, 15 July 2007 <http://www.chinatownconnection.com/ taiwanese-society-martial-law.htm> (last accessed 23 December 2012).

18. See Zhang, Yingjin and Xiao, Zhiwei (eds). *Encyclopedia of Chinese Film*. London: Routledge, 1998.

19. The Taiwanese New Wave (or Taiwanese New Cinema) is typically defined as the brief period between 1982 and 1987 (Neri 30–1). The Second New Wave is defined, loosely, as the period beginning in the early 1990s and extending, more or less, to the present (32).

20. Yinjing Zhang has argued that, thematically, Taiwanese films of the 1980s are linked by the tendency either to confront the island's colonial past or to contend with the anxiety of modernisation (57). I would add that Hou is usually associated with the former and Yang the latter.

21. See the introduction to his book *Cinema Taiwan: Politics, Popularity and the State of the Arts* (4).

22. In *Film Theory*, 2000. 'The nation, like a film, is a "projected image", partly phantasmic in nature. Any definition of a filmic nationalism, then, must see nationality as partly discursive and *intertextual* in nature, must allow for racial difference and cultural heterogeneity, and must be dynamic, seeing the nation as an evolving, imaginary, differential construct rather than an originary essence' (Stam 290, my emphasis).

23. Hou Hsiao-hsien, for example, also receives funding from French production companies and has shot his films abroad, in both France and Japan. The last example of this was Hou's 2007 film, *The Red Balloon/Le voyage du ballon rouge*.

24. Zhang worked as a farm labourer and cotton textile mill worker; Chen joined the Red Guards.

25. The movement would not have been fully recognised by international art-house film circles until the early 1990s.

26. See Crespi article.

27. *Quand j'étais élue, tout a changé . . . enfin vous préférez mieux avoir une voiture ou passer le bac? Ah, je suis contente parce que j'en ai les deux.*

28. Bloom explains that these terms are not self-evident in themselves, and she goes on to define each one carefully. 'Metropolitan France', she explains, is historically defined as France proper and does not include 'overseas France', that is, France's colonies in Africa, and so on. While she is careful to define 'China' rather broadly – 'Greater China' would include the PRC, Taiwan, Hong Kong, and the Chinese

diaspora – 'China' in the context of her article refers predominantly to the main-land (4–6).

29. See <http://www.taipeifilmcommission.org/en/LoveMovie/Taipei> (last accessed 28 February 2013).

30. In her book, *Melancholy Drift*, Jean Ma states that Taiwanese film-makers, such as Tsai, have: 'negotiated between the movements' increasingly negative reputation at home and the momentum of its enthusiastic reception abroad' (4).

31. Zhang notes that this fact is especially surprising given the immense popularity and cultural dominance of Taiwanese-language films during the 1950s and 1960s.

32. From *The Cinema of Small Nations* (eds Hjort and Petrie), Indiana University Press, 2007.

33. I should add here that I am sceptical even of Song's claim that the national cinema model has been contested only in recent years. It seems misleading chronologically to categorise film theory trends in this way, that is, as the period pro- and post-national cinema.

34. I will grant that Guo-Juin is attempting to make a more metaphorical point, perhaps, about Taiwan's identity crisis. But for the purposes of clarity I intend to justify, define and distinguish my own terms from those of other scholars.

35. Theodor Adorno similarly observed that works of art can be thought of as 'after-images' or replicas of life; it is by virtue of its separation from the world that art reaches a 'higher order' of being (Adorno 6).

36. See also Song Hwee Lim, in *The Chinese Cinema Book*, 2011.

37. A term that, Higbee acknowledges, Novak uses to describe architecture, not film.

38. In Lu's 1997 book *Transnational Chinese Cinemas: Identity, Nationhood, Gender*.

39. Tom O'Reagan in Hayward (2000, 91), as quoted by Higbee (81).

40. In his case, the rise of the Nazis, pre-World War II.

41. The Lumière brothers went on tour around the world – to London, New York, Bombay and Buenos Aires – with their films.

42. Higbee is himself citing Susan Hayward's *French National Cinema*, Taylor and Francis, 2000.

43. See Lu's *Transnational Chinese Cinemas* (1997) and Zhang's *Screening China* (2002).

44. The term 'Chinese' is itself problematic and perhaps 'Sinophone' (not as defined by Shu-mei Shih) is more accurate. I shall discuss this debate later on.

45. In Zhang's newest book, he goes one step further and calls for the term 'polylocal-ity' to take the place of 'transnationality' in Chinese cinema studies.

46. A Deleuzian analysis of a cinematic text, for example, would be entirely different from a Bordwellian analysis, and both might be equally controversial.

47. It is not even entirely clear by its very definition that the 'Francophone' does not include France, as Shih suggests. 'The Anglophone' seems obviously to include the United States and Britain.

48. See Bloom's 2005 article, 'Contemporary Franco-Chinese Cinema: Translation, Citation and Imitation in Dai Sijie's *Balzac and the Little Chinese Seamstress* and Tsai Ming-liang's *What Time is it There?*'

49. Bernardo Bertolucci's *The Last Emperor*, Agostino Ferrente's *L'orchestra di Piazza Vittorio*, and, most recently, *Un cinese a Roma* by Gianfranco Giagni.

50. Furthermore, the usage of the dash denotes equality as opposed to the slash which tends to denote dichotomy.

51. My notion of hybrid cinema is also, in part, inspired by Hamid Naficy's model (see Naficy, 2001).

2. TAIWANESE–ITALIAN CONJUGATIONS: THE FRACTURED STORYTELLING OF EDWARD YANG'S *THE TERRORIZERS* AND MICHELANGELO ANTONIONI'S *BLOW-UP*

Frederic Jameson describes Edward Yang's (楊德昌) films as miniature show-cases for alienation in a modernised Taipei – as spaces in which conventional plots and characters no longer exist – spaces in which linear narrative is replaced with moments of coincidence and points of intersection. Yang also makes explicit use of voiceovers and dialogue to express the 'heaviness' of life in modern-day Taipei, unlike other Taiwanese art house directors, such as Tsai Ming-liang. The combination of these factors forms the basis of Yang's style: though he does film space unconventionally, as Jameson suggests, he also relies heavily on dialogue or 'words' more generally. My analysis of Yang's films within this chapter, therefore, relies on a careful consideration of both these aspects: camera movement and dialogue. I also analyse a case study for comparative purposes, in response to questions such as: why is Yang so frequently compared with Italian director Michelangelo Antonioni? Is there any validity to this comparison? Premised on the assumption that is Yang a 'universal' film-maker, I argue that Italian director Michelangelo Antonioni's *Blow-Up* and Yang's *Terrorizers* contain overlapping themes and plot devices to such an extent that they can be considered analogies for modernism more generally. I return to these connections shortly.

We must first go back to the early 1980s to see how Yang entered the scene. Yang was talented but he was also lucky. In 1982, four directors were chosen by Taiwan's Central Motion Picture Corporation to contribute to a special anthology of short films, entitled *In Our Time*, which were supposed to represent everyday stories of Taiwan from the 1950s to the 1970s. The resulting anthology contained the films of four young directors: Chang Yi, Ko I-chen, Tao Te-chen, and Edward Yang. Yang's short film, entitled 'Expectations' (also translated as 'Desires'), tells the story of a young girl, entering puberty, who discovers her sexuality while lusting after her handsome college-age neighbour. In one particularly noteworthy scene, the young teenage girl, Fen, discovers that she has her period for the first time. Though one might expect such a scene to be dramatic, on the contrary, the scene is extremely low key and contemplative. Film scholar Edmond Wong, in his book on Yang (*Edward Yang,* 1993), notes that this scene from 'Expectations' exemplifies the central difference in style between Yang and more traditional directors. With reference to the scene in which Fen makes her 'discovery', Wong comments: 'different from other directors, Yang moved the camera slowly to record the sudden incident and showed a gentle care for [Fen] the protagonist' (Wong).

Instead of an overreliance on melodrama or character expression, in other words, Yang relies on the juxtaposition of images to create emotion. This reliance on mundane objects in the world – a breeze blowing through curtains, a pipe dripping water into a puddle – separates Yang from his mainstream counterparts who might choose instead to rely on reaction shots. From the very beginning then, Yang showcased his ability to mask commentary of larger social trends, in an era of extreme social change in Taiwan, in the telling of individual stories. Unlike his colleague and contemporary, Hou Hsiao-hsien, Yang was known for his serious, wise demeanour and, occasionally, for his temper tantrums. Unlike Hou, however, Yang was neither frank nor blunt. Yang's goal overall, as a film-maker, was to create realistic, believable characters. An added benefit, perhaps, was that the lives of these characters came across as emblematic of the class struggles associated with modernisation in 1980s-era Taipei.

BIRTH OF A MOVEMENT

Yang was born in Shanghai in 1947 but grew up in Taipei after his family moved to Taiwan during the Chinese Civil War. Though he was interested in drawing and architecture while growing up, his father discouraged him from following a 'creative path'. Thus, in an effort to please his father, Yang attended university in Taiwan and specialised in electrical engineering. In the early 1970s, however, Yang left Taiwan and moved to Florida where he completed a master's programme in computer design. After the master's programme, Yang moved to Los Angeles where he attended film school at the University of Southern California. He dropped out after only a year. For the six to seven years after that, between about 1974 and 1980, Yang lived and worked in Seattle as a software designer. But Yang felt unsatisfied with his life and with his job during these years despite the fact that he had spent much of his life being educated and trained to work with computers. 'By the time I was thirty, I felt so old' the director recalled in a 2001 interview with the *New Left Review* (Anderson 6). He was restless to an unbearable extent.

One day, says Yang, as he was walking down the street in Seattle, he noticed that Werner Herzog's *Aguirre, the Wrath of God* (1972) was playing and he bought a ticket to see it. Herzog's historical fiction film, a masterpiece of minimalism set in 1560, is about a conquistador (Klaus Kinski) who goes slowly insane in the jungle. The film was shot entirely on location in the Peruvian rainforest, where Herzog and Kinski nearly killed one another.[1] Watching the film changed his life, Yang recalled, to such an extent that he convinced himself to leave his job and return to film-making. In 1980, then, Yang returned to Taiwan. Just after his return, he was lucky enough to find work as a scriptwriter and television director for a popular television series. Soon afterwards, the CMPC commissioned Yang to direct 'Expectations' for *In Our Time* (Berry 2005, 273). *In Our Time*, explains an *Economist* reporter, was the first government-sponsored effort to showcase the efforts of four native directors. More importantly, it was the first successful effort to introduce the idea of 'personal cinema' to Taiwanese audiences (90). The reporter realised the significance of this step for the industry only four years after it had begun.

In that same 1986 *Economist* article, entitled 'New Wave Brings Realism', the reporter describes Yang and other New Wave film-makers as rebellious geniuses. Certainly the New Wave directors were rebellious in the sense that they were fed up with current rules and regulations, and they were reacting against an out-of-date, overly commercialised industry. Many of these directors, Yang included, had either lived or studied abroad before returning to Taiwan to make films. The experience of living abroad, then, though by no means a 'rite of passage' for Taiwanese New Wave directors, was certainly not a negative. Living abroad offered Yang an invaluable perspective. His experience working for a software company jaded him but it also turned him back towards his creative side. Not everyone was convinced that the movement was important, especially critics in Taiwan. In 1983, a year after *In Our Time* was released, critics were divided. Many critics did not see that New Wave cinema was a worthwhile trend. Critics in Taiwan either believed in the need for change or they did not. The older generation, dominated by those who had been born in China and remembered the Communist victory in 1949, tended to be reactionary while younger critics were on the side of change. The older generation complained that the New Wave was not real 'Chinese' cinema because it was designed to appeal to 'foreign audiences'. Younger critics, meanwhile, praised the cinematic style of New Wave film-makers because it was fresh, internationally minded and sophisticated. Younger critics in Taiwan, in other words, approved of the fact that New Wave film-makers had been 'weaned' on a steady diet of both Asian and international cinema (90).

International critics heaped praise upon New Wave film-makers, especially Edward Yang. Even in 1986, the journalist for the *Economist* practically gushes over the New Wave movement and the prospects for its future. Unlike the Hong Kong cinema produced only a few years earlier, notes the reporter, this cinema does not reek of 'phony internationalism' – it possesses an authentic quality to it. Taiwan, he observes, is aided by its geography. While Hong Kong is landlocked and in close proximity to China, Taiwan's isolation imbues it with its own cultural values, separate from those of the mainland. The New Wave movement is small, admits the reporter, but the directors and writers 'pop up' in one another's films, offering the viewer an 'intertextual reward' for simply being a fan. The New Wave movement, moreover, offers the viewer a genuine sense of the collaboration that takes place behind the scenes.

Nevertheless, even in 1986, critics were aware of the potential risks associated with cinema that could be deemed 'too sophisticated' by the masses. Regardless of the CMPC's support of the industry overall, local audiences had not fully embraced the movement. Taiwanese audiences still greatly preferred paying to see either American box office successes or lighter domestic entertainment (as opposed to art house cinema with weightier messages and longer running times). Though this anti-intellectual sentiment might appear counter-intuitive in many ways, the situation is similar in many other film industries, especially Hollywood. Winning a Golden Horse Award, though prestigious, might actually turn local audiences against a particular film-maker, causing his or her future films to fail commercially with local Taiwanese audiences. This was the fear in the late 1980s. Unfortunately, this journalist predicted one of the central problems for Taiwanese film directors – a problem that continues to plague the Taiwanese film industry in 2013.

Turning back to the early years of a revitalising industry, we can see how the movement evolved, and how Edward Yang became a leading figure in its development. After the termination of martial law in 1987, democratisation loosened regulations on all forms of media in Taiwan which, for thirty-eight years previously, under the KMT, had been regulated by three government agencies (Curtin 134).[2] Edward Yang's early films: 'Expectations' (sometimes translated as 'Desires' (1982), part of *In Our Time*), *That Day, On the Beach* (1983), *Taipei Story* (1985) and *Terrorizers* (1986)[3] coincide with the moment of transition out of the martial law era and into a new era of freer media. It would be difficult to classify Edward Yang's films into any one genre. Though his films often portray the alienation of modern-day life in Taipei, they also showcase heartfelt family stories. The four-hour-long historical epic, *A Brighter Summer Day/Gu ling jie shaonian sharen shijian* (1991), for instance, was inspired by the same real-life stabbing incident that intrigued Yang when he directed *The Terrorizers*. *Brighter Summer Day* is also an autobiographical story for Hou in other ways. After the first scene of the film, a series of title screens describes the historical context, as if Hou imagines that his viewers might wonder who these characters are and why they should be interested in them. The silent titles seek to answer these questions:

> millions of mainland Chinese fled to Taiwan in 1949 with the Nationalist government after its civil war defeat by the Chinese Communists. Their children were brought up in an uneasy atmosphere, created by their parents' own uncertainty about the future. Many formed street gangs to search for an identity and to strengthen their sense of security.

As viewers, we now have much of the information that we require to understand the film's set-up.

Yang was required to work within the specific constraints of the Taiwanese system, though the quality of his work did not suffer from it. In a 2002 interview, Yang commented that film distribution companies in Taiwan have always been, and continue to be, seriously flawed. Yang alleged further that money-laundering was a common occurrence in the 1980s and that distribution companies took profits from successful Taiwanese films to finance films in Hong Kong (289). These long lists of rules and regulations prevented early Taiwan New Cinema films from being distributed in the first place. In response to these difficult conditions, Yang dedicated his career to creating films that would be both interesting and compelling. According to his own statements, he did not create films to profit from them (Berry 288). When asked by film journal *Cineaste* to describe mainstream film-making in Taiwan before the New Wave, Yang commented: 'The Taiwan film business was very much like China's. It was for propaganda. They spent millions and millions to make a film, say, about a certain national hero. It praises a guy who sacrificed his life to save a bridge during the war and protect the nation' (Sklar). When asked whether or not he tries to create 'a portrait of Taiwan' in his films, Yang responded that by simply creating a compelling story, he does not need to add his own viewpoint into the mix.

Nevertheless, it is obvious that Yang both had an opinion and that he did incorporate a certain viewpoint into his films. Again, in the beginning of *Brighter Summer Day*, two young boys from the street gang are playing truant from school to 'crash' a film shoot. The film studio is shot only from a bird's-eye view, from the perspective of the boys who are looking down from the balcony. The set looks artificial; there is a proliferation of lights, costumes, cranes, and people. The director is angry and does not seem to care much for his work: 'This is our last shot, let's get it over with!' he barks at the actors. The shoot is interrupted, and chaos ensues, when the kids are discovered in the balcony. These opening scenes emphasise the authoritarian, stuffy nature of the time. This particular scene also implies disdain for the overly melodramatic and artificial film-making techniques that were prevalent in the late 1950s and early 1960s in Taiwan.

Unfortunately, *A Brighter Summer Day* was released as the first New Wave movement was imploding. The movement dissolved in the late 1980s, leading to a sudden loss in talent. Thus, though Taiwan's film industry had been gaining strength in the mid- to late 1980s, it collapsed again in the early 1990s. This collapse forced directors such as Yang and Hou to take on many of the roles that had once been handled by the larger film crew. They 'became their own producers, production managers, acting coaches, editors and unit publicists' (25). Yang himself estimated that about 60 to 75 per cent of his entire film crew for *Brighter Summer Day* had never made a film before (Charity 47). Despite the fact that the industry was in such a troubled state at the time, reviewers praised *Brighter Summer Day* for its rich, complex storytelling. One particular critic laments the fact that the film had been restricted to a brief seven-day release in London.

After a *Brighter Summer Day*, an immense project film with little to show for it, Yang had become desperate to find collaborators who would be able to take on some of the workload. Therefore, 1994's *Confucian Confusion/Duli shidai* was the product of Yang's new effort to collaborate more deeply with his film crew and his actors. Unlike his contemporary, Hou Hsiao-hsien, Yang had an advantage after the collapse of the New Wave movement. Because he worked simultaneously as a lecturer in film in the Department of Drama at the National Institute for the Arts (run by Stan Lai), Yang continued to have access to the best young talent in the industry.

By the early 1990s, Yang's 'Atom Films' had become trendy again. The offices were situated in a central area, next to a café named 'Youguan Danwei' (translated as 'The Department Responsible'), where the fashionable people of Taipei went to hang out and share ideas. The café's name – 'Youguan Danwei' – is a reference to, and parody of, the government department that had been responsible for censoring arts and media during the martial law period. According to *Sight and Sound* writer Tony Rayns, who wrote an exposé on Yang during this crucial period, anyone who had grown up in the Taiwan of the 1950s and 1960s would have been familiar with the 'Youguan Danwei'. As Rayns reports in his 1994 *Sight and Sound* article, 'Yang's Comedy: On the Set of *A Confucian Confusion*', the café was a hangout for the crew working for Yang at Atom Films. In the article, Rayns recounts his visit to Atom Films, the café, and the set of Yang's *Confucian Confusion*. He observes: 'both the place and its customers embody a mood that's new in Taipei: too cool to be rebellious, but cynical about politics, disrespectful of the old order, and wryly detached from the city's assertive affluence' (27). It is clear from his description of the working conditions on the set of *Confucian Confusion* that Rayns was extremely impressed with Yang's film-making technique. He describes Yang as a thoughtful director who respects the craft and the process of acting. He marvels at the fact that Yang allows his actors to reshoot scenes ad nauseam until their gestures lose any hint of the unnatural. Because Rayns writes for an English-speaking readership (in the early 1990s when the English-speaking world knew little about Yang), Rayns anticipates the need to justify to his readers *why* his experience with Yang was so remarkable. Anticipating specifically that his readers will wonder why Yang's interest in the performance aspect of his film should be seen as anything 'new', Rayns explains that *the interest in an actor's performance is new* for Taiwan. There has never been a star system or even a professional training school for actors until recently, explains Rayns, and these facilities were normally located in China or Hong Kong (25). In fact, he notes, when Hou directed *The Puppetmaster/Xi meng rensheng* (1993) only a few years earlier, the director had complained that his actors did not have adequate film acting experience. Most of Hou's actors had appeared only in Taiwanese television shows but had never worked on film sets.

Though Yang maintained a relatively small following throughout the 1990s, the director is still best known for the final full-length film of his career: *Yi Yi* (2000), a three-hour-long family epic about life and death in the Jian family. Yang has described the international success of *Yi Yi* as 'luckily unlucky' (288). Though the film won a number of prestigious awards, including the award for Best Director at the 2000 Cannes Film Festival, it was not distributed or shown in Taiwan. *Yi Yi* was a success for Yang despite problems with the Taiwanese film industry.

Though Yang died of colon cancer in 2007, he is still recognised as one of the primary 'authors' of the New Cinema movement that began in the 1980s. In their book on Taiwanese cinema (*Treasure Island,* 2005), Yeh and Davis describe Yang as 'foremost among the New Cinema directors who asserted their authorship over the authority of the genre, stars, and studio politics' (Yeh and Davis 7).

TERRORIZERS AND *BLOW-UP*: A CASE STUDY

Humanity has also invented, in its evening peregrinations – that is to say, in the nineteenth century – the symbol of memory; it has invented what had seemed impossible; it has invented a mirror that remembers. It has invented photography. [Benjamin 2002, 688, ln (Y8a, 3)]

Watching a film like *Terrorizers*, it is easy to see why Yang has been described as 'foremost' among New Cinema directors. The Taipei that we see in Yang's films is a city of 'boxed-in dwellings' (Jameson 154) but it is also a city that is ripe for people watching. Yang's films contain child or adolescent characters that come to learn about life through death (Yang-Yang in *Yi Yi*, the street gang in *A Brighter Summer Day*). Though Yang's Taipei is often portrayed as a dangerous space – a space in which conventional plots and narration are called into question – it is also an expressive space. The characters in Yang's films use words to express the difficult nature of life in the city. Unlike Hou or Tsai, Yang's films are not taciturn or uncommunicative. Analysis of Yang's films must not rely solely on camera movement because the words and thoughts of his characters are equally meaningful.

Yang's aesthetics are compared most frequently with those of Italian director Michelangelo Antonioni who is best known for the films that he made in the 1960s. Antonioni is especially famous for his loose trilogy, starring Monica Vitti, which consisted of: *L'avventura/The Adventure* (1960), *La notte/The Night* (1962), and *L'Eclisse/The Eclipse* (1963). Later in the decade, Antonioni directed his first English-language film, *Blow-Up* (1967) which was a surprise box office success. Thus, while Antonioni travelled to a variety of countries to shoot his films, Yang always remained in Taiwan. Many of Yang's films contain interior shots of apartments: shots of bedrooms, bathrooms, and living rooms that overlook other apartment buildings. Characters view other 'boxed-in' dwellings from their own claustrophobic dwelling. In the first scene of *Taipei Story* (1985), for example, a young woman, Chin, played by singer (and Edward Yang's future wife) Tsai Chin, and her boyfriend, Lon (played by Hou Hsiao-hsien), are looking at an apartment. Lon, a former baseball player, stares out of the living room window as Chin half-heartedly evaluates the apartment. The interior space of this apartment is markedly similar to the apartment in *Terrorizers*. John Anderson notes this similarity as well, commenting: 'Even the shape of the room is the same, as if to suggest that the limits on the options open to Taiwanese youth extend to the architecture itself' (34). These 'boxed-in dwellings' contrast with the empty space that can be seen from the outside looking in; when Chin is at work, we see her walking around the large impersonal office space. From above, office workers look like ants in a maze; and from the outside looking in, the mirrored windows of bland office buildings reflect light so that the movements of the people inside are always obscured. To the eye of the viewer, these mirrored windows are the visual equivalent of empty space.

This Jamesonian notion of 'empty space' is also prevalent in many of Antonioni's films which is one of the reasons why the two directors are so frequently compared. The final scene of Antonioni's 1962 film *L'Eclisse* is particularly demonstrative of these aesthetic similarities. In this final scene of *L'Eclisse*, nondescript landmarks in Rome become characters unto themselves; these are the settings for a romantic encounter that never occurs. Because these geographical spots do not necessarily serve as the eventual meeting place for the film characters, the looming presence of the cityscape emerges menacingly into the foreground. In the final scene of this film, the viewer's expectations are challenged when the protagonists never reunite as they had planned. The viewer is a witness to a romantic rendezvous that was planned but never actually takes place. Since neither character arrives at the agreed-upon spot, waiting for the other to arrive, the viewer can safely assume that neither of the lovers is aware that the other one never turned up. The absence of both lovers is almost more disappointing, from the viewer's standpoint, than the absence of either one or the other. Because neither bothered to make the date, the viewer is faced with the unpleasant realisation that neither character was invested in the relationship. As viewers, we might feel cheated, and justifiably so. After all, what is the purpose of watching a love story that fails? Further, what is the purpose of watching the failure occur if we are never even given a reason why the relationship failed? The flakiness of the characters almost feels like an insult to the viewer. In another sense, the open-ended, unresolved ending could be liberating for viewers who are accustomed to the typical happy endings of romance films. Now, instead of being able to file away the film in our minds as simply 'another great love story for the books', we are required to contend with the open-endedness and ambiguity of the narrative. Stories do not always begin or end neatly.

This principle is also apparent in films such as Yang's *A Brighter Summer Day/Gu ling jie shao nian sha ren shi jian* (1991). Just as *L'Eclisse* begins in the middle of a lover's quarrel, *Brighter Summer Day* begins in the middle of an unpleasant conversation between a father and his son's teacher. After the fade-in, the viewer is able to make out the man, at fairly long distance from the camera, with his back to us. As soon as the dialogue begins, the viewer is quickly able to read the situation. A father is at school contesting his son's exam results while his son waits in the corridor. Though the father is speaking with a teacher, her figure is obscured from view. The scene in the school cuts to a street shot. Figures slowly walk towards the camera in the distance. The viewer can hear the sounds of cars but it is almost impossible to make out the figures in the distance. Eventually, two bicyclists ride towards the camera and, when the scene cuts again to the father and son sitting across from one another in a café, the viewer is certain that there were the two figures on bikes that we saw only a moment ago. The son and father eat ice cream in silence. The waitress watches them from the side.

In his article, 'Remapping Taipei: in The Geopolitical Aesthetic: Mapping Space and Time in the World System' (1992), Jameson comments on this idea of empty, unfulfilled space within modernist narratives. He observes:

> These known misunderstandings bring into being a new kind of purely aesthetic emotion . . . that it is purely aesthetic, however, means that this effect is conceivable only in conjunction with the work of art, cannot

take place in real life, and has something to do with the omniscient author. These occurrences remain disjoined, unknown to each other, their interrelationship, casual or other, being a non-existent fact, event, or phenomenon, save when the gaze of the Author, rising over miniature roof-tops, puts them back together and declares them to be the material of story-telling, or Literature. (114)

Jameson is commenting more broadly on the advent of modern storytelling. When a film-maker tells a story with his camera, he or she creates a plot that may contain aspects of realism but which could never be duplicated in real life: 'conceivable only in conjunction with the work of art'. He/she compares this newer, 'modern', and alienating aesthetic with a more 'holistic', pre-modern aesthetic. In the Victorian era, Jameson notes, plot formation seemed to reunite isolated monads. Unification of multiple destinies and strands in Victorian-era storytelling was reassuring to readers. The ultimate unity of the story and the illusion of social totality were indicative of God's design. Now in modernity, says Jameson, everything that is stunning about these accidents and points of connection seem, because of their ephemerality, to drive us more deeply into individual isolation. The Providence effect is an aesthetic one (115). Urban spaces work well in assembling the empty spaces of such meetings or missed encounters. Jameson explains this effect: '. . . the urban seems propitious to it, infinitely assembling the empty spaces of such meetings or missed encounters; while the modern (or the romantic) seems to supply the other vital ingredient; namely, the sense of authorial function or of the omniscient social witness' (114).

Jameson further offers the example of the omniscient reader: that is, the idea that the reader can 'know things' that the characters cannot know. Lovers miss each other by minutes (or both fail to arrive, as in the case of *L'Eclisse*), murders are committed in the darkness of apartment buildings, couples cheat on each other, and so on. The viewer is allowed to peek into the lives of 'anonymous' city dwellers within the context of a fictional narrative, set in urban space. This ability to spy on the mundane lives of urbanites is the phenomenon that Jameson refers to as synchronous monadic simultaneity or SMS (116).

In a film such as *Terrorizers*, argues Jameson, the viewer is not interested in the separate lives of each of the characters as much as in how these lives come to intersect and overlap during the course of the film. The plot itself becomes intertwined with the idea of spatiality. The drama of the film is inextricably connected to both the specificity of Taipei as a space unto itself and to the more abstract idea of urban space more generally. Jameson's boxed-in dwelling analogy is meant to parallel the idea of Taiwan as a traditional yet non-traditional, a national yet multi- or transnational space. The city of Taipei, Jameson remarks, functions as a 'non-national nation state' (154). For

Jameson, the enclosed spaces within Taipei are emblematic of the inequality that is inherent to globalisation on an international scale. Though city dwellers may become more prosperous overall as a result of international globalisation and capitalism, they are nevertheless trapped within the walls of city life itself. An increase in personal wealth is not the equivalent of freedom, as Yang clearly shows his viewers in *Taipei Story* and in *Terrorizers*.

Yang's film-making style has been consistently compared with that of Antonioni in part because both directors make frequent use of *temps mort*, or 'dead time'. Despite the name, argues Hamish Ford, 'dead time' emphasises the fullness of life that exists both within and beyond the frame in a film. Ford describes *temps mort* as: 'the moments that occur when the image continues after the narrative usefulness has ended, or when people have left the frame, leaving us with a non-anthropocentric image of the world' (Ford, n.p.).[4] Film scholars are quick to point to the aesthetic similarities between Yang's 1986 film *Terrorizers* and Antonioni's 1967 film *Blow-Up*.[5] David Bordwell, for instance, comparing the two film-makers, comments: 'Antonioni plays things down, "dedramatizing" his scenes by keeping the camera back . . . (You see the Antonioni influence on similar strategies in the work of Edward Yang' (Bordwell, 'Two Chinese Men of Cinema' 2007, n.p.). Here, Bordwell is describing Antonioni's cinema of alienation (a part of this is *temps mort*): as the camera 'pushes backwards', the viewer is challenged to consider ontological questions related to metanarrative.[6] The spectator is encouraged to consider questions such as: why should we be interested in the fate of certain characters over others in the fictional, constructed world of one particular film? Most of Antonioni's films share the theme that Bordwell describes: de-dramatisation mixed with an emphasis on absence, empty space, and missed opportunities. Though Bordwell is comparing the two directors here, his remark about Yang is tacked on only parenthetically. Certainly, a more sustained comparative analysis of the two film-makers is warranted.[7]

Though he does not discuss Yang alongside Antonioni, Frederic Jameson has famously argued that *The Terrorizers* should be read in the context of modernity – or, what he calls 'late capitalism'. In 'Remapping Taipei'[8], a chapter in *The Geopolitical Aesthetic* dedicated entirely to an analysis of the film, Jameson notes: 'It does seem to be the case that *Terrorizer* . . . assimilates modern subjects, and the toll it takes on psychic subjects, more generally to urbanization than to Westernization as such. This lends its "diagnosis" a kind of globality, if not universality . . .' (117) Though Jameson is clear to state that Taipei does not resemble a modern 'Western-style' city, he suggests that it does represent a growing trend that is specific to what he calls: 'late capitalist urbanization' (177). Chris Berry takes issue with Jameson's reading of the film, arguing that, because Jameson is not able to view the film from within a Taiwanese context, he misreads the significance of many key aspects within the story. In response to Jameson's idea that the film laments the rise of a technologically superior but shallow image-based society, Berry comments: 'No locally informed contemporary viewer of the film could possibly miss the subtle sarcasm directed at the dominant role played by the *fukan* institution[9] in Taiwan's cultural life in the 1970s and 1980s' (17).

While Jameson provides one of the earliest analyses of the film, and Berry shows how Jameson misreads the film's critique of technology, both readings of the film fail to answer some of the most interesting aspects of *Terrorizers*. How are reality and fiction distinguished, or become indistinguishable, within the film? How do these juxtapositions of images, in certain key sequences of the film, create meaning? In one of the most sustained attempts at a comparison, Jim Weaver describes *Blow-Up* as 'the modernist spiritual predecessor' of Yang's film [in his video essay entitled 'Edward Yang's *The Terrorizers*' (2012) (8)]. *The Terrorizers*, argues Weaver, rejects the 'modernist interpretive temptation' (4, from Virilio 144), while *Blow-Up* ends with a clear conclusion: Thomas is able to realise and accept his inability to 'apprehend the world around him', which leads him to re-examine his 'subjectivity' (4). This modernist/postmodernist contrast is supposed to show us that, while the characters in Antonioni's film progress on a casual, 'modernist path', the characters in Yang's film are connected only contingently, in line with 'postmodern' form. Weaver argues that 'the juxtaposition of shots [in *The Terrorizers*] does not result in any new, clear meaning' (3), that Yang's film rejects the viewer's inclination to connect sequences of shots into a meaningful whole, that sequences of shots are connected only through graphic match, and that graphic match does not suggest causality. Though it is true that a 'graphic match' does not suggest causality, the technique does imply a visual correlation between certain compositional elements in two juxtaposed shots ('Glossary of Film Terms' 229).[10]

Though *Terrorizers* is by no means a remake of *Blow-Up*, the two films do share striking thematic similarities. On the most basic, superficial level, both films feature a protagonist (Thomas in *Blow-Up*, an unnamed photographer in *The Terrorizers*) who, as a result of his nosy picture-taking, becomes embroiled in a murder. Both protagonists then grow obsessed with reconstructing the scene with their photographs. In a broad narrative sense, both films deviate from the standard 'Hollywood formula': the stories aren't linear; the conflicts are never resolved; and the lives of the characters reflect the incompleteness of the writing process. Both films problematise the 'veracity of representation' – the idea that a photograph can fragment and warp reality such that the truth of the past becomes difficult to pinpoint. Characters in both films comment on the frustration associated with 'not being able to finish something' (Zhou Yufen in *The Terrorizers*, Thomas in *Blow-Up*). Writer's block spans across all forms of media, from photography to writing, and, in each film, the protagonists grow obsessed with the idea that writer's block can result in a potentially 'deadly' final product.

Contrary to Weaver, who states that *The Terrorizers* 'is not a meta-reflective film about the struggle to create art that mirrors life' (1), I would argue that both *Blow-Up* and *Terrorizers are* premised on the idea that photography can be deceptive, and, more generally, that art and reality *can* be mirrored and distorted by one another. Both films also function as artefacts – as reflections of a particular strain of political resistance that appears in art within a specific historical context. While Antonioni's film reflects the drugs and rock-and-roll counterculture of 1960s London, Yang's film critiques the empty materialism of the rising middle class in 1980s Taipei. While *Blow-Up* resists traditional, Hollywood notions of narrative (that is, stories progress in a linear fashion, they are bookended by clear beginnings and endings, and so on), *Terrorizers* resists both the Hollywood stereotype and the plush storytelling of Fifth Generation film-makers.[11] Neither film ends, of course, with any sort of satisfying 'resolution' by a standard Hollywood definition: Thomas is left by the camera in the middle of a field and Zhou is cut off by the end credits just as she is about to vomit.

Though Berry and Weaver (among others) have noted similarities between Yang's *Terrorizers* and Antonioni's *Blow-Up*, there are surprisingly few close-reading comparisons of the two films, especially with regard to the two endings. Many previous analyses rely on a superficial comparison between the modernist/postmodernist aspects of both films, a distinction that itself tends to be ill-defined and inconsistent. By comparing and analysing key sequences, I aim to shed light on the thematic similarities and modes of 'narrative fracture' that these two films share. I feel that close readings of individual scenes – rather than a broader political commentary – prove more fruitful in the case of these two films. In addition, I aim to define Yang in the context of Taiwanese New Wave and to distinguish his work from that of Antonioni. Yang and Antonioni's styles of film-making are very different but not in the sense that scholars such as Weaver might have us believe.

Though neither film is absolutely dependent on national setting, both films depend on characters that are themselves frozen in time and space and are in some way attached to their respective historical periods. Antonioni's *Blow-Up* is a veritable time capsule. The film is fascinating to watch because it captures the avant-garde, colourful mood of late 1960s-era London. The film's protagonist, played by actor David Hemmings, radiates this same inimitable quality. Hemmings plays Thomas, a character based on the real-life fashion photographer David Bailey.[12] Hemmings's facial features recall the boyish good looks of Beatles-era Paul McCartney; his innocent facade hides a misogynist undercurrent. As Thomas, Hemmings manages to craft a character who is both sympathetic (appealing even) and yet repugnant at the same time.

He barks commands at the models in his studio, seeing them only as objects in front of his camera. Even when 'seducing' Veruschka, Thomas holds the camera firmly over his face. This oddly likeably unlikeable character – a sort of Alex DeLarge 'light'[13] – might have been a difficult role for anyone but Hemmings.

Though Antonioni foresaw the need to shoot his film outside Italy, the director did not want his film to be defined by its setting. In a 1982 interview with *Corriera della Sera*, Antonioni expresses the pressure he felt to break through notions of 'the national' in his film-making: 'While I was filming, I was hoping that no one seeing the finished film would say: "*Blow-Up* is a typical British film". At the same time, I was hoping that no one would define it exclusively as an Italian film' (Antonioni 89). Antonioni seems to have achieved his goal in the sense that the film did surprisingly well overseas. *Blow-Up* won the Grand Prix at Cannes and was an enormous box office success in the United States (which led to eventual changes in the Hollywood film rating system).

Antonioni was eager to capture a setting that did turn out to be ephemeral in many ways. The director knew that the film would not have worked as well if it had been shot in Italy. In the same interview, he comments: 'A character like Thomas doesn't really exist in our country' (89). He expands on this idea: though Thomas *could* have existed in either Rome or Milan, he does not. Though there were plenty of photographers who lived and worked in Rome and Milan in the 1960s, they would not have 'worked' as plausible facsimiles of David Bailey. For the project to 'ring true' for Antonioni, the film had to be set in London, at the centre of British youth culture.

If *Blow-Up* is biographical, then *The Terrorizer* is autobiographical in many ways. Yang's overall body of work is known to possess autobiographical elements: in *Yi Yi* (2000), for example, NJ (Nien-jen Wu) is unsatisfied in his career as a computer software designer (much like Yang was). Speaking about the personal, autobiographical nature of *Yi Yi*, Yang once commented in an interview: 'When you make a film like this . . . it's like writing a very intimate letter to a very good friend. The movie's success is not something that boosts my ego. But that there are so many friends in the world that understand you – that's a comforting feeling' (Anderson 4). The autobiographical aspect of Yang's films extends to the collective memory – the autobiography so to speak – of the Taiwanese population. In line with this idea, John Anderson describes Yang's *oeuvre* as a soul-search into the history of Taiwan, an exploration based on a 'lack of a traditional solid foundation' in a 'patchwork culture' (5).

In a very real sense, Yang's *oeuvre* is 'more Taiwanese' than any of the other New Wave directors. All his films are set in cities in Taiwan, and predominantly in Taipei. Though Edward Yang's *Terrorizers could* have been set in a city other than Taipei, the film reflects the political and literary climate of 1980s Taiwan. When Yang was asked whether or not he intended to make a statement about the alienation of Taipei specifically, the director replied that individuals can feel lonely and alienated in any city in the modern world. The American suburbs (as portrayed in films such as the 1999 Sam Mendes film *American Beauty*) are a much more frightening concept. '[The suburbs]', Yang laughs, 'are for people who want to be isolated in a very populated area!' (Berry 2005, 282). *Terrorizers*, notes Yang, incorporates elements that are both autobiographical and historically significant:

> . . . primarily I tried to relay what I witnessed. What I really wanted to do was reflect the variety of social phenomenon [*sic*] of that era in the structure of the film . . . the film is very much intertwined with the city of Taipei . . . what was happening in Taipei city was a very unique situation. (Berry 2005, 283)

Yang chose to set this film in Taipei, in other words, because the city was meaningful to both his own life and to the story of the film itself. The murder in *Terrorizers* is based on the Mao Wu Incident, a real-life stabbing that was etched into his memory as a schoolboy in Taipei. Yang explains that he wanted to 'leave behind a record' so that the impact of the event would not be forgotten by future generations (Berry 2005, 283).

The characters in this film, and in many of Yang's films, were reminiscent of real people but were always fictional. As Tony Rayns describes the characters in *Confucian Confusion*: 'None of these characters is based on an actual individual, but all of them are highly recognizable urban types, especially in Taipei. The key question in the months to come will be: to what extent will audiences beyond Taiwan relate to these characters and situations?' (26) Rayns concludes that because Warner Asia has been asked to oversee distribution, as well as foreign and international sales of the film, that *Confucian Confusion* would be an international success. Because Yang creates scenes that are representative of larger themes, his aesthetics work on a universal level.

Jameson describes the universality that is present in Yang's films, and he explains the appeal of the postmodern theme:

> In our own postmodern world there is no longer a bourgeois or class-specific culture to be indicted, but rather a system-specific phenomenon: the various forms which reification and commodification and the corporate standardizations of media society imprint on human subjectivity and existential experience. (Jameson 131)

Even small, seemingly unimportant scenes fit into the larger 'jigsaw puzzle' of a Yang film. Each of his films functions as a sort of 'social panorama' in miniature. By constructing realistic portraits of lower middle-class Taiwanese families, Yang manages – almost paradoxically – to create films with universal appeal.

Antonioni's characters, on the other hand, tend be members of the upper class. Plagued with the ennui of modern-day existence, Antonioni's characters are often less than sympathetic to the viewer upon first glance. Though the main character in Antonioni's film *Blow-Up,* Thomas, is based on a real-life, successful, celebrity photographer, the plot of the film is based on a fictional short story by Argentine writer Julio Cortázar entitled: 'Las babas del Diablo'/'The Devil's Drool.'[14] Though Antonioni's film is obviously adapted from Cortázar's story, many of the details differ. In Cortázar's story, Michel is an amateur photographer living in Paris. The narration shifts between present tense and flashback mode and, more strikingly, between first person and third person.

Michel recalls, for the reader, an event that permanently shaped his psyche. Wandering through Paris one day with his camera, he happens upon a suspicious occurrence: a blonde woman corners a nervous young boy as a man watches from his car. Reacting to the oddity of the situation, Michel reaches instinctively for his camera:

> I raised the camera, pretended to study a focus which did not include them, and waited and watched closely, sure that I would finally catch the revealing expression, one that would sum it all up, life that is rhythmed by movement but which a stiff image destroys, taking time in cross section, if we do not choose the essential imperceptible fraction of it. (Cortázar 123)

As Michel fumbles to document the scene, the woman angrily confronts him, and the young boy is able to run away. Though the man in the car does not speak, he emerges, menacingly, from it. In that moment, Michel is able to catch a glimpse of the man's eyes which he describes as bottomless holes. Later, after enlarging the photo in his darkroom, Michel quickly realises that he has captured a crime: an attempted sexual assault orchestrated by the frightening-looking man in the car.

Antonioni's film contains a similar plot intrigue: Thomas photographs an odd-looking couple – a younger woman and an older man – while walking through Maryon Park in London. The young woman (Vanessa Redgrave) confronts Thomas angrily and insists that he provide her with the negative (he refuses). Thomas returns to his apartment and enlarges his photos which appear to depict a murder-in-action. In the photos, the woman is coercing the man into the target range for an unseen sniper. Later in the film, Thomas finds the dead body in the bushes. Unfortunately, it is now night-time, and he is not carrying his camera with him. When Thomas is finally able to return to the spot to 'record' the image with his camera, the body has mysteriously disappeared. The mystery of the missing body is never explained within the film, an unsatisfying ending by most standards, but typical for Antonioni.

If there is any 'lesson' to be learned so far, it is that crime and art do not mix. When the creation of art – taking photos, writing novels – is combined with crime, the results are deadly. The artist becomes embroiled in a story that was not preconceived, that he has happened upon by chance. That moment – the moment that the artist decides to put an end to his writer's block by document-ing the crime – is a dangerous one. The documentation of this dangerous new reality causes the artist to enter into a world in which fiction and non-fiction are no longer distinguishable. Once the picture has been taken or the words have been written, the artist is inevitably damned to exist in the fictional world that he has created for himself. Like Cortázar's narrator, who views the pho-tograph as a 'stiff image' that 'destroys movement', Walter Benjamin describes the 'captured moment' of a photograph as a 'dialectic at a standstill'. We are able to 'seize' a moment by viewing an image, an image that is in itself dream-like and elusive: 'this standstill is utopia, and the dialectical image, therefore, dream image' (Tiedemann 943). Film captures movement, whereas photogra-phy captures static images.

Terry J. Peavler, in his article: 'Blow-Up: A Reconsideration of Antonioni's Infidelity to Cortázar' (1979), offers a similar interpretation of Thomas's fate:

> . . . with the pressing of the shutter something mysterious happens in the world of technology: instead of the image before the lens being frozen on film while life behind the camera goes on, the photographer himself becomes eternally frozen, as if on film, while life in front of the lens con-tinues. (Peavler 889)

In modernist fiction, the description of feeling detached from one's own body, reflected real-life worries. Compelled to capture the brutality of reality, the 'photographer in fiction' experiences life as a hand cranking a machine rather than as a human being. In the early days of photography and cinematography, artists and critics worried that both life and art had becomes too mechanical for comfort. The 'photographer in fiction' figure is the Modern Man in crisis. This association can be traced back to Serafino Gubbio, the cinematographer protagonist in Luigi Pirandello's 1915 novel Shoot![15] In Pirandello's novel, Gubbio often asks himself: 'If it is mechanical, how can it be life, how can it be art?' (Pirandello 88) In the final scene of the novel, Gubbio films a scene in which the actor is supposed to shoot a caged tiger. Suddenly, the stunt goes terribly wrong, and the actor is brutally ripped to shreds by the huge beast. Perhaps most disturbingly, Gubbio is unable to stop filming in order actually to help the man. Gubbio, another 'photographer in fiction' is a slave to his beastly camera: '. . . that machine had in its maw the life of a man; I had given it that life to eat to the very last . . .' (Pirandello 332)

The fate of the twentieth-century 'photographer in fiction' is equally beastly. In a final, frustrated attempt to capture an interesting image, to escape from the drudgery of everyday life, the photographer searches for inspiration on the streets of the city. The photographer happens upon (perhaps even 'lucks into') the middle of a dramatic event that he or she is compelled to document. First, the photographer feels as if it is his or her 'moral duty' to capture the crime in the act; then the photographer feels obliged to take on the detective role and to solve the mystery. Though the photographer is certainly not a trained detective, he or she must attempt to solve the mystery using familiar methods. The photographer is trained to enlarge images, to 'zoom in' on dark corners, and to reproduce negatives in an infinite variety of ways. As the photographer enters into the dark room, the ability to reproduce and manipulate images ad infinitum leads the photographer further away from reality. The photographer's all-encompassing obsession to solve the crime leads to a disruption of personal relationships.

Cortázar's narrator comments: 'I'm telling a truth which is only my truth, and then is the truth only for my stomach, for this impulse to go running out and to finish up in some manner with this, whatever it is' (115). When Michel says that his story is the 'truth only for my stomach' he is admitting that the telling of the story is what has become important – he must confess and remove it from his consciousness. In recounting the story, Michel alleviates the knot in his stomach that was caused by him witnessing the event in the first place. But the confession is not inspired by a noble cause: Michel admits that the telling of his story is motivated by his desire to get it out of his system, not by his desire to serve as a witness in a murder trial. In a literary take on the liar's paradox (that is: 'this sentence is false'), Michel admits to his outright unreliability as a narrator. By shifting the perspective between first and third person throughout, Cortázar signals to his reader that his narrator is erratic and untrustworthy. Michel's 'confession' requires only that the reader willingly accepts the falsity of his story; nothing that he has said, or will say, should be taken as testimony. Michel is aware that his desire to confess does not outweigh his moral obligation as a witness to a crime. Nevertheless, he consciously places morality to the side because the burden of keeping the story 'within his own stomach' has become too overbearing. He knows that if he begins to question himself, he will no longer be able to rid himself of it. The act of telling is, therefore, a selfish one: 'If I begin to ask questions I'll never tell anything, maybe to tell would be like an answer, at least for someone who's reading it' (116).

The male protagonist of Yang's *Terrorizers* is, similarly, a photographer who unwittingly captures still images of a crime scene in action. The still photos that Yang's protagonist captures recall the photographs that comprise Chris Marker's film *La Jetée* (1962). Marker's film is composed entirely of still photographs, pasted together to create the alienating feeling of a post-apocalyptic future in which humans are forced to live underground like rats. The stillness of the photographs gives the film an eerie, timeless quality – as if the present, past and future can no longer be distinguished because everything that was going to happen has already happened. There is only one moving image in the entire film: the woman (Hélène Chatelain) is lying in bed and blinks her eyes. This is the only moment in the film in which the present tense exists. In this moment only, the viewer enters into this new form of reality, this new dimension in time, that the still photos cannot provide. In this moment, the woman comes to life, breaking free from the 'stiff' timeless infinity of the photographic medium. If photography is like death, if the photograph is like a corpse, then the moving image is like a breath of life.

Corpses and sleeping bodies are a consistent visual theme in *Terrorizers*. The images of dead bodies are burned into the mind of the viewer, visually juxtaposed with shots of characters who are sleeping or lying in bed. The images at the beginning of the film are carefully constructed into a series of graphic matches – the young photographer's girlfriend has fallen asleep while reading a book, a dead body lies in the middle of the street outside, Zhou is asleep in bed, but suddenly awakens, the White Chick collapses in exhaustion in the middle of the road.

In the first of a sequence of shots, we see a hand appear, shooting a gun from an apartment balcony. In the next shot, we see a dead body sprawled

Figure 2.1   An anonymous dead body, a victim of the shoot-out.

Figure 2.2 White Chick, collapsed in the middle of the street.

Figure 2.3 Zhou Yufen, awakened from sleep and worried about her novel.

in the middle of the street. These subsequent images are combined and juxtaposed, linked causally in the mind of the viewer. The man in the street, we assume, was killed by the gang's gunshots. Sounds are juxtaposed as well: the sound of gunfire is replaced with the sound of rapid picture-taking. The young photographer is snapping pictures of the horrific scene. Though the police chief is unfazed by gunshots, he does not seem to appreciate having his own picture taken. Pointing directly at the photographer (and simultaneously at the viewer), the police chief motions for the young man to exit the premises. Like the photographer, we have been caught in our shameless voyeurism, and we have been warned to leave the scene.

But the photographer does not heed the policeman's warning. As he continues to snap pictures of the crime scene, two policemen attempt to confiscate his camera. Fortunately, the young photographer is able to wrestle his camera from the policemen's clutches when they are momentarily distracted by an escaping gang member. A young, tomboyish woman is left behind in the wake of the gang member's attempt to flee from the police. The woman tries desperately to escape as well, despite her injuries. As we come to find out later, the woman (nicknamed 'White Chick' because she is ethnically Eurasian), is a part-time prostitute and member of the gambling ring.[16] The photographer, meanwhile, intrigued and infatuated by the girl, snaps a series of pictures of White Chick as she limps, with her back to the camera, down the alleyway. At the end of the sequence, White Chick collapses in the middle of a busy street.

David Bordwell, who describes this sequence as one of the 'most enigmatic and elliptical opening sequences in modern cinema', notes that Yang often breaks his scenes into emotionally forceful fragments. He describes the series of image fragments that the viewer sees as White Chick staggers and falls, commenting: 'I imagine these as forceful, laconic comic-book panels' (2007, n.p.). Bordwell's description of this sequence fails to account for Yang's use of film as a medium distinct unto itself. As spectators, we are drawn into the action of this scene because of camera movement – much more so than we would be if it had been broken up into a series of comic-book panels. In fact, it is precisely because we are watching a film (as opposed to looking at a series of pictures) that we are made to feel like witnesses to a crime. As Julia Round notes: 'the reliability of the medium [of film] is seldom compromised . . . however, comic's use of overtly stylized art subverts this (as there is no truth or realism in the mode)' (Round 325). As film spectators, we are made uncomfortable by the possibility that we are the sole witnesses to the White Chick's accident, and that no one has seen it or will stop to help. Yang adds to our discomfort by leaving the scene unresolved. In fact, we do not find out until a few scenes later that the photographer did actually witness White Chick's fall, and that he saved her life by taking her to a hospital.

In his chapter 'Le Grand Imagier Steps Out: The Primitive Basis of Film Narration', in the larger volume *The Philosophy of Film and Motion Pictures: An Anthology* (2006), George M. Wilson argues, contrary to Round, that the reliability of the film medium, as well as the comic book medium, are frequently compromised. In both forms of media, the viewer can imagine that the frames that comprise the story have been selected by an unreliable narrator.

Wilson comments on this phenomenon in terms of 'fictional showings'; the idea that fictional narratives imply the existence of a narrator or 'show-er':

> It is easy to think of possible comic strips in which a fictional showing would be implicated. The frames of the comic strip could be rendered in such fashion that they are themselves represented as being, say, photographs taken by a witness to the events depicted . . . one can conceive of ways in which the represented character of the frame and the nature of their selection could convey fictional facts about the personality and sensibility of the 'implied' photographer. In this example, there is plainly a fictional activity of showing the story that the viewer is to imagine, that is, the fictional activity of taking and assembling the photographs. And here there is a fictional agent of that activity, that is the fictional eyewitness and photographer. (Carrol and Choi 188)

Wilson argues that the text's medium offers clues that allow the viewer to imagine the appropriate type of fictional showing. He argues that detailed facts within the text itself allow the viewer to understand the text as well as to imagine the appropriate context of the 'fictional showing'. Whereas in a piece of literary fiction, argues Wilson, where representational strategies tend to be fixed and familiar, '. . . in other cases – the comic strip is a good example of this – rather special strategies of implicit representation of the text have to be more distinctly set in place' (188). Wilson's observation leads the film viewer to wonder: could White Chick's fall have been re-assembled to appear 'real' by the photographer? As witnesses to the fall, we are certainly left with feelings of discomfort. If, as Bordwell suggests, the scene is reminiscent of assembled comic-book panels, and if, as Wilson suggests, both the film text and the comic strip can be imagined as fictional 'showings' then how might we account for the difference in our emotional response to the immediacy of Yang's camera movements? The ambiguity of this scene suggests that narrative unreliability can appear in a variety of media and, moreover, that the film and comic strips, as media forms, may not be so distinct from each other.

Meanwhile, the young photographer's girlfriend, angry with her boyfriend when she discovers his obsession with White Chick, rips down all his photos and negatives. Yang's choice of shot pattern is unusual in this sequence: the camera shifts between the angry girlfriend and the astonished boyfriend in a typical action–reaction, ABAB pattern. In the last shot of the sequence, the girlfriend turns around one last time to glare at her boyfriend. When she looks towards the balcony, we expect that the boyfriend will appear in the next shot, resolving the sequence. A final shot of the boyfriend at the balcony would have resolved the sequence, allowing the viewer to see his final reaction. Instead, the shot is empty, except for the wind blowing through the curtains. The photographer has already left the apartment, returning to the crime scene with his camera slung over his shoulder.

Like Thomas, the young photographer is dedicated to his camera at all costs, even at the expense of his relationship with his girlfriend. Concerned only with the elusive idea that he can 'capture' truth with his photos, the photographer ignores the reality that exists beyond the frame. Later in the film, the young photographer sits with White Chick, and she asks him: 'what pleasure do you get from pictures?' The young photographer, who is about to enlist in the army, tells White Chick: 'I'll bring your picture with me to the army, you'll stay with me and wait for me.' Unable to differentiate life from the reality of his photos, the young man knows only the image of White Chick that he has created. When we find out later that White Chick was never serious about her relationship with the photographer, her photograph appears – in pieces – blowing apart in the breeze.

Zhou (Cora Miao), meanwhile, comments to her husband Li (Lichun Lee) that she cannot sleep because of her compulsion to rewrite her novel. The fact that the deadline is looming only makes her writer's block worse. In response to Zhou's complaint, her husband replies: 'writing a novel shouldn't be so deadly'. Unknown to him, the action of writing the novel turns out to be most deadly for Li. Zhou is able to escape her writer's block only by escaping from the 'prison' of her real-life situation. The characters in her novel mirror events in the film: a woman leaves her husband for an old flame. Similarly, Zhou leaves her husband for a man who is both her former lover and her publisher. When the husband in Zhou's novel finds out that his wife has been unfaithful, he kills his wife's lover and then kills himself.

Zhou, on the brink of leaving her husband, asks him: 'can't you separate fiction from reality?' The question, however, is directed as much at the film viewer as it is at her husband. As Yang shows us, we are not able to separate fiction from reality, at least not within the context of this film. We watch as Li shoots Zhou's lover; then, in the second to last scene, he shoots himself. Strangely, though, Zhou and her lover appear together again in bed, in the final scene of the film. We are now no longer certain whether or not the murder has actually taken place or if the murder sequence was meant to represent the imaginary world of Zhou's novel.

Unlike Weaver, therefore, I am unconvinced that the scene must be inter-preted as a representation of Li's dream. There are too many other possibili-ties: on the one hand, the final sequence reads as an alternate ending, a piece of the narrative puzzle that has been inserted out of chronological order; on the other hand, as I mentioned, the murder scene could be a filmic representa-tion of Zhou Yufen's novel. Though 'imaginary' in some respects, the world of Zhou's novel has become inseparable from reality, for Zhou and for the film viewer. Like Thomas, who freezes himself into a limbo between reality and fiction in the moment that he snaps the picture, Zhou traps herself in the fiction of her own story in the moment that she rewrites it. Her decision to leave her husband for her former lover allows her to escape from her writer's block and to find success but it also seals her fate as prisoner within her own narrative.

Life's 'rhythm of events' cannot be reproduced with photography because the photograph is a cross-hatched representation of time. Though this is a simplified version of the idea that cameras distort the veracity of representation, this is not the equivalent of the claim that either *Blow-Up* or *The Terrorizers* denies epistemic certainty. This conflation has led critics to identify *The Terrorizers* as the epitome of a 'postmodernist film', while *Blow-Up* is deemed 'modernist'. Weaver, for instance, writes:

> This troubled relationship between the real and the mediated, a thoroughly postmodernist trope, is perhaps best exemplified by *The Terrorizers'* main cinematic intertext: Michelangelo Antonioni's *Blow-Up* ... yet Antonioni's film, like Zhou Yufen's novel, refashions incidents into patterns to reach a conclusive, if enigmatic ending ... (Weaver)

It is not clear that the relationship between the real and mediated is a 'thoroughly postmodernist trope', rather than simply a modernist trope, as Weaver argues. Certainly it is clear, as Weaver contends, that, after watching *Blow-Up*, the viewer is not sure if the murder was ever committed or if Thomas ever had evidence of it. It is not clear, on the other hand, as Weaver contends, that Thomas's subjectivity has 'been examined' and that he has 'reached new conclusions' about his capacity to 'apprehend the world around him'. The film's final message *can* be read in this way, but it need not be. In fact, *Terrorizers* is more interesting if it is read – not as the cinematic intertext of Antonioni's film – but as a *second* modernist iteration of it. That is, both films cause the viewer to ponder the relationship between reality and art by showing the protagonist cross between those very lines. Thomas is frozen in time as life continues around him. By taking the photo of the couple in the park, Thomas freezes himself into the image. Meanwhile (and ironically), though they have supposedly been 'caught' in the image, the couple now seem to transform and move as they please. The message of *Blow-Up*, therefore, is not: 'we have no idea what happened in the park; therefore, we must accept that everything in life is relative. Like Thomas, we must re-examine our own subjectivity, accepting our inability to "know" the truth.' The message, rather, is that by writing a story, by taking a photograph, an author feels as if he or she is capable of telling some sort of truth to the audience. What happens, instead, is that the author becomes stuck in the telling of the story or, in Thomas's case, in the frame of the picture itself.

Thomas involves himself in the imaginary tennis game at the end of the film because he accepts his fate as the ghost behind the camera – caught in his role as the 'photographer in fiction'; he has no capacity to communicate reality through art. But Thomas's 'acceptance' of his situation does not necessarily have to be read in a positive light. Either we interpret Thomas's so-called 'acceptance' as a healthy, life-improving revelation or, on the contrary, we interpret it as his final departure from whatever sanity he may have had left. Photos cannot communicate in place of experience, just as language cannot always communicate experience. This does not mean that the murder did not happen, nor does it mean necessarily that Thomas is crazy – only that our modes of communication and mediation can freeze us, causing us to become ghosts in the lively world around us. We do not know whether or not Thomas has personally reached these conclusions. It is up to the viewer to interpret the film's message about the complex relationship between art and life.

Like the young girl in the *Twilight Zone: The Movie*[17] who is willed into a television set by her evil brother and gobbled to bits by a cartoon character, Thomas, Zhou Yufen and the young photographer are trapped in dangerous fictional worlds. In some cases, these are the worlds that they have created for themselves. Li, who expressed his desire early in the film to have nothing to do with his wife's writing, is the most serious victim of his wife's act of fiction. Dead by his own hand, Li is the final, most devastatingly real, casualty of the artistic process.

CONCLUSIONS

Towards the end of his own life, Edward Yang continued to create films on both death and photography. By the time that Yang directed his final three-hour film, *Yi Yi*, however, the tone had changed somewhat. Overall, *Yi Yi* contains a positive message about the nature of music, life, love and death. The film's title is untranslatable into English because the Chinese title, written – means 'one, one' when written side by side, but means 'two' – when written vertically. The film, set in Taipei, follows the lives of three members of the Jian family: middle-aged father NJ (Nien-jen Wu) who is married to Min-Min (played by Elaine Jin), young son Yang-Yang (Jonathan Chang), and teenage daughter Ting-Ting (Kelly Lee). The film is bookended by Min-Min's brother's wedding in the first scene and Min-Min's mother's funeral in the last scene. At the wedding, NJ runs into his former girlfriend Sherry (Ke Suyun) who is now married to a rich American. Seeing Sherry causes NJ to enter into his own existential crisis, and he begins to wonder whether or not he has made the right decisions in his life. Through a work assignment, NJ meets and befriends a Japanese game designer named Ota (Issey Ogata). The two men are able to communicate only in English, the language of business, and yet they pontificate on life and love in several poignant scenes. Western classical music pervades

Yi Yi. Besides *Moonlight Sonata*, the soundtrack features Beethoven's *Cello Sonata No. 1*, Bach's *Toccata in E minor*, and *BWV 914*.

In one such scene, NJ and Ota dine together for the first time as they attempt to negotiate a business contract. Ota steers the conversation away from work and offers advice to NJ as he reflects on the stress associated with life changes. 'Why are we afraid of the first time?' he asks. 'Every moment in life is a first time. Every morning is new. We never live the same day twice. We are never afraid of getting up every morning. Why?' The camera cuts from the restaurant and the two men get into a car. The cut in this moment suggests that NJ had been intrigued by Ota's philosophising at dinner which has led the two men to 'hang out' together in a more personal setting. In the car, the men bond over their love for classical music. NJ recalls that classical music had no meaning for him until he fell in love for the first time at the age of fifteen. 'Many people think that music is useless', NJ comments to Ota, '[because] you can't get any money from it.' NJ then reveals that he recently ran into his former girlfriend, Sherry, at his son-in-law's wedding. Sherry, he reveals further, was the girl that allowed him to fall in love with music. He had not seen her for thirty years until that night. Immediately upon learning this about his friend, Ota insists on taking NJ to a karaoke bar. At the karaoke bar, Ota shows off his piano skills. At first he accompanies drunk singers but ends the evening with an impressive rendition of Beethoven's *Moonlight Sonata*. Listening to Beethoven prompts NJ to call his former girlfriend later that same evening, after he returns from the bar. 'I was stupid to have left you' he says to her answering machine.

Placing *Moonlight Sonata* in this scene is a significant narrative choice. The original title of the piece, *Quasi una fantasia*, was a musical directive that translates imperfectly into English as 'to be played as if in a fantasy'. The original note for the piano player, as written by Beethoven, also reads: '*Si deve suonare tutto questo pezzo delicatissimamente e senza sordini*' (This piece is to be played very delicately, without any mute/with the sustain pedal pressed down the entire time). The sustain pedal prolongs every note so that the entire piece resonates as each note overlaps with the last. The echoing of the pedal creates the feeling, for the listener, of moving away from reality and into the world of fantasy. Classical music, for both NJ and Ota, is beautiful precisely because of its ability to carry the listener away from the mundane aspects of everyday life. NJ and Ota both believe that music allows people to rise above menial tasks, to see beyond the shallow desire to make money, and to find happiness in art. If art is fantasy, then fantasy is both life and death at the same time.

The film deals with death as much as it deals with life. In Yang's final film, however, death is not a frightening place but, rather, it is a place for the wise. In the last scene of the film, the youngest son, Yang-Yang, speaks at his grandmother's funeral. Yang-Yang's final speech to his grandmother comprises both the last words of *Yi Yi*, and the last words that any of Yang's characters would ever speak.

> They all say you've gone away, but you didn't tell me where you went. I guess it's someplace you think I should know. But, Grandma, I know so little. Do you know what I want to do when I grow up? I want to tell people things they don't know. Show them stuff they haven't seen. It'll be so much fun. Perhaps one day I'll find out where you've gone. If I do, can I tell everyone and bring them to visit you? Grandma, I miss you. Especially when I see my newborn cousin who still doesn't have a name. He reminds me that you always said you felt old. I want to tell him I am old too.

Yang has stated that the topics of his films were meant to be universal, though certain aspects of his films would have been most recognisable to Taiwanese audiences. Nevertheless, Yang explains, cultural forces and 'practical reality' can be combined to create a story with a 'larger force', a force that causes audiences to react in much the same way around the world (Sklar). Yang-Yang's speech, overall, functions as a eulogy to Yang himself – a sort of unintentional self-obituary. For this reason, among others, Yang-Yang's monologue seems all the more poignant since Yang's death in 2007.

After Yang won best director at the 2000 Cannes Film Festival for *Yi Yi*, he was poised to take his place among the most prominent world art cinema directors. Though *Yi Yi* was the first of Yang's seven feature films to receive commercial distribution in the United States, it was not released in Taiwan. This fact angered Yang because he felt that the Taiwanese media were continuing to demonise art house cinema. He worried that his own reputation in Taiwan would never change – that he would always be labelled by the general public as 'that guy who killed Taiwanese cinema because my work would never sell' (Sklar). The problem, explains Yang, is that people in general do not react well to those who paint bleak pictures of society. Negativity is not always a selling point. When Yang died in 2007, the *China Post* ran an obituary stating that it was Yang himself who pulled *Yi Yi* from Taiwanese theatres in protest against corruption in the local industry. In fact, this was true. Nevertheless, upon Yang's death, local film critic Huang Chien-yeh issued the statement: 'His death was a great loss to our film industry. He created a unique era with his poignant pessimism and cold rationality ... backing the uncompromising, sharp critique with his deep emotion' ('Taiwan Mourns'). Though the film was released on DVD for the Criterion Collection in 2006, *Yi Yi* has yet to be screened publicly in Taiwan.[18]

NOTES

1. According to the story, Herzog forced Kinski at gunpoint to continue acting for the camera. Herzog denies this story. Nevertheless, it is well documented that the two men did not get along.
2. The provincial government, the military, and the Kuomintang (Curtin 134).
3. Yeh and Davis refer to Yang's early *oeuvre* as 'Expectations' (92).
4. See Hamish Ford, 'Antonioni's *l'Avventura* and Deleuze's *Time Image*', *Senses of Cinema*, 5 October 2003, issue 28.
5. Bordwell <http://www.davidbordwell.net/blog/2007/08/11/bergman-antonioni-and-the-stubborn-stylists/> For a more in-depth analysis, see Weaver, *The Seventh Art*, section 3, issue 3 (also a video essay).
6. 'In *Red Desert*, I had worked hard to ensure flattened perspectives with the telephoto lens, to compress characters and things and to place them in juxtaposition with one another. In *Blow-Up*, I instead opened up the perspective, I tried to put air and space between people and things. The only time I made use of the telephoto lens in the film was when I had to – for example in the sequence when Thomas is caught in the middle of the crowd' (Antonioni 90).
7. Clicking the link that Bordwell provides to his commentary on Yang, entitled: 'Two Chinese Men of the Cinema', we find no further comparative analysis of the so-called Antonioni/Yang aesthetic. Weaver's video essay seems to be one of the only longer comparative analyses.
8. In *The Geopolitical Aesthetic: Cinema and Space in the World System*.
9. *Fukan*, or a literary supplement, is a journalistic phenomenon that is unique to modern China. Though *fukan* was considered 'leisure reading', it also contained cultural commentary. Most importantly, *fukan* supported many rising literary writers in the 1970s and 1980s in Taiwan, and sponsored an annual writing contest (Berry 17).
10. For the online glossary, see <onlinelibrary.wiley.com/doi/10.1002/9781444304794.gloss/pdf> (last accessed 25 February 2013).
11. Of course, both Antonioni and Yang were influenced by aesthetics that reach beyond narrative traditions, or aesthetics, associated with either the 'East' or 'West'. Antonioni was intrigued by China and travelled to the mainland to make a film documentary, *Chung Kuo*, in the early 1970s. Yang, meanwhile, lived in the United States, where he attended the University of Southern California, for several years before returning to Taiwan (Berry 273). Both film-makers, therefore, were used to working transnationally; that is, across borders.
12. Bailey worked in London throughout most of the 1960s where he took photographic portraits of celebrities such as (model) Jean Shrimpton, Catherine Deneuve and the Beatles.
13. Alex DeLarge (Malcolm McDowell) is the main character in Stanley Kubrick's *A Clockwork Orange*. His baby face belies an incredibly sick and twisted personality.
14. The story was originally written in 1959. After the success of the film, the story is also translated as 'Blow-Up' (probably for marketing purposes).
15. The full title is: *Shoot! The Notebooks of Serafino Gubbio Cinematograph Operator*, and was written by Pirandello in 1915, in the early days of cinema. The protagonist, Gubbio, is an early cinematographer who works for the Kosmograph studio during the infancy of the film industry in Europe.
16. Yang cast this particular actress because her life was similar to that of the fictional character she plays in the film. Yang heard from a friend that she was interested in the role (See Berry, *Speaking in Images*).

17. This occurs in the third segment of *Twilight Zone: The Movie,* entitled: 'It's a Good Life', directed by John Landis (1983).
18. At the current time of publication, 2013.

3. MAPPING HOU HSIAO-HSIEN'S VISUALITY: SETTING, SILENCE AND THE INCONGRUENCE OF TRANSLATION IN *FLIGHT OF THE RED BALLOON*

In his 2001 text, *An Accented Cinema: Exilic and Diasporic Filmmaking*, Hamid Naficy defines his concept of 'accented cinema' as: 'fragmented, multi-lingual, epistolary, self-reflexive . . . amphibolic, doubled, crossed' and so on. For Naficy, 'accented cinema' contains: '. . . lost characters; subject matter and themes that involve journeying, historicity, identity, and displacement' (4). At the end of this long list of adjectives, Naficy adds that accented cinema is often a collective undertaking (that is, it is often co-produced), and that the films themselves tend to reflect the film-maker's identity as an exile or migrant.

In an interview with French director Olivier Assayas, Hou Hsiao-hsien (侯孝賢) describes himself as a Taiwanese film-maker who is 'culturally Chinese'. Though this term, 'culturally Chinese' does create a misleading sense of the uniformity of culture, Naficy's terminology can be similarly misleading. Though Naficy's description of 'accented cinema' is helpful in that it contains a general list of qualities that most non-Hollywood films share, the term again reinforces a binary. If, on the one hand, 'dominant cinema' is 'considered universal and without accent', then, on the other hand, says Naficy: 'the films that diasporic and exilic subjects make are accented' (Naficy 4). Despite his beautifully rich and imaginative description of accented cinema, and despite his work to add pinches of ambivalence into the equation, Naficy has still, fundamentally, divided cinema into two classes: one 'dominant' and 'universal', the other 'exilic' and 'accented'. As we shall see in the chapter on Ang Lee, especially, this can be a misleading dichotomy. Similarly, when Shih describes the 'Sinophone' as a grouping of visual practices outside the mainland, we are left with a certain difficulty when attempting to describe Taiwanese cinematic tradition in relation to mainland influences. Though we certainly would not want to make the mistake of conflating separate traditions, it seems equally illogical to create unnecessary divisions.

It may, in other words, prove impractical to cut off possible channels of comparative analysis despite the fact that the channel of influence between the mainland and Taiwan is fraught with imbalance. For this reason, I have adapted and appropriated both Naficy's term 'accented' and Shih's term 'Sinophone' for the purposes of discussing Hou's films in the context of this chapter. I have revised the meaning of the term to encompass the idea of displacement in the context of the film narrative itself. While I agree with the majority of Shih's central arguments (that is, the idea that diaspora is temporally marked, that linguistic communities are open and constantly changing), the term 'Sinophone' (as defined by Shih) can be stretched to encompass all types of visual art, from films, to paintings, to photographs, to television programmes. Shih constructs a solid thesis about the displacement of the Chinese diaspora and how this relates to and enriches Sinophone visuality in general terms. In discussing Hou's films as incarnations of the New Cinema tradition, however, I have found it necessary to build upon Shih's definition of Sinophone visuality.

NATIVIST LITERATURE, NEW WAVE CINEMA

Taiwan's move towards independence, away from the mainland, was preceded by a long list of setbacks and political embarrassments. In the 1970s, Taiwan, not yet an industrial or 'commercial' society, was in a period of transition though this move towards change was not necessarily visible. Through the KMT government, the Republic of China still controlled Taiwan. The government figures at the time (Secretary General and Minister of Education, Chiang Yang-shih, in particular) were determined to trample progressive voices (Huang 2003). Domestic discontent fomented and bubbled up from beneath the surface, causing the ROC to react aggressively. One of the ROC's most aggressive moves was its withdrawal from the United Nations on 26 October 1971. The withdrawal came in response to a major protest organised by the Defending Diaoyutai (釣魚台), a pro-peace movement that was also nationalistic and pro-unification.[1] The movement originated as a protest against the increasingly violent disputes between China, Japan and Taiwan over a small group of uninhabited islands (the Diaoyutai). As a further result of these disputes, the ROC severed diplomatic relations with Japan in 1972, forcing Taiwan to do the same. Only a few years later, at the 1976 Olympic Games in Montreal, the ROC ordered the Canadian government to disqualify and turn away Taiwanese athletes. Taiwan was forced to sever diplomatic ties with the United States, Japan, and other major nations.

One of the most interesting, but less well known, of the clashes between the KMT government and peace-seeking citizens was the National Taiwan University Philosophy Department Incident (臺大哲學系事件). When a number of professors and students in the philosophy department at NTU spoke out in favour of peace for Taiwan in late 1974, the Taiwanese governmental authorities responded by dismissing the professors and forcing the NTU to close down the entire department. The professors were accused of being communists and extreme leftists and were not allowed to resume their teaching positions. It was not until 2003 that the university finally apologised for the incident and invited the professors back to their original positions – nearly thirty years later. The desire for peace, and the desire for Taiwan to move in a new direction more generally, were pervasive among the left, the educated, and Taiwanese students living abroad. The incident exemplifies the harsh authoritarian environment that had characterised Taiwanese society in the 1970s as well as the growing resistance against that authority. This series of political embarrassments in the 1970s led Taiwan into a new era of reflection in the 1980s. After this long period of domestic turmoil, martial law was lifted in 1987. Though the Democratic Progressive Party (DPP) had been formed much earlier (in the 1970s), Taiwan continued to have a multiparty system until 2000 when the DPP, which had advocated Taiwanese independence since the 1970s, finally gained formal control.

A newfound sense of pride, in combination with a shifting national identity, led to self-reflection and a renewed interest in local indigenous cultures. As scholar June Yip notes, this new sociopolitical awareness was first expressed most strikingly – not in the medium of film – but in nativist (*hsiang-t'u*) literature (Yip 711). *Hsiang-t'u* literature was not nostalgic, nor was it escapist. *Hsiang-t'u* authors wrote specifically from the perspective of Taiwanese natives, written for those who had come to self-identify as Taiwanese in the wake of the occupation. Some *hsiang-t'u* writers, such as Wu Cho-lui (1900–76), had lived through the Japanese occupation and were therefore positioned to reflect on the experience. Wu published his first novel in 1936 and he continued writing throughout his life. Wu's writing traces Taiwan's progression as it moved out of the colonial past and into an era of national reflection, embodied in art in both new literature and cinema (Tu 26). In a story from his larger collection, *Fig Tree*, Wu writes: 'The Taiwanese never looked upon the Ch'ing dynasty as their homeland. In the back of the Taiwanese mind there was their own nation. That nation was the Ming dynasty – the country of the Han people. This, then, was the homeland of the Taiwanese.' The statement is powerful and resonant. Taiwan, says Wu, belongs to the Han population – not to imperial rulers.

Other *hsiang-t'u* writers, such as Pai Hsien-yung and Chung Chao-cheng, wrote predominantly about the post-war period and openly expressed personal attitudes on controversial social and political topics. Taiwanese nativist writers of the post-war era adopted a blended style, taking pieces from modernism as well as from traditional Chinese literature. Nativist literature was specific to the Taiwanese experience, and writers such as Pai and Chung did not hesitate to recount gruesome aspects of their experiences. Pai's novel *Crystal Boys* (1983), for example, recounts the difficulties that are faced by a group of young homosexual men growing up in Taipei in the 1960s, and is written from the perspective of one of the men.

Many critics view the popularity of *hsiang-t'u* literature as the precursor to New Cinema. Yip describes New Cinema as the 'cinematic heir' to the nativist tradition, noting further that film director Hou Hsiao-hsien was at the forefront of the movement. Hou's films, Yip notes, deal with the same question that was raised by the *hsiang-t'u* writers: 'what does it mean to be a modern Taiwanese?' (Yip 712). Hou's *City of Sadness*, for instance, is a historical film that tells the story of a Taiwanese family's experiences from 1945 to 1949 – the violent years in which Taiwan emerged from the Japanese occupation and just before the arrival of the Kuomintang from the mainland. Before *City of Sadness*, the Taiwanese government had denied that the February 1947 incident had even occurred, despite the fact that tens of thousands of Taiwanese natives had been killed by the KMT. Hou's film daringly presented the corruption and horror of the incident – a decision that, on the film's release, resulted in major controversy.

This is, perhaps, why Hou Hsiao-hsien is one of the best known of the Taiwanese directors, both domestically and internationally. Born in Mei county, Guangdong province in 1947, Hou and his family quickly fled to Taiwan to escape the Chinese Civil War. Hou grew up in Taiwan, and studied at the National Taiwan Academy of the Arts. Though his early films: *The Sandwich Man* (1983), *A Time to Live, A Time to Die/Tongnian wangshi* (1985), *Dust in the Wind* (1986) and *A City of Sadness* (1989), are now associated with the realist, New Wave movement of the 1980s, it is important re-emphasise the idea that Hou's earliest films were very much influenced by nativist literature. Unlike Fifth Generation film-makers on the mainland, Hou was unfettered by censorship for most of his career. Even his earliest films deal with taboo subjects: in particular, the arrival of the Chinese Nationalists in Taiwan following the Japanese occupation (Berry 236).

Hou began his career before most of the other New Taiwanese film-makers and, even today, is still one of the most famous Taiwanese directors. As early as 1973, Hou was working in the film industry as an assistant director, screenwriter and producer (Berry 235). He had already been working in cinema for almost a decade when he directed his first full-length feature, *Cute Girl*, in

1980. Hou's first major film, however, was *The Sandwich Man,* a film that he co-directed with Wan Ren and Tseng chuang-hsiang in 1983. Greater success was soon to follow. Hou's 1985 epic *A Time to Live, A Time to Die* won the International Federation of Film Critics (FIPRESCI) Prize at the 1986 Berlin International Film Festival, and *A City of Sadness* (1989) (the first in a trilogy about twentieth-century Taiwanese history and national identity) won the Golden Lion at the 1989 Venice Film Festival. Hou continued to direct successful films into and throughout the 1990s. Most notably, Hou's *The Puppetmaster* (1993) won the Jury Prize at Cannes, and *Flowers of Shanghai* (1998), a historical drama about the lives of five courtesans in Qing Dynasty-era Shanghai, earned Hou a best director award at the Asian Pacific Film Festival.

In the 2000s, Hou directed *Millennium Mambo* (2001), *Café Lumière/Kohi Jiko* (2003), *Three Times* (2005), and *Flight of the Red Balloon/Le voyage du ballon rouge* (2008). In many ways, Hou's experience making *Café Lumière* prepared him for the challenge of *Flight of the Red Balloon.*[2] Hou travelled to Japan to shoot *Café Lumière* in Japanese, with Japanese actors, despite his own inability to speak Japanese fluently. The film was a tribute to Japanese director Yasujiro Ozu (best known for his 1953 *Tokyo Story*), pioneer of the low, 'pillow shot' camera angle, an unmoving camera, and a fragmented story-telling method. *Café Lumière* is the story of a young Japanese woman named Yoko Inoue (Yo Hitoto) who finds out, towards the beginning of the film, that she is pregnant with her Taiwanese boyfriend's child. She has a strange dream which leads her to a friend who owns a bookshop in the heart of Tokyo. At her friend's suggestion, Yoko conducts research on Taiwanese composer Jiang Wen-ye (whose musical imagery matches the imagery of her dream) for the remainder of the film. Unsurprisingly, *Café Lumière* is slow-moving. The plot consists of little more than has already been described. Tony McKibbin, in his *Senses of Cinema* article on the film, defends the slowness of the film. He remarks: 'An "innocent" spectator viewing Hou Hsiao-hsien's work might think they're watching "nothing" rather than witnessing the work of a master.' He explains that Hou's camera techniques comprise both an aesthetic and a philosophy. Hou prefers, or rather *insists*, upon leaving shots open to interpretation. Like Ozu's camera in *Tokyo Story*, Hou's camera actively avoids providing the viewer with all the required information within any one particular shot. This can be both a frustrating experience as well as a transcendent one.

Like Tsai, Hou prefers the long take, a still camera, and a noticeable absence of wordy dialogue. The lack of speech in Hou's films contributes to an overall feeling of non-ironic 'sweetness' and the hidden emotions of his characters. Unlike Tsai, however, Hou's films are self-consciously emotional. They are also less explicitly sexual. Emotions are expressed through subtle camera movements and the gestures of the actors. Overall, Hou's delicate camera work suggests that every small gesture is demonstrative of the untranslatable nature of love, fondness, and, at times, nostalgia for the past.

DOCUMENTING EARLY FAMILY LIFE

In the mid-1990s, French director Olivier Assayas (best known for *Irma Vep* with Maggie Cheung and Jean-Pierre Léaud, 1996) followed Hou back to his childhood neighbourhood to shoot a documentary portrait of him (entitled *HHH: A Portrait of Hou Hsiao-hsien)*. Since the two directors were on friendly terms, Hou offered to take Assayas on a tour of his old neighbourhood on the southern coast of Taiwan in the small town of Fengshan. As Assayas and his camera operators follow him through the town, Hou pauses at various monuments, reflecting on his early life. He explains that his parents did not expect to remain in Taiwan permanently, so they bought cheap, bamboo furniture. The family graveyard was never moved from Guangdong. Hou's own film *A Time to Live, A Time to Die* (1985), especially the opening sequence, is highly autobiographical. Scenes from *A Time to Live, a Time to Die* were actually shot in Hou's childhood home (76). Watching the film, then, allows viewers an insight into the director's personal childhood experiences in Fengshan. The title character is a little boy nicknamed 'Ah Hao', a shortened version of Hou Hsiao-hsien (Zhang and Xiao 338).

In the opening scene of *A Time to Live*, the voiceover narration speaks to the autobiographical nature of the film. The narrator explains that the film consists of 'memories from my youth; particularly impressions of my father'. In the second shot, a long take reveals the interior of Ah Hao's childhood house. The camera remains still for so many moments that the shot begins to resemble a framed painting. Approaching the vanishing point of this 'painting' is the kitchen area. On the right side of the frame is a door leading outside. Pots are casually strewn about the kitchen area as if someone is cooking on the other side of the wall. Children play outside but the door is open as if they might run through the house at any moment. Overall, the interior of Hou's quasi-fictional childhood abode looks lived-in but comfortable – open to the outside world but, at the same time, impermanent.

The third shot of the opening sequence of *A Time to Live* features an empty chair and desk made from a bamboo-like material. In case the viewer may wonder why no one inhabits the desk, Ah Hao's voiceover narration resumes, explaining why the father – and eventually the entire family – ended up moving to Taiwan. His father ran into an old classmate on the mainland who turned out to be the mayor of Fengshan. When Ah Hao (and Hou) would have been born, in the late 1940s, many families were trying to leave the mainland because of the Chinese Civil War. The narrator explains that, by running into his former classmate, his father found the perfect opportunity to relocate to

Figure 3.1   A cinematic recreation of Hou's childhood house (from *A Time to Live, A Time to Die*).

Taiwan: 'In Ghuangzhou [my father] met an old classmate from Chung-shan University . . . he asked if my father would move to Taiwan to be his Head Secretary.' The voiceover sets the scene and, with a subtle cut, the father suddenly inhabits the shot, reading casually at the desk. This almost seamless cut leaves the viewer with the impression that the father could have been sitting there all along. The narration, in other words, functions as a sort of cue that allows the viewer to detect the father's presence in the Fengshan house.

Overall, the sequence functions as a cinematic recreation of Hou's early memories, albeit an imperfect, slightly skewed recreation. Though these memories are, of course, specific to Hou, the presentation of those memories contains elements of universality. There is a sense in which Hou's childhood memories are emblematic of a larger, collective experience. Commenting on this impression of universality in *A Time to Live, A Time To Die*, Xiao and Zhang, in their *Encyclopedia of Chinese Film*, explain that: '[even though it tells] such a personal story . . . the film resonates with the life experiences of many other Taiwanese people' (338). Despite potential risks, Taiwan represented an improved living situation for those still living on the mainland around the time of the Chinese Civil War. This idea is reflected in the film when the narrator explains that Ah Hao's father quickly grew accustomed to his new lifestyle. After only a year living in Taiwan, Ah Hao's father writes to his wife, instructing her to bring his mother and children over to the island. Taiwan is 'a good place,' he writes, 'there's tap water'.

Though not quite so autobiographical, Hou's *Dust in the Wind* takes place in a historically significant era for Taiwan. Set in the early 1970s, *Dust in the Wind* is the story of a young boy, named Wan, who leaves his home in a northern mining town and searches for work in Taipei. After moving from job to job, Wan reunites with his girlfriend Huen who has also come to Taipei to find work. She takes a job as a seamstress. Wan is then conscripted into the army and remains in Kinmen for several years. The major turning point in the film occurs when Wan (and the viewer) find out that Huen has married someone else. At the end of the film, Wan returns home, and the relationship is never restored. Because of the minimalist storyline, *Dust in the Wind* has been described as 'light' but, at the same time, 'deep'. Udden, for example, describes the film as universal because, with clever camera work, it manages to move beyond the so-called Taiwanese experience. Though the storyline is simple and relatively uneventful, the combination of long shots and long takes creates a structure that is interesting in itself (78). Though the film is not particularly eventful, Hou plays with the expectations of his audience. The viewers do not expect that Huen will leave Wan because the film is told from Wan's perspective. When she does, this comes as a major surprise. The combination of the slow-moving, fragmented narrative – in addition to a plot centred on the 'Taiwanese experience' – came to embody the ideal of the New Wave.

The New Wave was an exciting movement for everyone involved. It was during this period, Hou explains to Assayas, that he came to realise that film could function as the 'carrier of serious ideas'. Before the 1980s in Taiwan, notes Hou, literature held this role. Though Hou claims that he intended that *A City of Sadness* would open up a space in which taboo subjects could surface, he also claims that the film was meant to represent historical events from an objective perspective. After the success of *City of Sadness*, Hou remarks with pride, a code of silence (in some pockets of the population, at least) was finally broken. The film generated a reaction; some of that reaction was positive and some of it was negative. Nevertheless, the film functioned as a catalyst; the subject of the KMT takeover after the fall of the Japanese empire shifted to the forefront of the collective consciousness. Now, Hou explains to Assayas, it is at least possible to engage in discussion. Now, Hou remarks: 'a lot is outside'.

In different conversations with Assayas, Hou has commented on the conflicted nature of his relationship with the mainland's cinematic tradition. He reflects on his formative experiences as a child, going to see mainland Chinese films in secret (Bale, n.p.). When asked by Assayas whether he views himself as a Chinese or Taiwanese director, Hou responds: 'A Taiwanese director, but culturally, I can't deny the fact that I'm Chinese' (Bale). In fact, Hou has collaborated with many other directors, from Taiwan and from the mainland. There is one concrete example of cross-strait collaboration: though he worked as a producer on Zhang Yimou's *Raise the Red Lantern* (1991) (M. Berry 262), Hou claims that he did not influence Zhang's artistic vision. Though not an example of cross-strait collaboration, Hou and Edward Yang were also frequent collaborators throughout the 1980s. In 1985, for example, Hou starred as Lung, the lead role in Yang's *Taipei Story*. In a 2001 interview, Hou's screenwriting partner Chu T'ien-wen describes the alliance between Yang and Hou as a 'magical moment' for the Taiwanese New Wave: 'As soon as they came together, everything fell into place. The birth of New Taiwan Cinema boils down to these two forces running into each other at the perfect time – it really all was timing' (Berry 245). Hou's work is, of course, also informed by a vast array of international directors. Hou has mentioned, in particular, that his major cinematic influences include: Pasolini, Ozu, and Wong Kar-wai (Berry 2005, 242).

James Udden, in his book *No Man an Island: The Cinema of Hou Hsiao-hsien*, argues that Hou is 'at his best' when he focuses on the colonial era in Taiwanese history (170). Udden further argues that, while the New Wave movement (beginning in 1982 with *In Our Time*) 'marked the key transition from cinema as a largely commercial enterprise to a more cultural endeavour', the 1989 release of Hou's *City of Sadness* changed history. The film's release was, according to Udden, '[the] single most important event in the history of Taiwan' (153). It was, he adds, the first Taiwanese film openly to depict the White Terror and 228 Incident. On the other side, Udden's remark implies that Hou may not have been 'at his best' when he chose not to focus on Taiwanese colonial history. Though Udden's implication is debatable, it is not difficult to see why critics would feel nostalgic for the 'glory days' of the New Wave.

Despite the provocative subject matter of many of his films, Hou depicts stories and characters from a quiet distance. He prefers to remain at this 'objective distance' at all times; violent scenes are frequently depicted with long shots so that the spectator will not be overwhelmed (Zhang and Xiao 338). Hou also prefers long takes, a still camera and limited dialogue. Hou's films do not rely on dialogue or wordiness at all; on the contrary, many are built around the notion of silence. In *City of Sadness*, for instance, Tony Leung's character, Lin Wen-ching, is both deaf and mute. Interestingly, it was decided that Leung's character would be 'mute' in the film because Leung did not speak either Japanese or Taiwanese. This decision reflects Hou's overall willingness, as a director, to use language sparingly and only when necessary. As a result, the lack of speech in Hou's films contributes to an overall feeling of non-ironic 'sweetness' and the hidden yet strong emotions of his characters.

Dialogue is so unimportant to Hou that he does not even necessarily rely on scripts. David Bordwell, writing about the making of Hou's most recent film, *Assassin*, notes that the actors are never given their lines before a scene:

> Hou never uses storyboards or shot lists. He does not even write out
> dialogue beforehand for the actors. His scenes have always grown out

of the specifics of *a setting* . . . his modus operandi is to then respond directly to the *atmosphere* he finds himself in, no matter how long it takes. Everybody who works for him seems to understand this. (Bordwell 2013, n.p., my emphasis)

Hou's films are built around atmosphere. Fast-moving plot development is almost always rejected in favour of narrative fragmentation, the illusion of objectivity and an almost obsessive preoccupation with objects and settings. Quite a few of his films begin with a shot of a lamp or a light. *A City of Sadness* and *Three Times* (2005) begin this way; *Millennium Mambo* (2001) begins with a shot of a neon light on the ceiling of a passageway in Taipei. Lamps function as a marker of place but they also establish the so-called 'objectivity' of the director's perspective. By focusing initially on the environment of the setting, and on the inanimate objects within that environment, Hou achieves two goals: he establishes distance from the action, or 'objectivity' and, secondly, he relinquishes responsibility for the (occasionally disturbing) events that his camera portrays.

Watching a Hou film is a bit like watching a puppet show. Much like a puppeteer showing off his dexterity by manipulating a gloved body with his hand, Hou inserts characters into settings and tells them how to move. The space that a puppet inhabits is an ontologically ambiguous space. The audience is never sure where to look: at the puppet or in the direction of the voice? Hou's characters inhabit this same dual, ontologically ambiguous space: though a certain amount of Hou's film-making is autobiographical, it is difficult to tell where 'truth' ends and where the fiction begins. In fact, many of Hou's films are connected to the idea of puppets, in both a literal and a metaphorical sense. Hou's interest in puppets can be connected back to his earliest childhood experiences growing up in Taiwan and sneaking into puppet shows or *budaixi*. Speaking about his early interest in the performing arts, Hou recalls: 'Most of the performances I saw were of puppet theater . . . these are some of my earliest impressions of the theater' (Berry 237). Usually, Hou explains, he was able to catch only the last half of the show and, even then, he would have to sneak in.

One of Hou's earliest projects, *The Sandwich Man,* was adapted from a story by Huang Chun-ming entitled 'His Son's Big Doll'. In the story, a Taiwanese sandwich-board man looks for a better paying, less humiliating job to enable him to support his family. At the beginning of his story, Chun-ming describes his protagonist as 'a puppet on a string' (34): dressed like a clown, carrying film ads on his back, he is hunched over with fatigue and embarrassment. *The Puppetmaster* is a biographical film about the life of Li Tian-lu (played by himself), the Taiwanese puppeteer whose theatre was taken over by the Japanese during the occupation. As mentioned previously, Hou's most recent film, *Red Balloon,* tells the story of yet another eccentric puppet-show worker.

From New Wave to Second Wave

HHH, the Assayas documentary, contains interviews with many of the people who worked with Hou in the 1980s. Over the course of his film, Assayas gathers the founders of the Taiwan New Cinema (separately) and asks them to reflect on their experiences. These figures include: scriptwriter T'ien-wen Chu, actor and writer Nien-jen Wu, and writer and director Chen Kou-fu. Chen, in particular, offers a clear vision of what it was like to be a part of the New Wave movement: '[We had] a driving impulse to change' he says, 'the feeling was absolutely incredible'. Chen describes the experience as collaborative – all the New Wave directors, writers and actors would hang out together in one house. Everyone in the house would jot down ideas on a large white board, Chen says, and it was there for everyone to see. He describes the excitement and the anticipation of the time: 'you definitely sense that things are going to happen but you don't really know what' (Assayas).

Many years after making the documentary, Assayas gave a speech to a French audience, justifying his decision to chronicle the life of Hou Hsiao-hsien in the first place. In the mid-1990s, Assayas explains, French critics did not understand why he was interested in Taiwanese film. The movement, he continues, was 'complètement nouvelle' for both Taiwan and for China. Films were made outside studios in opposition to the established government. 'Ce n'existais pas,' he explains, 'J'ai compris que quelque chose se passait.' Though he explains it as if he discovered the movement, Assayas was clearly impressed by Hou and the other New Wave directors. He felt that the movement was a reflection of the sociopolitical environment of that particular era in Taiwan but it was also an expression of a universally 'human' experience, outside the problem of cinema altogether. Assayas explains that he made the documentary because he wanted French audiences to understand and appreciate Hou – and Taiwanese cinema more generally. Despite the arrogant assumptions of his remarks, Assayas did help bring Taiwanese cinema to France in the 1990s.

As a founder of the New Wave movement, Hou Hsiao-hsien may have been 'at his best' in the 1980s and 1990s when he was attempting – through cinema – to recreate a bygone era in Taiwanese history (170). Nevertheless, after the turn of the past century, Hou's films have become particularly inter-textual, self-reflexive, and transnational. Though many of his films are based on historical events with serious content, Hou is also a fan of simple love stories. His 2005 film *Three Times*, for instance, is a love story told in three separate periods (the late nineteenth century, the 1960s, the 2000s). Each segment portrays a different couple; though the couple is played, each time, by the same two actors (Shu Qi and Chang Chen). The catchphrase for the film: 'I want to be with you anytime', can be interpreted as either 'all times of the day', or throughout history, 'in all time periods'. The film falls squarely into the romantic genre. In the first scene of *Three Times*, for example, the camera movement combines with music and the subtle gestures of the actors to create a powerfully sentimental mood. The film begins with Hou's signature shot: an illuminated ceiling lamp. As the camera pans down to Shu Qi's character, the sound of the Platters 1958 rendition of 'Smoke Gets in Your Eyes' fills the non-diegetic soundtrack. The camera rests on Shu Qi's face for a moment before panning over to a handsome man (Chang Chen), who is shooting pool. In what could be described as a 'reaction' shot, the camera pans to the pool balls as they hit one another. Shu Qi's character smiles. The scene continues in this manner, and for the entire length of the song. The two lovers are not in the frame together until the final moment of the scene, as the song ends. Where other directors might have chosen a close-up, Hou chooses a medium shot, remaining at 'arm's length' from the action at all times. In this remarkably subtle shot, she glances at him stealthily but then looks away.

Interestingly, Edward Yang uses the same rendition of 'Smoke Gets in Your Eyes' in the break-up scene in *Terrorizers*. This is the dramatic scene in which the young photographer is confronted by his angry girlfriend who has discovered his pictures of White Chick. In Yang's film, the song signifies hurt and anger: a breach of trust has been discovered, and now the break-up is inevitable. In *Three Times*, on the other hand, the song emphasises the romantic quality of young love, in spite of its potential for foolishness. Lead singer Tony Williams's wailing voice tells the story of a young man in love but blinded by naivety: 'they asked me how I knew my true love was true. I, of course, replied, something here inside cannot be denied . . . yet today my love has flown away, I am without my love.' In the context of *Three Times*, the song functions as both an ode and a response to Yang: Hou pays his respects to Yang while proving his own dexterity with sound and image. The scene feels romantic. Meanwhile, the pain and suffering of Yang's young protagonists seem to have faded a little.

The small gestures which are captured by Hou's camera evoke the untranslatable nature of first love, ill-fated romance and nostalgia for the present. In the opening shot of *Millennium Mambo*, the camera follows Vicki (Shu Qi) in a long shot as she skips in slow motion through a covered Taipei elevated walkway. Smoking a cigarette, she occasionally looks over her shoulder but never directly into the camera. Though Vicki's voice narrates the sequence, she speaks about herself in the third person; though she wants to break up with her lover, Hao-Hao (Chun Hao-tuan), she keeps going back to him. The slow-motion movement, combined with the techno beat and voiceover narration creates a mood of fleeting ephemerality, a sort of nostalgia for the present. The narration reveals an interesting detail: 'this happened ten years ago', she states, 'in 2001 . . . the world was celebrating the new millennium'. Audience members in 2001 might have been amused to imagine their future selves looking back to the then present. In 2013, however, we have passed the 'future' (2011) from which this flashback is supposed to occur. Watching the scene in 2013 feels a bit like watching a film, now somewhat dated, about the past. Though the idea is clever (nostalgia for the present), the effect of the film's original conceit has changed, arguably for the better but arguably for the worse.

Hou's *Flight of the Red Balloon* (2007), shot in Paris, is one of the best examples of Hou's transnational dexterity though it also serves as a testament to his limitations. *Red Balloon*'s two women protagonists Suzanne (Juliette Binoche), the eccentric French woman who performs in puppet shows, and Song (Fang Song), a Taiwanese film student hired by Suzanne to babysit her son Simon, represent this communicative fluidity/untranslatability. Hou's film oscillates between French and Chinese, revealing and celebrating instances of non-translatable, imperfect correspondence between cultures. Though Jean Ma describes Hou's *Red Balloon* as a 'remake' of Albert Lamorrise's *The Red Balloon* (*Le ballon rouge,* 1956) (83), the film is more accurately described as a 'tribute' to Lamorrisse layered in cross-cultural hybridity.

The decision to shoot *Red Balloon* in Paris was not haphazard. Hou had been invited to contribute to a series of films that would be shot, at least partially, in the Musée d'Orsay in Paris. The film series was commissioned by Musée d'Orsay president, Serge Lemoine, in honour of the museum's twentieth anniversary celebration. As part of the deal, Hou was required to film at least one scene of the film in the museum though he was not required to shoot any more than one. In line with those requirements, Hou shoots the final scene of *Red Balloon* in the museum but the rest of the film is shot in other locations around Paris (and includes a large amount of indoor scenes). Nevertheless, Hou decided that the film should be shot almost entirely in French, even though he himself does not speak French, whereas Mandarin is spoken in only a handful of scenes. As a result of this linguistic decision, the film itself represents an interesting case of identity confusion. As Michelle E. Bloom eloquently observes, in her [unpublished] article on Hou and *Red Balloon*: 'The displacement of a director from his native language as well as from his national "home" contributes to the hybrid identities of transnational cinemas' (Bloom). Though this was not the first time that Hou had received financing from abroad, this was the first time that he had shot a film in Europe. Critics worried that Hou's decision to make the film in France, with French-backed financing, would further alienate the director from domestic audiences in Taiwan.

The critics were probably correct and Hou has apparently returned to Taiwan to shoot his forthcoming film, *The Assassin* (set to be released in 2013). *The Assassin* is a historical drama set in ninth-century Tang Dynasty era China. The film, when completed, will represent Hou's first venture into the martial arts or *wuxia* genre.

James Udden has argued that Hou's post-2000 films are not as 'striking' or original as his earlier work, even though they are visually interesting (170). On the contrary, however, Hou's twenty-first-century films – *Millennium Mambo*, *Café Lumière* (2003) and *Flight of the Red Balloon* (2007) – are visually 'ground-breaking' but in a different sense. These post-millennium films document Hou's ability to work on an international scale, to move fluidly across national boundaries and between languages and to work with an impressive variety of actors. *The Red Balloon*, in particular, expresses Hou's connection with France and with the French film-making tradition, while *Café Lumière* functions as a cinematic ode to Japanese director, Yasujiro Ozu. Jean Ma describes *The Red Balloon* as a 'remake' of Albert Lamorisse's *The Red Balloon/Le ballon rouge* (1956). The film, for Ma, exemplifies Hou's move away from the local in an effort to gain funding at all costs (83). I would not describe Hou's *The Red Balloon* as a 'remake' nor would I describe it as a desperate attempt to please French tastes. *The Red Balloon* showcases Hou's ability to build a film using the specificity of a particular setting, in this case Paris. *The Red Balloon* is also a multilingual, hybrid film. Oscillating between French and Mandarin, it reveals (and celebrates) moments of non-translatable, imperfect correspondence between cultures.

As I have mentioned throughout this chapter, Hou's cinema encourages his viewer to contemplate taboo subjects and to revisit historical wounds through the almost paradoxical assumption that communication works better through silence. Hou's willingness to confront the past while remaining at arm's length exemplifies his connection with Taiwanese New Wave and Second Wave aesthetics on the one hand, his divergence from the mainland (and even the Hong Kong) aesthetic on the other.

Through 'narrative objectivity', film-makers can create characters who appear displaced in time. Hong Kong auteur Wong Kar-wai uses a similar technique (to that of Hou Hsiao-hsien in *Flight of the Red Balloon*) in his 1994 film *Chungking Express*. In both these films, the accented quality that Naficy describes is expressed cinematically through the films' development of characters. The protagonists in both films, furthermore, are reflections of Naficy's concept of the 'accent' but in contrasting ways. In *Chungking*, Cop 663 and Faye are displaced within their own surroundings, namely in pre-handover Hong Kong, and yet the film is shot entirely in Hong Kong. In *Red Balloon*, meanwhile, Song is thrown into the midst of French culture, displaced from her home town of Beijing.

In the introduction to *Sinophone Articulations Across the Pacific*, Shih contends that one of the Sinophone's favourite modes is intertextuality, and that this sort of intertextuality is meant to construct new identities and cultures. By this definition, Wong Kar-wai's *Chungking Express* is an eloquent ode to the Sinophone in terms of both intertextuality and heteroglossia. The film consists of at least three audibly distinct languages: Cantonese, Mandarin and English as well as less clearly audible languages such as Hindi and Japanese. *Chungking* was filmed in two very distinct areas of Hong Kong: inside and around the Chungking Mansions, and in Central, another well-known neighbourhood. The Chungking Mansions location was hand-picked by Wong because it is filled with a diverse crowd of people from around the globe on a day-to-day basis – this is one of its most distinguishing factors. The Mansions are located on the island of Kowloon, an island that is filled with cheap residential accommodation, a spectrum of ethnic restaurants and exotic shops. The film's soundtrack is also incredibly diverse and covers an enormous range of eras: at various points throughout the film we hear Indian music, synthesisers, the song 'California Dreamin'' by the Mamas & the Papas, 'What a Difference a Day Makes', by Dinah Washington, and Faye Wong's own Cantonese cover version of 'Dreams' by the Cranberries.

The narrative is divided into two stories: the first story centres on the Taiwanese-born policeman, He Qiwu, who is struggling to get over the fact that his girlfriend May recently broke up with him. He Qiwu is lonely, alienated and essentially trapped by time (he is obsessed with expiration dates, and decides to wait until 1 May 'formally' to get over his girlfriend). It is the second story in the film, however, that makes up the bulk of the film. The second section of the narrative centres on the relationship, or lack thereof, between a snack-bar server, named Faye (Faye Wong), and another policeman (#663) who remains unnamed, played by heartthrob Tony Leung. Like He Qiwu, Faye and Leung's characters are trapped in their respective temporal and spatial realities though they occasionally overlap. In one noteworthy scene, Faye and Leung stand alone in the snack bar; Faye rests her hand on her face behind the counter and remains still while Leung stands a few feet away sipping his coffee. Alienated within their fast-moving environment, Leung and Faye remain trapped in slow motion as the anonymous figures of Hong Kong flit through the frame.

Faye is in love with Leung's character but is too shy to tell him. Instead, she sneaks into his apartment while he is out and plays around inside, jumps on his bed and sings. Among the central visual themes of the second half of the film are aeroplanes: real aeroplanes, model aeroplanes, paper aeroplanes, and flight attendants (Leung's first girlfriend is a flight attendant). Faye longs to leave her isolating job as server, fly away to California and become a flight attendant herself, which she does at the end of the film. In this sense, she escapes. Leung's character, meanwhile, remains trapped in Hong Kong. We watch him as he waits, for hours and hours, for Faye to meet him at a restaurant but she never does because she has already left for California. This scene is similarly marked by the slow-motion/fast-motion technique that Wong uses throughout the film: Leung's character remains fixed while the rest of the world rushes by.

As Shih notes, Hong Kong culture tends to be regarded as a culture of 'dis-appearance'. Around the time of the 1997 handing-over by the British, scholars begin to look back nostalgically at Hong Kong's colonial era. Many Hong Kong cultural theorists wondered what would come next after this final parting glance of nostalgia. What, they wondered, would come after the handover? Shih describes this nostalgia as: 'Fetishism of the present, whereby the most mundane of everyday practices becomes immediately imbued with historical and symbolic meaning, would have to be replaced with a different temporal logic as the present will no longer be a site of nostalgia' (141). This observation also describes the general aesthetic and theme of *Chungking Express*: fetishism of the present moment mixed with apprehensive worry about the future. The characters in Wong's film search for a means of escape, and the image of the plane symbolises the possibility for departure. As Shih maintains, the political situation of Hong Kong immediately prior to 1997 (this film was made in 1994) is clearly entangled with the artistic concerns of Hong Kong film-makers, Wong Kar-wai in particular. Though Wong does not specifically address the British handover in this film, his characters can be seen as metonymic representations of larger sociopolitical issues.

Hou's films tend to be metonymic in this way as well. Hou has been, and continues to be, a vocal critic of government regulations on the film industry. In 2007, for example, Hou told reporter Sandra Shih that directors in Taiwan still face several obstacles when attempting to shoot films out of doors because there is no one agency that controls the application procedure. Though this might not matter for established film-makers, such as Hou himself, newer producers might have a hard time establishing themselves. If the structure were more transparent, Hou comments, investors might be more attracted to the industry as well. In this same interview, Hou suggests that it will be necessary to set up an agency to help new film-makers with the application process for permits and with government regulations in general.

By this same year, 2007, France and South Korea had already established their own agencies for this very purpose: to help potential new film-makers navigate the bureaucratic process that is required to shoot a film on location. Meanwhile, the process remained difficult in Taiwan. While in France, for example, Hou was allowed to finish shooting his scene in the Paris *Métro*, even though he was not scheduled for that hour. In Taipei, however, a long list of regulations prevents most film-makers from shooting in the Taipei underground. Whereas in South Korea, city governors provide helicopters for film-makers to use to shoot panoramas of Busan, the Taipei city government did not have the same resources. Waiting in the wings, Taipei City Government Department of Cultural Affairs commissioner Lee Yong-ping apparently decided to set up a film commission in Taipei with Mayor Hua Lung-bin as the chairman. This film commission would then handle most of the pre-production tasks. They would contact the local agencies and aid film producers in the bureaucratic process of obtaining a permit. Next year, Lee comments, the film commission would serve mainly as a professional group of location scouts who would then set up a database for film-makers to make use of. 'Through the platform of a film commission, the film industry chain would be integrated', she promises. She is referring to the Asian Film Commission Network that was established so that Asian member countries could share resources and collaborate. At this time, Taiwan was not part of the network (Shih).

Hou's *The Red Balloon* can also be read in sociopolitical terms and in relation to Shih's notion of the Sinophone. Again, however, I have appropriated Shih's term to describe character development and narrative themes within the film. The first point concerns self-orientalisation and the second concerns the problem of translation. Shih mentions the phenomenon of Sinophone film-makers who are criticised for attempting to cater to Western tastes in order to garner a bigger box office success (directors like Zhang Yimou and Ang Lee, for instance). Such directors have been criticised, in particular, for creating films that condemn the Chinese government while simultaneously exoticising Chinese cultural symbols. The problematic of self-orientalisation can also be connected to Hou's *The Red Balloon*, because one might justifiably wonder whether or not the director engages in it (either consciously or subconsciously).

In one of the first scenes of the film, Suzanne (the puppeteer) and Song (the Taiwanese film student) drive together in a car, presumably after meeting for the first time, though we cannot see either of the two characters. Instead, Hou's camera shows only the road in front of the car; the sequence, in other words, is shot from Suzanne and Song's perspective. Though her face is not visible, we can hear Suzanne's voice: 'Vous ne semblez pas timide' ('You don't seem shy'), she tells Song, who replies: 'Oui je suis timide' ('Yes I am shy'). In response, Suzanne attempts to comfort her new nanny: 'Vous devez être à l'aise' ('You should feel at ease'). Though Suzanne tries her best to make Song feel comfortable, her blatant comments have a note of judgement in them, and they are, perhaps, presumptuous-sounding to someone who is not used to enduring a personality critique. Unfortunately, this initial conversation characterises the rest of the conversations that occur between Song and Suzanne in the film. The two women never seem to 'connect' on a deeper, human level.

Ella Shohat and Robert Stam's discussion of cinematic techniques of separation based on cultural differences provides a helpful point of entry. In their book: *Unthinking Eurocentrism: Multiculturalism and the Media* (1994), Shohat and Stam are particularly interested in comparing the social portrayal of Europeans and non-Europeans in cinema:

> To speak of the 'image' of a social group, we have to ask precise questions about images. How much space do they occupy in the shot? ... How

often do they appear compared with the Euro-American characters and for how long? . . . Do the eyeline matches identify us with one gaze rather than another? Whose looks are reciprocated, whose ignored? . . . How do body language, posture, and facial expression communicate social hierarchies, arrogance, servility, resentment, pride? (Shohat and Stam 208)

If we were to attempt to answer these questions in relation to Song, we might initially conclude, based on the aforementioned scenes, that Hou engages in (self-) orientalism. Song is, after all, depicted as timid compared to the Parisians; her body language connotes passivity, and she describes herself as 'timid'. According to Shohat and Stam's criteria for evaluation, her passive body language might suggest that Hou 'places' her on a lower social hierarchy relative to Suzanne and the Parisians that surround her. Yet Hou's cinematic language functions on a more complex level, such that we would need to reach beyond an initial interpretation based solely upon Shohat and Stam's criteria.

The visual distinctions are even more pronounced between Shiang-chyi, one of the main characters In Tsai's *What Time is it There?*, and the Parisians that surround her. In Tsai's film, this visual separation points to Shiang-chyi's lack of cultural fluency. In Hou's *Red Balloon*, the visual and linguistic differences between Song and Suzanne are similarly emphasised. These differences, however, are not necessarily portrayed in a negative light. This is an important distinction. Watching the film, the viewer may wonder: could Hou be making some sort of cultural comment? Is there a suggestion that, because Song and Suzanne come from two very different cultures, they are never truly capable of connecting on a human level? Perhaps but, even if he does, Hou certainly does not paint Suzanne in a more flattering light. Though she is passive and timid, Song is also intelligent, talented and interesting. By the same token, though Suzanne is overbearing, crass and often angry, she is also depicted as warm-hearted. I am not convinced that Hou intentionally self-orientalises Song. In fact, Hou has described Song's character as a representation of his own alter ego. Using Shohat and Stam's criteria, we might be led to believe that Song's passivity represents weakness. On the contrary, Hou privileges Song's perspective and emphasises her strengths. She is calm and she is wise, qualities that become readily apparent when contrasted with Suzanne whose loquaciousness and eccentric mannerisms become increasingly irritating over the course of the film.

In her article on the 'Sinophone', Shih's point about translation relates nicely to the themes of *The Red Balloon*. Insofar as the 'Sinophone' is an imperfect copy of 'Chinese culture', it is also a form of translation. She remarks: 'translation is not an act of one-to-one equivalence, but an event that happens among multiple agents, among multiple local and hegemonic cultures, registering an uncertainty and a complexity that require historically specific decodings'

Figure 3.2   The puppeteer with Suzanne in the role of translator (right);
Song observes.

(5). In *The Red Balloon,* the 'translation scene' (which is actually two scenes pasted together) functions as a cinematic representation of this aspect of the 'Sinophone'. As the sequence begins, the camera is focused on a puppet in the form of a Chinese man dressed in traditional garb. As the camera pans over the audience, who are all mesmerised by the show, we can hear the sound of the puppeteer's monologue as it is spoken in particularly theatrical-sounding Mandarin. It is only later in the sequence that the camera pans toward the stage so that the film viewer can finally catch a glimpse of the puppeteer's face. After the puppeteer has finished reciting his poem, the camera moves to Suzanne who proceeds to translate and explain the cultural context of the Chinese poem to the French audience (and also to the non-Mandarin-speaking film viewer, because there are no subtitles during the actual reading).

The sequence then fades into the inverse mode of translation. In the second half of the sequence, the puppeteer and Suzanne are now sitting on a train, and Song, who has joined them, is now placed in the role of translator. Suzanne hands the puppeteer a postcard, one that supposedly represents something 'profoundly Chinese' for Suzanne even though, as she explains, she purchased it in a British museum. Song translates Suzanne's rather inane comments for the puppeteer who responds politely with a simple 'merci beaucoup'. As Song continues to translate and carry on a conversation in Mandarin with the puppeteer, Suzanne smiles pleasantly but blankly and looks out of the window.

This is the one scene in which Suzanne replaces Song in her role as the 'displaced' non-native speaker. This is, however, the only scene in the entire film in which Song is placed in the position of mastery over Suzanne.

CONCLUSIONS

Hou's film thus functions as a negotiation between French and Chinese, as an imperfect correspondence between cultures. In a certain sense, *The Red Balloon* seems to fit with Shih's paradigm of non-Chinese-centrism, and Song's character in particular seems to fit with Naficy's concept of the accented subject. On the other hand, these two paradigms neglect to account for the myriad ways in which a film-maker's narrative objectivity also does 'the work' of explaining why characters appear displaced and alienated. In the sense that these phenomena can be described without sole reliance on sociopolitical forces, Hou's *The Red Balloon* reaches beyond both paradigms.

So far, as we have seen, film-makers Edward Yang and Hou Hsiao-hsien employ cinematic (and narrative) devices that are unique to their trademark directorial style. In Yang's *Terrorizers*, for example, we saw how writer's block can be deadly and how 'photographers in fiction' freeze themselves in time, doomed by their own photographic curiosity. In Hou's films, in *Red Balloon* in particular, characters become displaced, from their surroundings and from one another, and are left with the inability to communicate. Like puppets within Hou's larger puppet show, Song and Suzanne cannot communicate beyond a superficial level. As Shih rightly notes, translation does not mean 'equivalence'. In the act of translation, misunderstandings and power struggles are inevitable.

Hou's films are built upon atmosphere, place and objects. Close-ups are shunned in favour of long shots, creating an 'objective distance' between the viewer and the action. As 'puppet master', Hou distances his camera from the *mise en scène* as if to suggest that he cannot be blamed for the chaos that ensues therein. Though many directors remain 'distant' from the action by keeping the camera still and far away, this technique can be used for a variety of effects. In the next chapter, I use the phrase 'disjointed connectivity' to describe Tsai's blend of cinematic methods, as well as the social and psychological states of the protagonists in his films. 'Disjointed connectivity' refers to a peculiar cinematic phenomenon: displaced characters that seem to be in a state of isolation and uncertainty while simultaneously being connected to each other through the use of cinematic devices such as parallel cuts. Thus, each film-maker so far allows the audience to step outside the frame, to catch a glimpse of non-diegetic space. The constant 'in-between', displaced status of the protagonists – neither entirely within the space or outside it – allows for this possibility.

NOTES

1. The movement began when Chinese students living in the United States protested against Japan's claim to the Diaoyutai Islands and, over the course of the decade, became a movement in favour of reuniting the mainland with Taiwan.
2. From an unpublished Michelle E. Bloom article describing Hou's experience making *Café Lumière* and *Flight of the Red Balloon*.

4. TSAI MING-LIANG'S DISJOINTED CONNECTIVITY AND LONELY INTERTEXTUALITY

> Tsai's central subject is the loneliness of the human condition ... his characters are invariably profoundly sad and alone but, seen from afar, the absurdity of their existence emerges, the tragicomic truth that, as lonely as they feel, they are always much closer to each other than their limited awareness allows them to recognize. (Rapfogel 26)

Tsai Ming-liang's inclination towards loneliness, alienation and 'slowness' in his films can be traced back to the earlier years of his life and career. Born in Kuching, Malaysia in 1957, Tsai spent a great deal of his youth attending local screenings of international films with his grandparents (Hughes, n.p.). Tsai has commented that his 'slow-paced childhood' allowed him to observe life in his home town from a leisurely perspective, arguably, according to Darren Hughes,[1] the same perspective that characterises the slow style of his films. At the age of twenty, Tsai moved to Taipei and entered the Chinese Culture University where he studied film and drama and was exposed to the most famous of the European auteurs such as Michelangelo Antonioni, François Truffaut and Robert Bresson. In 1982, the year that Tsai graduated from the Chinese Culture University, Taiwan was in an era of transformation: America had passed the Taiwan Relations Act in 1979 and democratisation was in sight. The nineteen-eighties was a decade of change for Taiwan generally and for the Taiwanese film industry in particular.

With little support from the Taiwanese government, film-makers such as Tsai (as well as Hou and Yang, as we have seen) were forced to seek funding from international sources. In a certain way, this allowed these film-makers stylistic flexibility, especially Tsai who was able to 'find his voice' by experimenting with a variety of cinematic techniques.[2] Between 1989 and 1991, Tsai wrote ten teleplays, eight of which he directed himself (Editions Dis Voir). The 1991 teleplay *The Boys* marked Tsai's first collaboration with Hsiao-kang (playing the character of Lee Kang-sheng) with whom he continues to collaborate to this day (Hughes). Tsai's first three films: *Rebels of the Neon God* (1992), *Vive l'Amour* (1994) and *The River* (1997) were funded by Taiwan's Central Motion Picture Corporation (the CMPC). Commissioned by French distributors and a French–German television network, Tsai's fourth film, *The Hole* (*Dong*) (1998) was funded only in part by the CMPC. This film therefore represented a shift for Tsai from a national to a transnational production model, the model that continues to characterise his work. Tsai's next films represent varying degrees of transnational influence: both *What Time is it There?* (2001) and *Visage* (2009) were shot in Taiwan and in France, while *Goodbye Dragon Inn* (2003) and *The Wayward Cloud* (2005) were shot in Taiwan. *I Don't Want to Sleep Alone* (2006), commissioned as part of an international series for the New Crowned Hope festival in Vienna in 2006, was shot in Malaysia (Ma 83).

Later in the chapter, I analyse Tsai's *What Time is it There?* in some depth, and to a much lesser extent *The Skywalk is Gone/Tianqiao bujian le* (2002) and *Visage* (2009) in relation to this terminology. I focus on these films in particular, not because they are more worthy of study than his earlier work but because these films represent Tsai's first real 'foray' into the transnational production model. The films also serve as a nice introduction to the themes and aesthetics of Tsai's work, more generally, for those who may not already be familiar with his *oeuvre*.

CINEMATIC TIME AS 'REAL TIME' IN TSAI'S FILMS

Cinematic theories of time have existed even before the advent of cinema studies as an academic field. Henri Bergson's notion of the *durée*, for example, questioned Kant's account of how human subjects experience time. I have coined the term *disjointed connectivity* in reference to Tsai's mode of representing cinematic time. *Disjointed connectivity* can be understood in relation to Bergson and *durée* more specifically.

Bergson asks a phenomenological question: how can the same image belong in two different systems at once, namely in my body and in the universe? If my body perceives an image, how is this different from an image 'existing' as such outside my own subjective position? Bergson attempts to explain the phenomenon by dividing the perception of images into two categories and puts them in contrast to one another: *subjective idealism* versus *material realism*. In

Bergson's understanding of subjective realism, the images that we perceive are variable: they can change depending on certain conditions, the person viewing them, etc.; hence, in this sense, they are subjective. On the other hand, in his understanding of material realism, images 'exist' in the universe regardless of whether or not we perceive them and, in this sense, these images are invariable or material, so to speak. Bergson makes a further distinction: if perception can be defined as something external to the body, affection should be defined as something that occurs within the body.[3] Bergson thought that the relationship between subjects and objects should be discussed in terms of *temporality*, not spatiality. This idea, that subjects and objects, the perceiver and the perceived, must be thought about in terms of their temporal relation to one another, is extremely important to our understanding of how more recent film theorists view cinematic time.

Gilles Deleuze's reformulation of film studies into a new mode of viewing the world, and as a way of mapping the movement of images in time, is no less than remarkable. In his *Cinema* books, Deleuze uses Bergson's concept of pure perception to redefine the idea of the simulacrum for his own philosophical purposes. For Deleuze, the simulacrum is not an impression or re-creation of life that is secondary or once removed from life, the simulacrum *is* life.[4] He posits that nothing we perceive in the world (as humans) is more than a subjective image. He posits further that there is nothing particularly stable about objects in the world, and that humans stabilise the objects they perceive to make sense out of them. When we think, we are maximising the power of the virtual because there are only simulations and no 'proper images' as Claire Colebrook calls them.[5]

It is easy to see how such a phenomenological view of the world might lend itself well to the study of film. The belief that technology is an invaluable tool for humans is by no means new but Deleuze views technology as positive for somewhat unconventional reasons. He does not think that the camera (a piece of technology) supplements humans but, rather, that technology approaches the inhuman. This follows from Deleuze's logic because, if all seeing is a form of technology, then the camera eye allows us access to an alternative way of seeing; time in its pure state, outside the taint of human perception. Consequently, Deleuze rejects entirely the idea that cinema is a manifestation of the human subject. Deleuze goes one step further and calls for a certain type of cinema, one that is powerful enough to shock the film viewer out of a lazy state of mind and towards a world in which human movement does not always map directly on to time. The powerful cinema of the time image executes precisely this move (as opposed to the cinema of the movement image which, generally, does not move beyond linear movement).

In her book *The Emergence of Cinematic Time: Modernity, Contingency, the Archive*, Mary Ann Doane, unlike Deleuze, offers us a clear historical context in which to situate the early development of cinema as a new art form in the late nineteenth and twentieth centuries. She grounds her study in the work of a multitude of thinkers from the time, such as Bergson, Etienne-Jules Marey (the inventor of chronophotography), Charles Sanders Peirce (a semi-ologist) and Sigmund Freud. She argues that with the advent of film came a renewed attention to Zeno's paradox and the problems associated with apply-ing it to camera movements.[6] She also argues that there are two competing, yet not irreconcilable, tendencies within modernity: 'abstraction/rationalization and an emphasis on the contingent, chance, and the ephemeral' (Doane 10). Her central contention within this book is that it is, indeed, possible and, moreover, fruitful to demonstrate the inextricable connection between these two tendencies. As society becomes increasingly industrialised, so does the necessity to rationalise time into even, measurable units. Yet, at the same time, this overwhelming need for structure is accompanied by a competing need to offer the subject a feeling of freedom from excessive structure and rationalisa-tion. Though this new sense of freedom, which arises within modernity, can be refreshing and liberating, it also has the potential to be dangerous and threatening. Doane believes that it was this very concept of the 'contingency of time' that allowed for, and helped along, the development of creative cinema throughout the past century.

These three theoretical models lead me to my own understanding of how time functions in cinema. The Wilson theory is a hybrid theory: I propose that film directors employ certain particular cinematic techniques (that is, varying lengths and types of shots, differing narrative structures) for the purposes of manipulating the spectator's subjective notion of cinematic time. I am sceptical of Deleuze's notion that the camera as a technological apparatus encroaches upon the inhuman simply because there is no way to watch a film through any-one's eyes but one's own. Perhaps one might be able to claim that a film 'exists' in some abstract sense outside the realm of human vision but, as I see it, there is no way to escape the fact that the experience of cinema is necessarily mediated by human subjectivity. Though I might be inclined to describe film viewing as a subjective experience, this *does not* mean that film is without structure. This is an important distinction. As Doane argues, there are two conflicting tendencies within time in cinema: on the one hand, directors create structure (either intentionally or not) in order to create a certain effect for the viewer. This structure might have an unintended effect, no effect or an opposing effect on the viewer but this does not mean that it is not 'present' in some significant sense. On the other hand, the masterful film-maker will be able to give us the illusion that we are free from structure – this relates back to Doane's 'contin-gency of time' concept.

Tsai Ming-liang's *What Time is It There?* exemplifies the idea that cinematic time can be contingent on the perspective of the spectator or film viewer. Luis

Buñuel's *Andalusian Dog*, Varda's *Cléo de 5 à 7*, and Resnais's *Hiroshima mon amour* exemplify the idea that cinematic time can be contingent in many ways as well, and in different ways. In each of these films, slightly different (but, at times, overlapping techniques) interact and play with one another to form a specific illusion: as we become immersed in the lives of these fictional characters, we come to believe that time is passing for them in some sort of 'true'[7] sense. Yet at the same time, if we are distracted from the film for even a moment, we might become aware that time is passing for us as we sit in the theatre, and that our idea of time diverges tremendously from that of the characters. Nevertheless, there is a strong illusion of what I call 'true narrative time'. How, then, does each of these films construct or deconstruct the illusion of 'true narrative time'?

In *What Time is it There?* Tsai employs two important methods of cinematic time manipulation: (1) the gratuitously long take with an absolutely still camera; and (2) the division of simultaneous time into two parallel stories between two central protagonists, Hsiao-kang and Shiang-chyi (and occasionally three at once if you count the mother character). When he uses the first method, Tsai positions the camera in a particular spot to film the 'private moments' of his characters. The camera is so static, yet so carefully positioned, that it often seems as if we are watching surveillance footage of these characters as they move in and out of the frames of their private worlds. We must, for instance, watch Hsiao-kang as he pees in random things that are everything but toilets, has sex with a prostitute, drinks from a water bottle and watches *The 400 Blows*. These unfathomably long takes serve to make us, as spectators, feel as if we are observing the lives of the characters in 'real time' such that it is nearly indistinguishable from 'true narrative time'. The long takes also add to the overall cringeworthy factor of the film but, at the same time, they are eloquently and artistically framed. Of course, the long takes also fool us into believing that we are witnessing 'real time', but the film is divided and carefully manipulated by Tsai for a particular effect. The narrative is divided between China and France, a man's story and a woman's story, existing simultaneously within the context of the narrative; strangers whose lives intersected for one brief moment, 'caught' in turn by the film apparatus. As much as Tsai might like us to imagine that we are viewing the lives of his characters in 'real time', the fact that we are witnesses to this highly privileged moment is proof that the film is a cleverly constructed illusion.

In *An Andalusian Dog*, the spectator is very much aware that time is not functioning normally throughout the course of this film. The film is punctuated by indicators of time that we, as spectators, grow to recognise as false. The opening words of the film are: 'Il était une fois . . .' as if Buñuel is beginning a fairy tale – the phrase connotes pleasant magical images and the whimsy of the distant past. But just a few minutes after the opening, we come to realise that the film is, in fact, filled with disturbing images of violence and sexuality. If there were any doubt, the famous eye-slicing scene puts a swift end to any remaining hopes for a fairy-tale film. There are four other time punctuations or markers in the film: 'eight years later'; 'at about three in the morning'; 'sixteen years before'; and finally 'in spring'. We soon come to realise that these markers are meaningless and have little purpose except to confuse and disorient us.

Adding to the surreality, the characters in the film appear to have the ability to control the images that appear or disappear from the shot. For instance, a man gropes the main woman of the film and her clothes seem magically to disappear as he drools over her. Buñuel employs many special effects to create a self-reflexive film: the superimpositions, montage sequences, and gory fake body parts all call attention to the camera-as-technological-apparatus and to the trickery of cinema in general.

Meanwhile, in *Cléo de 5 à 7*, the pendulum swings to the opposite extreme, and 'true narrative time' becomes almost undistinguishable from the spectator's experience of time. The narrative is constructed such that the spectator feels as if he or she is following a chunk out of the life of the protagonist, Cléo. We are never allowed to forget that time is passing because the film is divided into 'chapters', or five- to seven-minute segments. In the opening scene of the film, we hear a clock ticking in the background as the Tarot card reader tells Cléo her fortune. At the end of the film, we hear the chime of the church bell as Cléo hears her final diagnosis from the doctor. The entire film is based around the premise that Cléo is waiting in suspense from five o'clock to seven o'clock in the evening to find out the results of her biopsy. Yet the film's title is intentionally misleading because, in spectator time, the story really only follows her from five to six thirty (the film is only ninety minutes long). So, even though Varda wants us to imagine that we are watching a two-hour-long chunk of Cléo's life, in reality she is manipulating our sense of 'true narrative time'.

Hiroshima mon amour is similar to *Cléo* in that there is a similar feeling of inevitability, a similar sense of impending doom, associated with the representation of time. In *Hiroshima*, however, time is not presented in a linear fashion and is, instead, broken up by constant flashbacks. The flashbacks are, of course, related to the idea of history as it links to memory: they dominate the narrative so that we, as spectators, become psychologically invested in the unnamed French woman, called simply 'Elle'. At one point in the film, Elle is roaming around the streets of Hiroshima, thinking about Nevers. A succession of street shots of Hiroshima and Nevers appears one after the other as Elle thinks to herself in an interior monologue: 'A time will come. When we'll no more know what thing it is that binds us. By slow degrees the word will fade from our memory. Then it will disappear altogether' (English translation). These shots, in combination with the monologue, indicate to the spectator that, even though Elle is walking in the streets of Hiroshima in the present, she is simultaneously still living in Nevers in her mind. The film functions non-linearly for two reasons: (1) so that we, as spectators, will become familiar with Elle's past at the point that she is revealing it for the first time, and we will feel sympathetic; (2) so that historical memory becomes inevitably tied to private memory within the context of the film. In other words, though 'true narrative time' does not diverge much from 'real time', real time is divided between diegetic (or narrative-driven) and psychological events.

Loneliness abounds in all Tsai's films, and his 2001 film *What Time is it There?*[8] is certainly not an exception. Yet, unlike Tsai's earlier films, such as *Rebels of the Neon God, Vive l'Amour,* and *The River*, which take place in and around Taipei, *What Time* is shot in both Taipei and Paris. The narrative is divided into parallel stories: the lives of two strangers intersect for a brief moment when the woman, Shiang-chyi (Chen Shiang-chyi) buys a dual time zone watch from the man, Hsiao-kang (Lee Kang-sheng). After Shiang-chyi buys the watch, she travels to Paris for an indeterminate length of time, and for no clear reason. Meanwhile, Hsiao-kang, grieving over the death of his father (Miao Tien), remains in Taipei with his mother.

Though the two characters never meet again within the context of this film,[9] their lives appear to be almost uncannily interconnected, even across a time difference of seven hours and a distance of several thousand miles. Hsiao-kang becomes neurotically obsessed with changing every clock – even the enormous one on the outside of a large city-centre building – in Taipei to Paris time.[10] He also becomes obsessed with 'all things French' (Martin 2), including wine and French cinema (François Truffaut's *Les quatre cents coups/ The 400 Blows*, in particular). Though it remains unclear why Hsiao-kang has become so enthralled by French things, the most obvious explanation is that he is obsessed with Shiang-chyi, even though he met her only twice. Shiang-chyi, meanwhile, is embroiled in her own set of problems in Paris.

Tsai likes to film scenes in small, interior spaces, such as hotel rooms, bedrooms, bathrooms, cars and underground stations. He uses this technique when filming Hsiao-kang in Taipei and Shiang-chyi in Paris to suggest that these characters are metaphorically entombed. The scenes in *What Time* that are filmed in these spaces do arguably contribute to an overall sense of ahistoricism and placelessness, but not entirely. In *What Time*, Paris – a 'globalized' city in many respects – is far from unrecognisable. We are still able to recognise the Tuileries garden, the Métro, and the Père-Lachaise Cemetery. We are also easily able to distinguish the contrast in customs and language among Taiwan, France and even Hong Kong throughout the film. Similarly, Tsai's Taipei is not the equivalent of Edward Yang'sTaipei,[11] a city stifled by homogeneity and ill with modernity. As James Tweedie points out in his essay 'Morning in the New Metropolis: Taipei and the Globalization of the City Film', Tsai purposely documents recognisable buildings and public spaces in Taipei, such as the Fuhe Theatre and the Taipei railway station skywalk. Notes Tweedie:

> Taken together, Tsai's films become an ongoing attempt to document both the development of the modern city of Taipei, as reflected on the glass facades of buildings or in illuminated cityscapes at night, and to collect traces left behind by its decay. (121)

The 'traces' that Tsai 'collects', therefore, become part of a set – or a common thread – that connects Tsai's films to one another. This is the same thread that connects, however disjointedly, Tsai's recurring characters to one another and to themselves.

As a director, Tsai demonstrates what I shall call 'disjointed connectivity'; and so, in turn, do the protagonists in his film. I coined this phrase while attempting to describe Tsai's blend of cinematic methods, as well as the social and psychological state of the protagonists in his films. 'Disjointed connectivity' refers to this uncanny cinematic phenomenon that Tsai employs: displaced characters are in a state of isolation and uncertainty while simultaneously being connected to one another through the use of cinematic devices such as parallel cuts. Characters can also, of course, be connected intratextually, or from one of his films to another. The concept of 'disjointed connectivity' also relates to Tsai's overall project as an auteur: through his ability to weave intertextual references and interconnected stories and characters within his films, Tsai manages to reach a kind of 'meta-auteur' status. Thus, though Tsai's cinematic style is *connected* to the work of his cinematic predecessors, he is able to disconnect himself (become *disjointed*) with equal precision.[12]

Frederic Jameson describes a similar phenomenon when he compares Taiwanese cinema[13] to a recipe composed of equal parts empty space and equal parts modernity. His description allows for the possibility of both missed encounters *and* fortunate chance meetings within the context of modern cinematic representation. He refers to these missed encounters as 'known misunderstandings' which, in turn, create a special type of 'aesthetic emotion' in the external spectator (the film viewer, in other words) (Jameson 114). Jameson further observes:

> That it is purely aesthetic . . . means that this effect is conceivable only in conjunction with the work of art, cannot take place in real life, and has something to do with the omniscient author. These occurrences remain *disjoined*, unknown to each other, their interrelationship, casual or other, being a non-existent fact, event, or phenomenon, save when the gaze of the Author, rising over miniature roof-tops, puts them back together and declares them to be the material of story-telling . . . (my emphasis, 114)

Jameson is clear to delineate the element of the authorial in his description of cinematic urban spatiality. The film spectator, in other words, views both the space and the characters within that space through the eyes of the omniscient narrator. In *What Time*, Hsiao-kang and Shiang-chyi are unaware of the occurrences that connect their lives. These perceived connections serve the aesthetic satisfaction of the spectator, and of the Author. Shiang-chyi and Hsiao-kang are serial amnesiacs who do not remember themselves from previous films in which they played the same characters. Yet, though they are different people in every film, traces of their former characters remain. *Disjointed connectivity* is Tsai's conscious placing of intertextual, cinematic references from the work of other auteurs (Truffaut especially) into his films. *Disjointed connectivity* is the haunting of ghosts, the serial amnesiacs that are his characters as they appear and reappear throughout his body of work.

Throughout *What Time*, as mentioned previously, Tsai employs two important methods of time manipulation to carry out this odd effect that I am calling *disjointed connectivity*: (1) the absurdly long take with an absolutely still camera; and (2) the division of simultaneous time into parallel, yet converging, stories between two central protagonists. These cinematic techniques combine to create for the audience an overall feeling of discomfort mixed with intrigue because they serve to fragment time and space while simultaneously lingering on minute details. When he employs the first method, Tsai positions the camera in a particular spot – often in a hallway, a bedroom, or peering into a car – to film the characters moving in private space. As I mentioned previously, the motionless, unflinching camera eye makes us feel as if we are spying on these characters as they enter and exit the frames of their private worlds. These long takes are cringeworthy because, as spectators, we feel as if we are observing the lives of the characters in 'real-time'. In reality the film narrative has been carefully edited; we can do nothing but squirm in our seats.

Fran Martin, in her article: 'The European Undead: Tsai Ming-liang's Temporal Dysphoria' (2003), notes that it is Tsai's overt and self-conscious use of intertextuality and self-reflexivity that allows us to read the film through a global lens (Martin 2). Martin, in line with my own argument, warns against a pure formalist reading of the film, and stresses the need to view Tsai's extensive use of European pastiche (François Truffaut, in particular) in the light of 'transcultural citation':

> I think that addressing the complex question of what is signified by such transcultural citation necessitates a 'move outside the frame', as it were, to consider the wider contexts in which *What Time* is produced and consumed: contexts crucially conditioned, as I will argue, by Taiwan's cultural post-coloniality, and the place of Taiwan cinema within global film networks today. (Martin 5)

But 'moving outside the frame' is merely a preliminary analytical step. It is essential to realise that Tsai's *What Time* reflects more than the director's strong ties to both his Taiwanese and European cinematic predecessors,[14] the film exemplifies a turning point, even within Tsai's own career.

In a similar vein, Michelle E. Bloom, in her article 'Contemporary Franco-Chinese Cinema: Translation, Citation and Imitation in Dai Sijie's *Balzac and the Little Chinese Seamstress* and Tsai Ming-liang's *What Time is it There?*', points out that Tsai is more interested in commenting on *film*, in general, than he is interested in making a statement about Paris or Taipei. *What Time* is, indeed, a 'film about a film' (Bloom 2005, 319); it reaches beyond the local to find its own unique niche within the global cinema landscape. Partially because of Taiwan's volatile relationship with the mainland, the local cinema has become more internationally fluent. Convergence, rather than separation, seems to define the Taiwanese Second Wave, as intertextual citation of European auteurs becomes the norm among post-Taiwan New Cinema directors.

Some of Tsai's earlier films – *The River*, *The Hole*, and *Goodbye Dragon Inn*, for instance – are less obviously transnational, yet they all express the theme of loneliness in similar ways. Like Hou, Tsai prefers to use extremely limited dialogue, long takes and limited camera movement. Unlike Hou, however, there is not an underlying 'sweet' quality to Tsai's films. The characters that appear and reappear in different forms throughout Tsai's *oeuvre* are isolated from themselves and from others and, for this reason, his films are read as sad and depressing. Tsai himself characterises his own work best, perhaps, when he comments: 'My films have no climax and they are not dramatic, and not very complex. I replace narrative pleasure with the detail of life. But it is hard to get close to reality. I try to provide ridiculous elements, which are part of reality itself.'[15] Yet these ridiculous elements are precisely the elements that other critics have read as hauntings, as ghosts that reach into the frame, as parallel universes that open up within 'banal reality'. These are the elements that Tsai places into his films: intertextual and intratextual references that allow him to connect, in a disjointed manner, to his own fans.

STEPPING OUTSIDE THE FRAME: DISJOINTED CONNECTIVITY AND AUTEURISM

Tsai finds his niche even within a bevy of equally talented Taiwanese auteurs, specifically within the 'Sino-French' (Bloom 2011).[16] Despite the fact that much has been written on this particular film within the last decade, a close reading of individual scenes, based around the concept of *disjointed connectivity*, has not been attempted. I plan to show, therefore, that, as a film, *What*

Time signals more than just a shift in aesthetic taste for one particular director. Insofar as it functions on intertextual and intratextual levels,[17] the film requires a critical reading that will 'move outside the frame', as Martin puts it.

By many film scholars' accounts, Tsai's *What Time* is a film about alienation in the context of present-day city life that describes 'our postmodern condition'. In her article: 'Cinema as Heterochronos: Temporal Folds in the Work of Tsai Ming-Liang', Andrea Bachner, for instance, observes: 'If there is something that can be (il) legitimately called a "postmodern condition", both Tsai's life and his films embody some of it in their own oblique ways' (2004, 62). Certainly, it is true that Tsai critiques modern life without much recourse to historical foregrounding but, at the same time, his nostalgia can be linked to Taiwan as a post-colonial space. While it would not be inherently problematic to rely on Jameson's theoretical apparatus as a means of describing Tsai's depiction of Taipei, we must be clear not to conflate the aesthetics of Taiwan New Cinema (as exemplified by Edward Yang and Hou Hsiao-hsien) with the aesthetics of Tsai's cinema, which are not so easily categorised.

Despite the intense proliferation of scholarly articles on this (by now) ten-year old film, we have yet to adequately and accurately situate the film in a meta-cinematic context. Though I am certainly not claiming that it would be incorrect to discuss Tsai's film in terms of postmodernism, it is my contention that we need to rethink and re-analyse *What Time* in more tangible language, and with a nod towards auteur theory, as Song Hwee Lim argues in his article, 'Positioning Auteur Theory in Chinese Cinemas Studies: Intertextuality, Intratextuality, and Paratextuality in the Films of Tsai Ming-Liang' (2007, 230). Lim argues that, despite the continuing influence of postmodernism and post-structuralism on current film theory, it is difficult to argue that the auteur is completely and utterly dead, as a Barthean[18] would have it (225). Barthes, in fact, states in his 'Death of the Author' essay that 'To give a text an Author is to impose a limit on that text, to furnish it with a final signified, to close the writing' (Barthes 147). In the case of Tsai's *oeuvre*, however, ignoring the auteur might actually limit the cinematic text. Intertextual citation by film-makers such as Tsai cannot always be interpreted as a confirmation of postmodern, 'anti-authorial' aesthetics. Notes Lim: '. . . to the contrary . . . intertextuality, by invoking works of previous auteurs, precisely highlights a deliberate attempt at establishing a network of authorial association and, in the process, serves to enhance the status of the belated filmmaker by such association with former masters' (230).

This observation exhibits why the conceptual 'stakes are high' so to speak. If we are precluded, in some a priori sense, from relying on auteur theory when analysing Tsai's *oeuvre*, we shall have difficulty adequately reading Tsai's films in terms of *intra*textuality. I would argue that it is still possible to analyse Tsai's idiosyncratic use of space and time in *What Time* without relying too heavily on the discourse of postmodernity. In fact, when analysing *What Time*, we really cannot rely solely on the assumption that postmodernity frees us from history, time or even authorial intention. It would, therefore, be misleading to describe the space in *What Time* only in terms of the supernatural. In other words, though the film is filled with the themes of supernatural space, ghosts and resurrection, these phenomena can be more accurately described, within the context of the film, in terms of Song Hwee Lim's notion of intratextuality, and my notion of disjointed connectivity.

To clarify, I am not arguing that the themes of ghosts, reincarnation and the fantastic are not enormously important to the film. Rather, I am arguing that, if we read the spatiality of the film only in terms of this particular paradigm, we risk losing an overall grasp of how the film functions on a metacinematic or intratextual level. Building on Lim's contention, I would add that, if we say that Tsai's *What Time* exemplifies our postmodern condition and simply end there, we miss a large part of Tsai's authorial function.

Moreover, unlike Tu Chao-mei, who has argued that Tsai should be classified as an 'accented' or 'displaced' film-maker whose aesthetics reveal his struggle to reconcile space (Tu 2010), I would argue that, on the contrary, Tsai's aesthetics reveal his extraordinary capability of controlling the transnational cinematic space in which he is able to move with ease and fluidity. Tsai has said rather blatantly that he does not aim to please all audiences; on the contrary, he assumes that his audiences will keep up with him. In a question and answer session after a screening of *Rebels of the Neon God* in 2010, Tsai commented:

> We have the same audience around the globe. Some people won't even watch my films; they will see my name on the marquee and turn away . . . I use the same cast over and over again. This is not entertaining for most people. It is hard to say who likes my films, some PhD students fall asleep and some high school students love them. If you see film as conceptual, then you like my films. I don't always get a lot of applause at the end of my films. (Q & A, 2010)[19]

Fundamentally, Tsai's *What Time* (more so than his previous films) functions as an interweb of connections through which the director establishes himself as a 'knower of film' and, in an important sense, as a patriarch. As Lim accurately points out, Tsai wants to establish himself as a brand, as the 'surrogate father' of Hsiao-kang, just as François Truffaut was the 'surrogate father' of Antoine Doinel (233).

Figure 4.1   Lee Hsiao-kang and Tsai Ming-liang, in 2010, at the University of
Southern California Cinema School.

TIEN MIAO: THE GHOST IN THE FILM APPARATUS, HSIAO-KANG:
THE WATCHED BECOMES THE WATCHER

The first scene of *What Time* serves as a kind of prologue to Shiang-chyi's and
Hsiao-kang's parallel stories. Hsiao-kang's father, played by Tien Miao, is pre-
paring food in the kitchen; he then walks squarely into the frame and sits at the
dining table, facing the camera. A few moments pass, he walks to the doorway
and, after a futile attempt to call his son for the meal, he ambles back to the
table, lights a cigarette and then steps outside to finish it. This opening scene
endures for a total of three minutes and twenty seconds. Though this may not
sound like a long time, perhaps, the combination of Tsai's absolutely fixed
camera and his unapologetic refusal to cater to audience expectation creates
the illusion of stretched-out, slow-motion 'real time'. The entire scene consists
of one static shot that resembles a picture frame with definite boundaries. The
camera does not move to track Tien Miao's movements; on the contrary, Tien

Miao's movements are defined by the boundaries of the frame. When he walks outside, he moves towards the vanishing point of the 'picture' and hence away from our previously unhindered view of his face.

Tsai's camera, therefore, defines space in an unconventional way. The father's movements in this opening scene of *What Time* are not tracked by the camera but appear, instead, to be 'captured' by the camera. His decision not to provide a mobile camera in this particular scene creates uncertainty for the transcendental subject (namely, the subjects outside the frame, that is, the individuals in the audience and the director himself).[20] This same uncertainty is more or less equivalent to what Rapfogel calls 'omniscient distance' (26), that is, the ability to observe but only within certain predefined bounds.

Tien Miao moves around in a restricted space yet, when he sits at the dining table, he stares past the camera lens at something beyond that space, outside the shot. The only other scene in which Tien Miao appears is in the final scene of the film, and it is debatable whether or not he appears as the father character because he is, after all, supposed to be dead. These two scenes frame the film and are therefore isolated from everything in the middle. In this sense, they are 'exceptions' because, unlike the other scenes in the film, they remain open-ended. It is impossible to know, in other words, when the opening scene occurs in relation to the rest of the film. Is it a flashback? Does this scene occur towards the end of the father's life? In fact, it is entirely impossible to say with any certainty that the father is even *alive* in this scene. Because no one interacts with him, he could just as well already be a ghost who is visible only to us. Similarly, it is impossible to say with certainty whether or not Tien Miao's character is meant to represent the reincarnation of Hsiao-kang's dead father in the final scene of the film.

But there are other, less supernatural explanations for the father's strange relation to space vis-à-vis the other characters in *What Time*. I would suggest that Tien Miao's character is the only one in the film who is able to escape from the confining boundaries of the central narrative of *What Time* though not necessarily because he is a ghost. His character dies before the story begins and he never interacts with any of the other characters. Within this alternative, quasi-non-diegetic space, he becomes the surrogate patriarch of the film, a kind of metaphorical stand-in for the director himself. In *What Time,* therefore, as opposed to in Tsai's previous films, Tien Miao exists in a space 'outside the frame'.

Interestingly, Tien Miao died of lymphatic cancer in 2005 at the age of eighty. The last film that he appeared in was Tsai's *Goodbye Dragon Inn* (2003) which was shot in the Fuhe Grand Theatre in Taipei just before the site was demolished. In *Goodbye*, Tien plays a filmgoer sitting in the audience of the Fuhe on its last night of operation. In the fictional world of *Goodbye*, the final film to be shown at the Fuhe is King Hu's 1967 martial arts classic film *Dragon Gate Inn/Longmen kezhan* – not, coincidentally, the first major film to feature a much younger Tien. *Goodbye* therefore functions as a final vehicle of reincarnation for Tien as an *actor*. Here life imitates art: just as the Fuhe Theatre is preserved on film for all eternity just before its demise, so is Tien. Similarly, just as *Goodbye* functions as a filmic reincarnation of Hu's film through mise en abyme, Tien's life as an actor seems to have come full circle.

These facts become odder still when read in relation to the final of scene of *What Time*: after rescuing Shiang-chyi's suitcase from the pond, Tien Miao's character walks away from the camera and towards the giant, rotating Ferris wheel just outside the Tuileries garden in Paris. This final shot can be read as both a visual reference to the Buddhist Bhavacakra (aka the Wheel of Life) and also to one of the earliest manifestations of the film apparatus, the zoetrope.[21] The mysterious nature of this shot reflects the multilayered thematics of the film itself. On one level, there is an ambiguity with regard to whether or not the father's spirit has been reincarnated in line with the Buddhist belief. If one were to pursue this line of reasoning, it might follow that the superstitious beliefs of Hsiao-kang's mother turned out not to be so foolish after all.

Yet, on another, perhaps more interesting, level, Tien Miao's character walks towards the film apparatus itself and thus towards *cinematic* reincarnation. Why does he rescue the suitcase? If Tien can be interpreted as a stand-in for Tsai, then we might interpret this as a kind gesture on the part of the surrogate father, that is, the auteur. Through Tien, the auteur is able to step into the frame, perform a good deed for his poor, troubled protagonists without them even being aware, and then walk off into the figurative sunset. The final shot is, therefore, the ultimate self-reflexive filmic gesture – Tsai's fond ode to Truffaut – his acknowledgement that film itself is a construct that can be repeated and referenced in an endless cycle.

Tsai represents both Paris and Taipei not as open spaces full of life and vitality but, rather, as enclosed, deathly spaces in which movement and the possibility for change become highly restricted. In a 2002 interview, Tsai commented on his affinity for filming small confined spaces:

> On the one hand, it is a restriction; on the other it is very safe. Maybe I am always in search of a small confined space like this. I very much like to use them in my films. I like to film in hotel rooms, in elevators or on moving staircases. What counts is that the space itself is very clearly divided from the rest of the world. This might have to do with the subconscious. I do not like to have too many eyes focused on me. And I cannot feel safe until I have excluded these eyes. This means I have to create boundaries. In my work I can do this. (Leopold n.p.)

These comments help to explain, at least partially, why Tsai chooses to film interior locations as opposed to exteriors or establishing shots. I contend, in addition, that Tsai's cinematic manifestation of what he deems 'the subconscious' relates back to the phenomenon I previously referred to as *disjointed connectivity*. By creating boundaries, he is, somewhat paradoxically, able to express space freely. Private areas that are separated from the rest of the world serve as safe havens in which prying eyes can be averted. Though, on the one hand, Tsai's protagonists are limited by the void and emptiness entailed by urban existence, it is this same void that gives Tsai the freedom to emphasise points of connectivity between these protagonists.

The notion that camera shots are capable of expressing bounded space, as well as implied unbounded space (that is, all that lies outside the frame), is touched upon by Gilles Deleuze in *Cinema 1*, albeit with different terminology. What I have referred to as *disjointed connectivity* as it relates to *What Time*, complements Deleuze's concept of the 'out-of-field' [*hors champ*]. Deleuze questions the assumption that it is sufficient to distinguish between concrete, closed space and imaginary space, aka the out-of-field, as it relates to what is shown on the film screen. He also notes that, in film, apparently 'closed systems' are never absolutely closed because all space is related to other space by a fine thread that ties all 'sets' together and forms an integrated whole (Deleuze 17). He observes:

> In one case, the out-of-field designates that which exists elsewhere . . . in the other case, the out-of-field testifies to a more disturbing presence, one which cannot even be said to exist . . . a more radical Elsewhere, outside homogeneous space and time. Undoubtedly these two aspects of the out-of-field intermingle constantly. (17)

The idea that the 'out-of-field' points to more than a simple benign 'elsewhere' but, more significantly, to a disturbing presence that exists outside of homogeneous cinematic space and time resounds with what I conceive to be Tsai's aesthetic project. But there are ways to interpret the 'presence' that exists in the 'out-of-field' as more than a ghost or spirit in the literal sense. Tsai's representation of closed-off and confining areas implies a radical Elsewhere in the Deleuzian sense but there is no room for manoeuvring between the closed system and the imaginary space for Shiang-chyi and Hsiao-kang. The characters are, in a broader sense, confined by the *text* that they inhabit, and the 'disturbing presence' that 'haunts' them could well be thought of as the voyeuristic spectator or the omniscient Author.

I would not argue with the contention that, in a basic, literal and metaphorical sense, *What Time* is a film about ghosts and haunting, as Martin characterises it (1). I would say, however, that the 'ghosts' themselves, when brought to the light of day, can be interpreted as traces of intertext and pieces of the overall narrative device. In an intertextual sense, the film is 'haunted' by the cinema of Tsai's European predecessors, the cinema of his Taiwanese contemporaries, and his own cinema. *What Time*'s narrative deals with ghosts on a literal level, in the sense that it is, fundamentally, a film about death in the context of twentieth-century Taiwan.

For some reason, there has been little discussion of Tsai's representation of confined filmic space in relation to modern Taiwanese religious practices, particularly Taiwanese death rituals. In his essay on the subject, 'Identity and Social Change in Taiwanese Religion', Robert P. Weller notes: 'Most Taiwanese religious ritual involves spirits of the dead in one form or another' (Rubinstein 341). Weller adds that gods are believed to be spirits of dead men and women who were not able to pass into another realm because they lacked a younger generation of ancestors to mourn their passing. In the Taiwanese strain of the Buddhist religion, when an older loved one dies, it is customary for the younger generation to perform rituals for several days, if not weeks, until the soul of the dead has passed on to a 'happy place'. These rituals consist of bowing, chanting and offerings of incense. After the body has been frozen for several days, it is cremated and the ashes are sent to be stored in a receptacle inside a multilevel temple.

Those who remain behind in the land of the living are the unlucky ones, forced to practise these repetitive rituals. After the death of his father, Hsiao-kang is shown in a series of 'suffocating' shots: he rides, holding ceremonial offerings, in the back seat of a car which then enters a dark tunnel. In the very next scene, Hsiao-kang and the other funerary participants stand in the cramped, narrow hallway of the temple where they are performing the ceremony associated with the storage of his father's ashes. In the third of this mini-series of scenes, all related to the death of his father, Hsiao-kang appears in his underpants in the dark apartment that he shares with his mother. He looks frightened and disoriented as he moves carefully through the apartment. The camera remains static.

Meanwhile, on the right-hand side of the immobile shot, sits the large, white fish in a glowing tank. The face of the fish somehow, eerily, recalls the father's blank expression in the opening scene of the film. The whiskers and looming stature of the fish also recall the wise and stately stature of the father. Though the mother tries to communicate with the fish through the glass, she cannot. The fish, as it is represented in this film, inhabits a space that is beyond the reach of the characters in the film.[22]

I would suggest that it is of little importance whether or not we 'decide' to interpret the fish as the filmic, metaphorical reincarnation of the father. What is important about the existence of the fish, in general, is that, like the father, it occupies 'alternative' space – or using Deleuze's terminology – the 'radical Elsewhere'. Unlike Hsiao-kang, the fish is not confined by human concerns or superstitious rituals. As Nanouk Leopold characterises the fish in her 2002 interview with Tsai: 'He is like a silent spectator. Present, but unable to speak' (Leopold). The fish, in other words, functions less as a ghost and more as a witness or external spectator. As cinematic voyeurs, we, too, are silent spectators who watch and witness yet are unable speak.

Like the fish, Hsiao-kang's character within the film is also a cinematic voyeur. Unlike the fish, however, he does not inhabit the 'out-of-field'. After becoming obsessed with 'all things French', he rents Truffaut's *The 400 Blows* (1959) at an outdoor market and watches the zoetrope scene alone in his dark bedroom. Michelle E. Bloom has commented in great detail on this scene in *What Time*, noting, in particular, Hsiao-kang's corpse-like position and overall lack of movement as he watches the film. According to Bloom: 'Tsai portrays film spectators, exemplified by Hsiao-kang and *including us*, as passive, sleepy or sleeping, resistant to being woken up by demanding films (like his)' (my emphasis, 18) and, of course, like Truffaut's.[23] Hsiao-kang represents a certain type of film spectator who is simultaneously all-perceiving and passive. As Bloom points out, film spectatorship is not always portrayed as a passive activity; it can just as easily be thought of, or portrayed as, an engaging and lively activity. It is therefore important to attempt to understand why Tsai portrays film spectatorship in this way and, furthermore, what this portrayal suggests about us as viewers.

Bloom's assertion that Tsai means to include us, his audience, through his representation of Hsiao-kang is a provocative claim, and one with which I agree. Tsai creates a parallel between Hsiao-kang and his own audience using his signature static camera. The unmoving shot grants the spectators of Tsai's film the opportunity to contemplate their relationship, or *connection*, to Hsiao-kang during this relatively long scene. If we are inclined to regard film viewing as a fundamentally narcissistic experience,[24] I would argue that Hsiao-kang's lack of movement translates into ours, and that his corpse-like appearance reminds us of our own zombie-like stance as we stare at the film or television screen. This scene, therefore, works like a paternalistic, knowing, yet sly wink between Tsai and his audience.

These moments of disjointed connectivity between Tsai, his characters, and his audience, also appear in his 2009 film, *Face*. Though the film received mixed reactions at the Cannes Film Festival and other festivals worldwide,[25] the idea behind the film is immensely interesting, particularly for those audience members who are familiar with Tsai's earlier work. The film is filled with so many intertextual references that, according to Adrian Martin, who wrote on the film when it was first released: 'Each image throbs with a *latent* connection that could at any moment be made *manifest* . . .' (Hughes, his emphasis). Because the film is infinitely rich and complex, I explain only in basic terms how this film relates to *What Time* within the context of this chapter.[26]

The basic story of this film is as follows. The mother of a Taiwanese director dies (Lu Yi-ching reprises her role as the mother, and the director is now played by Lee Kang-sheng). In addition to having to deal with his grief, the director travels to Paris to shoot a film. The film-within-the-film is a cinematic remake of Salome, shot inside the Louvre museum. Salome is played by real-life supermodel Laetitia Casta, Jean-Pierre Léaud plays King Herod, and Fanny Ardant is both Queen Herodias and the French producer of the film-within-the-film. Jeanne Moreau (of *Jules and Jim* fame) shows up as well, as a character named Jeanne.

In one particularly interesting sequence, Ardant's character sits in a bedroom alone, leafing through a photo book. We soon realise that the book is made up of a series of stills, a flip book of the final scene in *The 400 Blows*. Antoine Doinel's young face now stares into Tsai's camera instead of into Truffaut's. Yet the image of his face is distantly removed from the boyish image that appeared at the end of Truffaut's film: his face appears in a picture book – a book of still images or frames – now only remnants of the original movie. Furthermore, we must imagine that Ardant is looking at his face and that we are therefore seeing the face through her eyes. As spectators of Tsai's film, we are witnessing Ardant's nostalgia for Léaud's face. Any nostalgia that we may feel for this iconic image is therefore being mediated, or channelled, through her gaze.

And in case we may happen to forget that Léaud is no longer a strapping young boy, caught in Ardant's vision of Léaud's iconic face, we are quickly pushed back into reality when, in the next shot, Léaud's withered body appears, burying ashes in a graveyard. Léaud is old and ugly; one might easily mistake him for a crazy man on the street. In any case, he is unrecognisable as the film star that he once was. His 'face' is no longer a focal point of obsession because the aura of his unreal persona has been wiped clean by Tsai.

In the very next scene, Ardant sits in the same kitchen that Tien Miao appeared in at the beginning of *What Time* – she is leafing through a book on Truffaut and eating an apple. To the right of Ardant, on the table, sits a framed picture of the dead mother. After a few moments, a hand reaches into the frame – from *outside* it – to grab an apple. Ardant does not notice but the effect is chilling. When the camera pans back, giving us a broader view of the room, the ghostly figure of the mother appears on the right side of the frame. Though it is difficult to tell, she appears to be sitting opposite Ardant on the other side of the table. Yet her image can be seen only through – or inside – the fish tank. The mother now occupies the space of the fish, that alternative space or Radical Elsewhere which was once occupied by Tien Miao. Fans of Tsai will, of course, recognise this fish tank from *What Time*; this is the fish tank that housed Fatty, the fish that the mother believed was her husband. Now, in the context of *Face*, the mother has switched places, so to speak, with the father in *What Time*. Just as Tien Miao's presence was disjointedly connected to the other characters in the film, off the screen but in the frame, the mother has moved to this parallel universe that has opened up within 'reality'.

This sequence is a perfect example of Tsai's disjointed connectivity. In the same film, these characters are unable to see each other despite the fact that they are intimately connected. Paris and Taipei, as cinematic urban spaces, have become interchangeable and indistinguishable – the two parallel stories of *What Time* have now collided in this film. In this sense, *Face* represents the ultimate cinematic dream for Tsai. The film represents a space in which public and private space collide: the public space of the Louvre becomes private while the private, intimate spaces of apartments become public, open to the spectator's viewing pleasure. With *Face*, Tsai suggests that cinematic space is, in a very fundamental sense, haunted. The space of cinema is haunted by the ghosts of iconic faces: the actors, the characters, and the directors who sat behind the camera. In this sense, *Face* represents Tsai's most ambitious project, an exercise in meta-cinema.

THE SKYWALK IS FALLING; STRANGER IN A STRANGE PARIS

In the context of *What Time,* Paris and Taipei are beautiful, yet abstract, in part because of Tsai's dislike of establishing shots. Though, as Bloom points out, Tsai does not erase or eliminate place entirely, he merely minimises it (2005, 18). Thus, though *What Time* is fundamentally a self-reflexive, intertextual, and complex transnational film, certain historical and spatial details tie the film to its Taiwanese landscape. In addition to the Fuhe Theatre (which Tsai uses for much of *Goodbye Dragon Inn* and a scene in *What Time*) Tsai is obsessed with another fated Taipei landmark: the Taipei railway station skywalk. According to Christopher Misch, the skywalk was demolished by the Taiwanese government soon after Tsai filmed *What Time* in order to increase the number of lanes along a heavily used roadway in central Taipei.[27] In addition, the skywalk became extraneous after the construction of a new underground tunnel was built for the Taipei Metro.

In the diegesis of *What Time,* the soon-to-be-torn-down skywalk represents Hsiao-kang's place of livelihood: this is where he sells his watches. The eradication of the skywalk, therefore, means that he will lose his place of business as well as his only source of income. Tsai directed a short film in 2002 entitled *The Skywalk is Gone* in which Hsiao-kang and Shiang-chyi reprise their roles in *What Time*. By 2002, the skywalk had already been demolished (both in real life and in the world of the film). Now that his watch stand is gone, Hsiao-kang turns to pornography and prostitution as a means to support himself. Upon her return from Paris, Shiang-chyi searches for the familiar landmark but a policeman confirms that a new underground tunnel has, in fact, replaced the walkway. Throughout the short film, using shots that linger on the void, Tsai emphasises the empty space that once contained the skywalk. Misch comments on the symbolism of the absent landmark in the 2002 film: '. . . Tsai's motif of the absent skywalk does not only represent the singular destruction of an urban entity, but rather it also symbolizes the unfortunate consequences of a constantly developing urban landscape' (Misch n.p.). The absent skywalk, in other words, points to urban renewal within a disposable society.

In the beginning of *What Time*, Shiang-chyi returns to purchase a watch from Hsiao-kang. The angle of the shot exposes the construction cranes looming in the background, threatening to overwhelm and take over. The sound of hammering construction workers punctuates their conversation. It is clear that the city of Taipei is in a constant state of incompleteness, or betweenness. Later in the film, Hsiao-kang's violent banging of the supposedly 'unbreakable' watch on the metal guardrail of the skywalk suggests that he knows his own fate but is powerless to change it. Though Hsiao-kang's frustrated banging is intended to be humorous, the movement also expresses the inability he feels to control the urban space that surrounds him or to halt the inevitable passing of time.

The present/absent skywalk also brings to mind and connects with *The 400 Blows*. Hsiao-kang's stance behind the guardrail connotes imprisonment; his repetitive movements recall a 'jail bird' slapping the bars of a prison cell with an object, in an effort to vent frustration and waste time. Like Antoine Doinel, Hsiao-kang's body language contains a quiet rebellious quality, suggesting that he is not well equipped to thrive in his own environment. But the latter's imprisonment is metaphorical. In *The 400 Blows*, as Antoine is carted off to jail in the back of the police van, he sadly watches the city lights of Paris pass by through the bars of the window. Arguably, Hsiao-kang's plight throughout *What Time* consists of an effort to connect with Paris by changing to Paris time all the clocks he encounters. Yet, like Antoine, he is not able to escape from the confining spaces or temporalities that surround him; he is often shown lying awake in bed, sitting or driving in his car, or attempting to turn back the clocks of Taipei by seven hours. His livelihood is tied to an area that has already been deemed useless by the Taiwanese government. As a result, Hsiao-kang, feeling worthless and desperate to make ends meet, becomes an underground sex worker.[28] One might imagine a much older Antoine Doinel following in similar footsteps.

The confinement that Hsiao-kang experiences is represented by Tsai's camera work which, in turn, parallels and echoes Truffaut's camera work, such that Hsiao-kang does metaphorically 'become Antoine' (Bloom 2005, 20). There are many obvious examples of these parallels, echoes and continuations throughout the film, though one subtler example seems to have gone unnoticed. In *The 400 Blows*, there is a scene in which Antoine lies in the small bunk of his prison cell. For a few moments, a blanket covers his face so that only his eyes can be seen. In Tsai's film, as Hsiao-kang is lying in bed, watching *The 400 Blows*, his face is similarly covered such that only his eyes can be seen. While the shot in Truffaut's film emphasises the loneliness and coldness of Antoine's cell, this parallel shot in Tsai's film works on multiple levels. On a simple level, the shot emphasises Hsiao-kang's loneliness, feelings of grief and confinement in a coffin-like space. On a more complex level, the image of Hsiao-kang's eyes peering out from a blanket connects him to Antoine as it simultaneously points to his role as a spectator or transcendental subject. Hsaio-kang's passive role as a transcendental subject in turn connects him to us, the spectators of Tsai's film, such that the watcher becomes the watched and the cycle of voyeurism continues indefinitely. Again, these complex relationships between the watcher and the watched can be thought of in terms of disjointed connectivity, a relationship through which Tsai self-reflexively acknowledges the position of his characters vis-à-vis his audience.

Tsai describes Shiang-chyi's character quite succinctly in the director's notes for *What Time*, when he comments: 'She is afraid of loneliness, yet she is content with being alone.'[29] Despite the fact that she is 'content with being alone', it is Shiang-chyi's loneliness that prevails. Her loneliness and subsequent despair arise as the result of a series of missed opportunities and failed interactions that occur on her visit to Paris. Even though it appears initially that Shiang-chyi and Hsiao-kang inhabit separate spaces – that their lives intersect at one point and then continue on parallel paths – these two storylines continuously intersect by way of disjointed connectivity. Not only do Shiang-chyi's actions often mirror Hsiao-kang's and vice versa but her actions also seem to be connected to his via cause and effect. Just as Hsiao-kang seems to be uncannily tied to Antoine Doinel, Shiang-chyi is similarly tied to Hsiao-kang. I shall highlight and discuss the many examples of these intersections and points of connectivity that exist between these two characters throughout the remainder of this chapter.

Many film scholars have commented on Tsai's overall depiction of Taipei as an ambivalent space that is defined as much by its colonial past as it is by its uncertain globalised future. In his essay 'Morning in the New Metropolis: Taipei and the Globalization of the City Film', James Tweedie, for instance, notes that Tsai attempts to document Taipei's continuing development, but also its simultaneous deterioration: 'No longer a utopian future glimpsed in the present, the Taipei of Tsai Ming-liang has outlived a modernizing era, and now faces a new wave of expansion, eviction, and demolition' (122). Though Tweedie does not specifically discuss *What Time* in this essay, his characterisation of Tsai's representation of Taipei works in the context of this film. Like Tweedie, I, too, do not see a utopian future inherent in Tsai's vision of Taipei and, moreover, I suspect that Hsiao-kang's obsession with turning back every clock in the city points to Tsai's own fascination with the notion of reversing the flow of time. Hsiao-kang's character is confined both metaphorically (through Tsai's use of claustrophobic shots or shots in which he appears to be corpse-like) and literally (his job has been indirectly eliminated by the municipal government). As the city rapidly changes and evolves and as buildings and transport systems are torn down so that new, more modern ones can be built, those living and working in Taipei are displaced (Hsiao-kang and his watch stand, for example), falling into a state of limbo from which it will be difficult to recover.[30]

In the same sense that Hsiao-kang becomes 'linked' with Taipei in the mind of spectator, Shiang-chyi becomes 'linked' with Paris. For some reason, while there has been a significant amount of discussion on Tsai's cinematic depictions of Taipei throughout the span of his directorial career, there has been much less discussion on Tsai's depiction of Paris in this particular film. Fran Martin argues that, although *What Time* might be interpreted as a postcolonial ode to European cinema of the past from a present-day Taiwanese director, the film's project is somewhat more sophisticated:

> . . . I think the film can be seen as problematizing its own westward trajectory, insofar as ultimately, as much as it appears as the locus of the characters' and the film's own desire, Paris is also figured, precisely, as *the land of the dead* . . . (her emphasis, 11)

Paris represents the land of the dead, Martin argues, because Hsiao-kang's dead father appears in the Tuileries garden at the end of the film and, furthermore, because Shiang-chyi meets Jean-Pierre Léaud (an iconic childhood star of the French New Wave) in the Père-Lachaise Cemetery.

I agree with Martin's assessment of Tsai's representation of Paris to the extent that the film 'problematizes its own western trajectory' by not privileging or romanticising Paris over Taipei. In fact, by way of Shiang-chyi's parallel storyline, Paris is represented as cold, unfriendly and isolating, perhaps even more so than Taipei. But I would argue that Paris represents, more precisely, the land of dead cinema. The reason for Shiang-chyi's trip to Paris is never explained because there is no diegetic reason for her to travel there. Yet Tsai must film her in Paris so that she can interact with the 'ghosts' of the French New Wave. The setting, therefore, functions in a certain sense as just another means for Tsai to showcase his penchant for complex intertextuality.

This intertextual interaction begins with the first shot of Shiang-chyi in Paris. Her appearance has been visibly altered from when she was in Taipei – she has been 'westernized' in the sense that she now resembles a European film actress from the French New Wave. She has cropped her hair into a short bob, reminiscent specifically of Patricia (Jean Seberg) in Jean-Luc Godard's 1960 New Wave film *Breathless*, also set in Paris.[31] Yet, unlike Patricia, who is confident, independent and fluent in French, Shiang-chyi is shy, dependent on others and unable to speak French. Also, unlike Patricia, Shiang-chyi never seems particularly interested in men or heterosexual pursuits, in general, even though it is clear that many men are attracted to her. Her inability to communicate on a meaningful level with others quickly alienates and isolates her. As observant spectators, we might notice that Hsiao-kang's actions are cleverly edited to juxtapose and mirror Shiang-chyi's even though he is thousands of miles away and she remains unaware of the connection.

Not coincidentally, many of Shiang-chyi's Paris scenes are shot in interior locations, even more so than Hsiao-kang's Taipei scenes. All of these scenes are tied together by a common theme: namely, they are marked by Shiang-chyi's incapacity to communicate on a 'meaningful' level with the people (men and women) that surround her. In the first such scene, Shiang-chyi sits alone drinking coffee in a café, facing the camera. A man sits at the bar in the foreground, though we can see only the back of his head. The man's head is positioned such that his line of vision matches up directly with Shiang-chyi's face – he is staring at her, much like we are. This scene which, unsurprisingly, consists of one long take, echoes the scene in which Hsiao-kang watches *The 400 Blows*. With a single long take, much like in Hsiao-kang's scene, Tsai highlights the role of the film spectator by allowing us to watch others watching – we observe others observing. The experience of spectatorship suddenly becomes self-reflexive again. Though she occasionally looks up from her coffee cup, Shiang-chyi avoids eye contact with the man. She stares out the window for a few moments while she finishes her coffee, then gets up and leaves while the man continues to look in her direction.

Scenes such as this underscore more than Shiang-chyi's inability to speak French. Shiang-chyi's submissive demeanour and her avoidance of the Western gaze show more than anything that she dislikes being regarded as some sort of 'exotic' object. In spectatorship terms, Shiang-chyi represents the inverse of Hsiao-kang; we watch Hsiao-kang watching others whereas we watch others watching Shiang-chyi. Thus, by refusing to reciprocate the Western gaze, she refuses to reciprocate our (the film viewer's) gaze, and is clearly made uncomfortable by the prospect of being voyeuristically watched.

While Hsiao-kang is shown performing many unsightly bodily functions, such as peeing into a bag, having sex with a prostitute, sitting on the toilet and guzzling a bottle of wine, Shiang-chyi's private bodily functions are more hidden from view. Although at one point she is heard vomiting in a bathroom stall, her back is turned away from the camera such that we are distanced from the action. Her vomiting in the Paris bathroom can be read as a symbolic reaction to Hsiao-kang's wine drinking in the previous scene. The juxtaposition of Hsiao-kang's consumption of the French wine and Shiang-chyi's subsequent vomiting underscores the connection between these two characters.[32]

Using a similar technique, Tsai juxtaposes Jean-Pierre Léaud's body with Shiang-chyi's as they sit on a bench in a cemetery. This scene further serves to deconstruct the image of Paris as a romantic city as it simultaneously shatters the image of the forever-young body of Antoine Doinel. Much like Marcello Mastroianni's 1987 appearance in Federico Fellini's *Intervista*[33] (and Léaud's own reappearance in *Face*), Léaud's appearance in *What Time* reminds the audience that all of us, even sex symbols, are not susceptible to the effects of aging. Martin points to the cinematic juxtaposition between Léaud and the previous shot in which Shiang-chyi gazes for nearly a minute at a stone sculpture of a human figure lying face down. This particular pairing of shots, Martin claims, combined with the fact that Léaud appears to be the less animated of the two figures in the frame, creates in the mind of the spectator a parallel between Léaud and death (12). I would say, more precisely, that these shots create a parallel between French New Wave cinema, as exemplified by Léaud, and death. Furthermore, because Hsiao-kang is metaphorically linked to Antoine Doinel in previous scenes, Shiang-chyi's failure to communicate with Léaud in this scene can be interpreted as another symbolic failure on her part to communicate with Hsiao-kang.

Shiang-chyi could be, in fact, unsuccessfully searching in her bag for Hsiao-kang's telephone number. By offering to replace the lost number, therefore, Léaud is attempting to 'fill the gap' of Hsiao-kang's absence. If one starts to think about the logic of replacing a phone number with another phone number, however, the gesture becomes nonsensical. Léaud's gesture implicitly assumes that communication is all that is essential, not the actual person being spoken to. He assumes that Shiang-chyi's loneliness can be remedied by communication with a stranger. In a broader sense, this scene functions on an allegorical level, a meeting between French and Taiwanese cinema. Léaud, the aged 'face'[34] of French cinema assumes that Shiang-chyi, the protagonist in many of Tsai's films, wants to communicate with him. But, as the painful, awkward silence becomes palpable as the two figures sit on the bench, it is clear that any fruitful communication between the two of them would be unlikely.[35]

In fact, the only person that Shiang-chyi does finally communicate with in Paris is a woman from Hong Kong who witnesses her vomiting in the bathroom and takes pity on her by offering her a cup of hot water. By way of this customary gesture, the two women strike up a conversation in the café and end up returning together to the Hong Kong woman's hotel room. When Shiang-chyi cautiously attempts to make a romantic advance at the woman, however, she is rejected and leaves the next morning in a state of utter embarrassment. The film concludes with a close-up shot of Shiang-chyi's immensely sad face as she sits alone on a bench in the Tuileries garden.

This 'final failure' is important because it emphasises the unfortunate notion that Shiang-chyi's series of miscommunications goes well beyond language or cultural barriers. As Bloom succinctly states, on the subject of 'Sino-French' film studies: '. . . speaking the same national language no more guarantees or even facilitates communication than not speaking or even understanding the same language precludes connection between people'.[36] Thus, even though Shiang-chyi is noticeably isolated from the Parisians that surround her, she is more greatly affected, in a profound emotional sense, by the woman from Hong Kong. This final scene, furthermore, underlines Shiang-chyi's departure from Hsiao-kang with regard to her 'trajectory' as a character. Even though Hsiao-kang is obviously distraught, if not somewhat damaged, by the death of his father, he still manages a reconciliation with his mother in his final scene of the film (we see him walk into the house and lie down next to her on her bed). Shiang-chyi, meanwhile, is last seen alone, cold and crying on a park bench in the middle of a city that has done nothing but isolate and alienate her.

More importantly, Shiang-chyi's set of 'failures' in Paris resonate with Jameson's concept of 'synchronous monadic simultaneity', and my notion of disjointed connectivity. These missed opportunities for communication and chance encounters seem, paradoxically, only further to isolate the characters from one another. Notes Jameson:

> Now in modernity, everything that is stunning about these accidents and points of connection, seem, because of their ephemerality, to drive us more deeply into individual isolation. The Providence effect is an aesthetic one. (1992, 115)

These accidental meetings serve as 'points of connection' only insofar as they function on an aesthetic level for the spectator. That which the Victorian-era writers may have deemed divine intervention is, in the current era, handed over to the realm of pure aesthetics. Disjointed connectivity, in other words, serves mainly to please the voyeuristic cinephile.

CONCLUSIONS

In *What Time*, Tsai proves that it is possible to produce a nostalgic ode to Truffaut (and European film in general) while simultaneously challenging the hackneyed conception of Paris as the ultimate romantic city. Not only does Tsai cite Truffaut and other European film directors but he also demonstrates respect for the films of his Taiwanese contemporaries, such as Hou Hsiao-hsien, as evidenced by his preference for the long take. Tsai's ability to create a complex cinematic pastiche allows him to resist being classified as an 'Eastern *auteur*' whose only goal is to resurrect the past influential movements of 'European cinema'. His related ability to envision and depict abstract urban space aids him in this endeavour.

As we have seen, *What Time* is divided into two distinct storylines, each one following the trajectory of two protagonists who are relative strangers to one another: Hsiao-kang and Shiang-chyi. Rather than keep them distinct, Tsai allows these two storylines constantly to interconnect and intersect. For the purposes of this chapter, I have labelled this particular phenomenon – the intermittent cinematic juxtapositions between Hsiao-kang and Shiang-chyi – *disjointed connectivity*. In light of the fragmented nature of Tsai's narrative, it is not difficult to see why so many films scholars have chosen to discuss Tsai's films in terms of postmodernity and the 'postmodern condition'. Perhaps the discourse of postmodernity is appealing because, in many ways, Tsai's use of inter- and intratextuality can be read as arrogant and even selfish. By employing these techniques, Tsai seems implicitly to assume that we are following his every move, we have seen all his films; 'collecting the traces' or 'breadcrumbs' that he leaves behind for his audience to find.

But, as Lim argues, there is no need to abandon auteurship entirely in favour of postmodernity, and I would add that the two are not necessarily mutually exclusive. If, as Lim suggests, we view auteurism as a critical discourse rather than as a film-making practice (as Andrew Sarris did) (240), it will become easier to reconcile these two seemingly competing discourses. Moreover, in many ways, the image of the pretentious and arrogant auteur is misleading, and it would be a shame to ignore the analytic possibilities that the framework of auteurism might have to offer. Lim comments: 'Knowing who is speaking *does* make a difference, as it can be an enabling and empowering source of identification and mobilization' (240). This is an important insight not only in terms of Tsai's film-making but, moreover, in the analysis of transnational cinema more generally.

Martin and others have deemed that *What Time* is a film about haunting, ghosts, death and the supernatural and, in a thematic sense, this is undeniable. But if we are to interpret this film in terms of Tsai's cinephilia and his penchant for 'showing off' his cinematic knowledge, then I would contend that the supernatural aspects begin to fade slightly. Once the Author comes to light, in other words, we no longer need to be afraid of ghosts.

ADDENDUM

On 18 November 2009, I attended a screening of Tsai's first film, *Rebels of the Neon God*, which was followed by a question and answer session, at the University of Southern California's Cinema School.

After the session, moderator and USC cinema professor, Akira Lippit, introduced me to Lee Hsiao-kang as he was exiting the theatre. At that time, my Mandarin was more or less non-existent. Flustered at seeing the real-life Hsiao-kang with no mediating screen to separate us, I mustered a 'nice to meet you'. Despite my own awkwardness, he was an exceptionally polite man.

I waited to meet Tsai. During the question and answer session, Tsai had mentioned that he could never tell whether or not an audience would find his films boring. 'Even some PhD students fall asleep watching my films!' he added.

My husband, who was standing off to the side, whispered loudly to me: 'Tell him that you are a PhD student who doesn't fall asleep watching his films!' I liked the idea. It was a compliment couched in a safe joke. As I finally shook Tsai's hand, I told him that I was a PhD student who was writing a chapter of my dissertation on him. Then I tried to pull off the joke, saying that I certainly don't fall asleep while watching his films.

Tsai completely misunderstood what I was saying. Thinking that I was referring to tomorrow night's screening of *I Don't Want to Sleep Alone*,[37] he suggested: 'Why don't you stop by?'

I thought afterwards that it was nice for him to have translated my banality into an intelligent reference to one of his films. In the end, this inability to communicate was not a blatant failure and at least I have a story to tell.

NOTES

1. See Hughes, *Senses of Cinema*.
2. For instance: mixing amateur actors with professionals, perfecting the long take, and integrating documentary-style camera work into a fictional narrative (Hughes).
3. Though it sounds contradictory to state that perception is something that occurs outside the body, I believe it makes sense when thought about in relation to Bergson's overall point. Perception is both internal and external to ourselves as subjects. On the other hand, when we talk about 'affection', I believe that we are talking about a much more personal experience, something that occurs within our subjectivity as we are absorbing images.
4. From Claire Colebrook, *Gilles Deleuze*.
5. Perhaps I am simplifying Deleuze here in the interest of time but this is his general line of thought as I have come to understand it (and interpret it for my own purposes).
6. Zeno's paradox posits that, because space is infinitely divisible, it is impossible to cross it with a finite number of steps.
7. Clearly this is a problematic term but, for the purposes of this paper, I shall stick to it.
8. From here *What Time*.
9. They do, however, meet again in Tsai's 2004 short film *The Skywalk is Gone*.
10. Fran Martin notes that the building stands opposite the Far Eastern Department Store which also happens to be flying the French flag. The Far Eastern group is a powerful retail force in Taiwan and, according to www.chinaretailnews.com the company plans to open twenty-five more department stores in Mainland China over the course of the next five years.
11. As evidenced in Yang's New Cinema film *Taipei Story/Qing mei zhu ma* (1986).
12. This concept is built upon and related to comments by other critics. Phelps, for

example, notes that Tsai's films often contain parallel universes, or: 'banal reality and another universe that opens up inside it' (see *Notebook* article online).

13. Though Jameson is referring to Taiwan New Cinema in this essay, I would argue that this portion of his analysis complements Tsai's film-making as well.

14. This trend continues to an even more dramatic degree in Tsai's newest film *Face/Visage* (2009) (Bloom JCC article, 2011).

15. From a question and answer session after the screening of *Rebels of the Neon God* at the University of Southern California Cinema School in November 2009.

16. In other words, a fusion or 'conjugation' of Chinese and French elements.

17. As Lim (2009, 237) notes, Tsai's films also work on a 'paratextual' level, meaning that his literal signature appears at the end of some of his films.

18. Lim is referring to Roland Barthes's well-known 'Death of the Author' essay which argued that textual analyses should not rely on author intention or biographical background (see Barthes 1977).

19. As translated from the Mandarin by an interpreter.

20. Tsai has been quoted as saying: 'The director is not God. This I have understood from the beginning' (see DVD commentary).

21. The zoetrope is also referenced earlier in *What Time*, intertextually, when Hsiao-kang watches the famous scene in *The 400 Blows* in which Antoine rides the anti-gravity machine.

22. Interestingly, the apartment in *What Time* was Hsiao-kang's real home, and the fish, named Fatty, really belonged to Hsiao-kang (Director's Notes, DVD). Fatty also appeared in Tsai's 1997 film *The River*.

23. This point is made partially to show the distinction between Tsai's representation of passive spectatorship and Dai Sijie's active and awake spectators in *Balzac and the Little Chinese Seamstress* (2000).

24. See Christian Metz in 'References' for an elaboration of this concept.

25. According to Bloom, a large proportion of the audience had walked out by the final scene of the film.

26. For a much more detailed analysis of the film, see Bloom's recent article in the *Journal of Chinese Cinemas*, 2011.

27. See Misch's article (no page numbers).

28. In *The Skywalk is Gone*.

29. From the DVD materials.

30. Tsai's representation of Taipei/Taiwan might be said to reflect his own attitude, particularly with regard to the 'sad state' of the Taiwanese film industry at that time. Tsai was more or less forced to look to French producers to finance many of his later films (unpublished Bloom article).

31. And also Mia Farrow whose hair was famously cropped by Vidal Sassoon for her starring role in Roman Polanski's 1968 film *Rosemary's Baby* (which was set in New York city).

32. This also relates back to the sequence in *Face* which I discussed previously (the juxtaposition of Ardant and Léaud, for example).

33. Mastroianni plays himself, and his appearance is meant to underscore his aging body and his fading status as a sex symbol. In one incredibly touching scene in the film, Mastroianni and Anita Ekberg gather with friends at her mansion to watch the famous Trevi fountain scene from *La dolce vita* (Fellini, 1959) and reminisce.

34. The title of Tsai's new film, *Face* (2009), arguably refers to that of Léaud.

35. Tsai has said that, while making *Face* (2009), he was most excited about shooting the scene in which Hsiao-kang and Jean-Pierre Léaud finally meet.

36. From an unpublished article.

37. Another Tsai film, from 2006, starring Hsiao-kang.

5. THE CHINESE/HOLLYWOOD AESTHETIC OF ANG LEE: 'WESTERNIZED', CAPITALIST . . . AND BOX OFFICE GOLD

'Thank you movie god!'
Ang Lee, winning the Oscar for Best Director for Life of Pi,
25 February 2013

Hollywood was kind to Ang Lee (李安) in 2013. At the 85th Academy Awards, Lee won his second Oscar for Best Director, since *Brokeback Mountain* in 2005, for *Life of Pi* (released in theatres in late 2012). Including the nomination of *Life of Pi* for Best Picture, this was the fifth Oscar nomination of Lee's career. The win was regarded as a triumph, not only for Lee but for Taiwan more generally. President Ma Ying-jeou thanked Lee for 'pushing Taiwan toward the world'; adding in the same congratulatory message, 'Taiwanese are proud of you'.[1] Towards the end of his acceptance speech, Lee thanked Taiwan for allowing him and his crew to film there: 'I could not make this movie without the help of Taiwan. We shot there. I want to thank everybody there who helped us, especially the seat of Taichung . . . Thank you academy. Xie xie. Namaste.' Chinese media outlets on the mainland, unlike in Taiwan, were quick to censor this part of Lee's speech. Online commenters on the popular Chinese microblogging site Sino Weibo expressed both pride and anger over Lee's win. 'Ang Lee is a good "hua ren" director, did you hear the word 'China' in it? Don't put feathers in your own cap,'[2] one Weibo user commented. Echoing the same sentiments, another user commented:

> Ang Lee's win for Best Director made some people so excited, they said it's China's pride. However, I feel a bit strange, as it's his own business. Even when it comes to pride, it's due to education in Taiwan and the US. How does it have anything to do with us?

Others disagreed with the idea that Lee's Oscar win meant nothing for China, arguing that the films feature Lee's thinking, which is bound up with Chinese culture, and that this is reason enough to feel pride: 'He used his method to present Chinese culture to the world, being Chinese I'm happy for him.'[3]

The controversy over Lee's Oscar win speaks to sociopolitical issues that are likely to remain unresolved into the immediate future. The controversy also speaks to a specific issue within Chinese-language cinema: on the one hand, the mainland Chinese censors are happy to express pride for Lee when he does not mention his Taiwanese heritage. On the other hand, the censors are quick to shun Lee when he does. In this sense, Lee is tied to his nationality whether he wishes to be or not. One comment on Sino Weibo summarises the issue succinctly. The commentator '夏商', points to the ridiculous situation that has arisen since Lee won the Oscar for a second time. While the 'other coast' calls him 'Son of Taiwan', says the commentator, the mainland debates Lee's Chinese ethnicity. The entire situation is absurd because: 'while the birth of a good work of art will always have a certain relationship to the system [country] and culture of one's person, it ultimately is the result of that person's own effort and talent'. The commentator, almost angrily, finishes his remark with a plea to stop equating an artist with his nationality: 'Stop dragging in country, nationality/ethnicity/blood/lineage, and other such "grand" things.'[4]

This 'problem' – the question of national authenticity – arises again and again among critics and scholars of Lee's films. While it would be difficult to argue with the idea that Hou Hsiao-hsien and Edward Yang create films that are inextricably tied to sociopolitical phenomena in Taiwan, it is much more difficult to argue the same about Lee's films. This is not to say that Lee's films are not tied to Taiwan identity in any way – in fact, many of Lee's characters grapple with this very issue. But Lee's career differs from Hou's and Yang's in a fundamental way. Lee began his film-making career and found success by creating characters who must come to terms with their Taiwanese identity in the face of change and, in particular, in the face of influence by the West. Many of the characters in Lee's early films move to the United States, for instance, and must cope with the loss of tradition in the face of modernity. In a fundamental sense, then, Lee's films have always been transnational and cross-cultural. Beginning in the 2000s, as Lee became more confident as a director, he began to shoot films in a variety of countries on a variety of topics. Many of his films have been shot entirely in English. For these reasons, Lee is often criticised for not being an 'authentic' Taiwanese director. As a case study in

the Taiwanese cinematic 'tradition', Ang Lee's successful career raises an interesting series of questions: what does it mean to be an 'authentic' director and,
further, is this a trait to be prized? Should artists be tied to, and defined by,
their national identities? In this chapter, I argue that to omit Lee's *oeuvre* from
the Taiwanese cinematic 'tradition' would be a mistake. I argue, furthermore,
that it would be a mistake to marginalise Lee's work simply because his films
tend to attract large international audiences and make money at the box office.
I argue, rather, that Lee's films problematise dichotomies such as blockbuster/
art house, national/transnational, authentic/inauthentic, and that Lee's films
are worthy of study for this very reason.

Success through Magic Realism

Ang Lee stands out as a film-maker because audiences find his films appealing and are willing to pay to see them. Has Lee found the Midas formula? In
many ways, it would seem that Lee has found the key to successful, universally
appealing film-making. Interestingly, many of Lee's most successful and critically acclaimed films – *Crouching Tiger, Hidden Dragon* (*Wo hu cang long*,
2000) and *Life of Pi* (2012) – fall into the magic realist genre. In a literary
context, magic realism is a continuation of nineteenth-century realism insofar
as the goal of writers, in both movements, is to describe everyday life in minute
detail. Unlike nineteenth-century realism, however, magic realism rejects
empiricism and, according to one definition: '[returns] instead to mythologies,
folklore and mysticism . . .' while at the same time, and almost contradictorily:
'the representation of historical conflict is central . . .'[5] Magic realist stories, in
other words, are 'magical' like fairy tales but 'realist' in accuracy and detail. In
this sense, magic realism is a bit of an oxymoronic genre.

In both *Crouching Tiger, Hidden Dragon* (2000) and *Life of Pi* (2012), the
magic realist qualities of the films are highlighted by the main characters. In
both films, in fact, the main characters either climb or fly into trees, and it is
within those trees that the magical aspects of the stories become apparent. In
Crouching Tiger, two of the main characters, Master Li and Jen Yu (Chow
Yun-fat and Zhang Ziyi), have the ability to jump and travel through treetops.
In one particularly famous scene, these two characters face off in a sword fight
on top of a forest canopy. Though at times throughout the fight they seem to
be suspended in mid-air, their bodies cannot defeat the laws of gravity entirely.
Though Master Li and Jen Yu appear almost weightless when perched on
the tiny branches of the trees, they still must cling to the trees to avoid falling
towards the ground.

When *Crouching Tiger* was first released, some critics complained about this
lack of realism: 'It is at this point that we realize that, like the major actors, we
have left the earth and will only touch down again when it is convenient for the

author.' This same critic complains that the actors do not jump high enough, so they are not able to fly like Superman. At the same time, he complains that their ability to jump is unrealistic because their movements are subject to the laws of gravity. Criticisms of this type fail, of course, to appreciate Lee's faithfulness to the magic realist genre.

Trees are also essential to the magic realism in *Life of Pi*. At the time of writing, Lee's most recent film, *Life of Pi* is based on a 2001 novel by Yann Martel. Recreated with stunning 3-D visuals, the film is about a sixteen-year-old boy named Piscine Molitor 'Pi' (Suraj Sharma) who survives a shipwreck in the Pacific Ocean and is stuck on a lifeboat with a Bengal tiger.[6] Though most critics have showered the film with positive reviews and although Lee has now won an Oscar for the film, not every critic is a fan. Dana Stevens of *Slate,* for example, writes: 'See it stoned.' Though the film is beautifully shot, Stevens explains: 'The story of the boy and the tiger in a boat wants to be both a magic-realist fable and a tense survival adventure, two modes of storytelling that undercut and sometimes undo one another' (Stevens).[7] Further, say critics such as Stevens, the last twenty minutes of the film are clichéd and didactic.

Overall, the film tends more towards the first mode of storytelling: a magic realist fable. Late in the film, this mode becomes more apparent when Pi's boat lands on an island that is, quite literally, made of trees; there is no soil. As he explores the island further, Pi discovers a large colony of meerkats that live on the island and that sleep in the trees and in the ponds below. In an effort to escape the meerkats, Pi climbs one of the trees, subsisting there for some time until one night when he discovers, to his horror, human teeth in the tree's fruit. Pi concludes that the island is an inverted version of his own world: instead of humans eating plants and fruits, the trees themselves feed on humans. Frightened by this realisation, Pi jumps on to the boat and flees the island with his pet tiger, Roger Parker, in tow. Not only do both of these films contain strong elements of magic realism but, moreover, the most significant magic realist scenes occur in and among trees.

The idea that trees are emblematic of the magic realist genre can be traced back to Italian novelist, Italo Calvino, who wrote stories and novellas throughout the twentieth century (in the 1950s and 1960s, in particular). One of Calvino's longest (but lesser known) novellas, *The Baron in the Trees (Il barrone rampante*, 1956), contains themes similar to those found in Ang Lee's films, especially in *Life of Pi*. The story of *The Baron in the Trees* is told through the eyes of a young boy, though the protagonist of the tale is the narrator's older brother, Cosimo. The action begins on 15 June 1767, the young boy recalls, when twelve-year-old Cosimo climbs a tree in protest when their father (the baron) scolds him for not eating his snails at dinner. Throughout the rest of the novel, and for the rest of his life, Cosimo remains in the trees. Though the story is told from the perspective of the younger brother, Cosimo is the hero. Cosimo creates a life for himself in the trees, a life that is more rewarding than if he had remained on the ground.

As Beno Weiss, author of *Italo Calvino* (1993), notes: 'He goes hunting and fishing, has a pet dog . . . becomes a scholar and author, falls in love and has sexual encounters with women . . . fights pirates, participates in the Revolution and Napoleonic wars . . . and is elected to public office' among other impressive accomplishments (48). Weiss concludes that the strange story of *The Baron in the Trees* 'works' because: 'The "lightness" and rapidity with which these events are presented by Calvino exhilarate the reader, precluding boredom and scepticism' (Weiss 48). At the end of Calvino's novella, Cosimo's fairy-tale world is gone. Cosimo is dead; his body is literally lifted into the heavens by a balloon: 'Ombrosa non c'è più. Guardando il cielo sgombro, mi domando se davvero è esistita' ['Ombrosa (the island on which Cosimo lived) is gone. Looking up at the empty sky, I wonder whether it had really existed at all'] (217). In the last paragraph of the novella, Calvino's narrator questions his own construction of the past. The intertwining branches and leaves of Ombrosa are like the words in this story that tangle together to form ideas and dreams, says Calvino. But now the story is over, just like Cosimo's world of trees and the narrator's childhood. Though the final paragraph of this story is filled with tragic and touching imagery, Calvino's humour remains apparent. The ending functions as a final 'wink' to his readers. Even if the entire story could not possibly be true, Calvino suggests, the words and images of that story were constructed to entertain.

In *The Baron in the Trees,* the older brother shapes and colours the narrator's world whereas, in Ang Lee's *Life of Pi*, Pi shapes the Writer character's worldview. The Writer (Rafe Spall) is a character substitute for Yann Martel, the original author of *Life of Pi*. In the context of the film, Yann is interviewing Pi about his life story for a new book that he is writing. At the beginning of the film, Pi promises that his story will convince the Writer that God exists. By the end of the film, it is unclear whether or not Pi has accomplished his task. Nevertheless the Writer does admit that Pi's more fantastic version of the story is more interesting even if it is untrue. Even if the tiger is a metaphor for Pi himself, the story is more interesting when the film viewer – embodied physically by the Writer – has faith in the fiction. Thus, even if the Writer – and, by consequence, the film viewer – remain unconvinced that God exists in some sort of strict sense, we must at least acknowledge that believing is more entertaining than not believing.

In Lee's and in Calvino's story, then, the central character departs magically on a voyage into the unknown. The narrator, meanwhile (the younger brother in Calvino's story and the Writer in Lee's film), is left to face 'adult reality' and the ordinary world. Ang Lee, like Calvino, winks at his audience through narration, daring the viewer to ask: where does reality end and imagination begin? Unlike the typical fairy tale, the magic realist tale does not need to end 'happily ever after' because the ending itself is open to interpretation. Both Lee and Calvino remind the reader/viewer that the magic of childhood will eventually fade and that we will all be forced to grow up and face our responsibilities to society. At the same time, we cannot always categorise existence into good or evil, real or imagined, truth or fiction, because that grey area of ambiguity between is usually more interesting. Similarly, one does not instantaneously transform from a child into an adult and there is no sharp dividing line between childhood and adulthood. For Ang Lee, like Calvino, time can be non-linear; the past exists in the present, the past is the future and the future is the past. Space can also be transformed in unusual ways; places and historical sites are described anthropomorphically and humans become animals. Though Lee does not view himself as religious, he does consider himself spiritual in many ways. In an interview about the film, Lee was asked to explain how *Life of Pi* explores spirituality. In response, Lee references Taoist thought, remarking: 'Sometimes (illusions) are more of life's essence, I can trust them more than real life that is full of deceit and covering up' (Kearney). The problem with this message, of course, is that the viewer need not be spiritual in order to believe that movies should contain interesting plots and impressive special effects. The viewer would simply have to prefer fantasy over mundane existence (which most of us do).

Is He a Sell-out?

Still, the question remains: how did a Taiwanese-American film-maker manage to attain such huge success – especially in an unaccepting and difficult climate such as Hollywood? First of all, Lee did not begin his career in Taiwan. In 1979, at the age of twenty-five, Ang Lee moved from Taiwan to the United States where he attended film school at New York University. After graduating with an MFA from NYU, Lee was a stay-at-home father for six years while his wife brought in money for the family. Lee's career as a film-maker did not pick up until 1990 when two of his screenplays, *Pushing Hands/Tui shou* and *The Wedding Banquet/Xi yan*, won first and second prizes, respectively, in a film competition sponsored by Taiwan's Government Information Office (Dilley 9). Producer and recently appointed studio head, Li-kong Hsu, impressed by Lee's talent, invited him to direct a full-length version of *Pushing Hands* for the Taiwanese market. *Pushing Hands*[8] became the first in the so-called 'Father Knows Best' trilogy, including also *The Wedding Banquet* (1993) and *Eat Drink Man Woman* (1994). Each film in the trilogy deals with the clash between older and younger generations, with actor Sihung Lung in the role of the patriarch. Though *Pushing Hands* (1992) was a success at the Taiwanese box office, Lee's next film, *The Wedding Banquet*, was nominated for both a

Golden Globe and an Academy Award for Best Foreign Language Film, securing Lee's status as a Chinese/Hollywood 'cross-over' film-maker.

Because of his success in Taiwan and in Hollywood, Lee has been forced, on several occasions, to declare his 'artistic allegiance' to one country over the other. When asked to which country he considers himself most culturally bound, Lee replied: 'I am not the father of American children. I have a connection with China, but it is most intimate with Taiwan . . . but I have a visa, so I work legally in the US' (Tyam). Though both the American and the Taiwanese media are eager to claim Lee for themselves, both describe Lee as a 'Taiwanese' director. When *Brokeback Mountain* won the Oscar for Best Director in 2005, for instance, Taiwan's president and vice president, Chen Shui-ban and Annette Lee, issued a joint statement: 'We extend our highest congratulations to director Ang Lee . . . He is the glory of Taiwan and we are proud of him' (Tyam n.p.). Despite the fact that the film was banned in mainland China for 'homosexual content', the Chinese government was more than eager to take credit as Lee's country of allegiance. But Lee is hesitant to declare his loyalties, and for good cause if he does not want to alienate potential industries or audiences.

Over the course of his career, Lee has directed both hits and misses. Some of Lee's critically acclaimed films (like *The Ice Storm*, 1997) did relatively poorly at the box office while others were moderate successes at the box office (*The Hulk*, 2003) but generated mixed to negative reviews.[9] Interestingly, Lee's 2009 comedy–drama *Taking Woodstock*, described by *Time* magazine as: '. . . a mess – Lee's first total miscalculation, his first wholly inessential film'[10] seems to be all but erased from public memory.

Lee's 'hits', on the other hand, are permanently ingrained into the public psyche, popular on an international scale that can only be described as unprecedented in the history of cinema. First and foremost on this list of 'hits', *Crouching Tiger, Hidden Dragon*, turned into the highest grossing foreign-language film in the history of American cinema.[11] Second on the list (at least from the 2000s) is Lee's 2005 *Brokeback Mountain* which was nominated for eight Academy Awards and won for Best Director, Best Adapted Screenplay and Best Original Score. On 24 February 2013, Ang Lee won the Academy Award for Best Director for *Life of Pi*.

From the standpoint of some scholars, Lee's desire to remain well liked by the majority has caused the quality of his film-making to suffer. In some cases, scholars appear to have deemed the entirety of Lee's *oeuvre* to be unworthy of critical analysis. Because Lee's film-making career has withstood a variety of criticism, from all sides, but particularly among the academic community, I have become interested in determining the value of these critiques, and reaching a conclusion about how Lee fits into the landscape of the Taiwanese cinematic tradition. To accomplish this goal, we need to answer the following questions: (1) what are the critical issues that are at stake? (2) are the criticisms that have been levelled against Lee fair in general? Lee's position, as a part of the Taiwanese cinematic 'tradition', is complex. In many ways, Lee inhabits the deadly grey area of film studies scholarship. On the one hand, many of his films are difficult to analyse in the same sense that a Hollywood blockbuster like *The Avengers* (2012) is difficult to analyse. What you see is, more or less, what you get: a highly structured, 'closed' découpage (Burch 14) (to borrow Noël Burch's terminology), or conventional camera work in combination with a straightforward narrative. On the other hand, it does not seem fair to omit an analysis of Lee's *oeuvre* simply because his films appeal to a wide audience. In their chapter on Lee, Yeh and Davis express this idea as well: 'It is too easy to confuse the categories of Hollywood film and popular film entertainment, imagining Hollywood has a lock on popularity' (190). Though Hollywood insiders may not risk pre-production money on foreign-language films, they will spend money on advertising for foreign-language films that they have a stake in promoting. As Yeh and Davis rightly point out, Hollywood insiders would love the world to believe that they have the know-how to endow a film with instant popularity and international appeal. The idea that 'Hollywood' is equivalent to mass appeal – or to mainstream film-making as a comfortable, 'known quantity' for that matter – is a conflation that Hollywood itself encourages.

Regardless, why are there all these competing claims to Ang Lee? To answer the question, one needs to reach back to the essence of the national/ transnational cinema debate. One may also wonder, of course: why should we have to answer the question at all? That is, why demand that Lee define his allegiance to one country over another? Why can we not just recognise that Lee has found success in both countries and leave it at that? Apparently, Lee's case seems to prove that we cannot.

Whitney Crothers Dilley, author of *The Cinema of Ang Lee: The Other Side of the Screen*, argues that Taiwanese film scholars are too quick to dismiss Lee, and that his strength as a film-maker lies in his ability to move above and beyond the boundaries of national identity. She writes:

> Ang Lee is a transcendent filmmaker who has not only brought worldwide attention and wider reception to Chinese cinema but has also gone beyond his Chinese roots to become a postmodern and post-boundaried artist who moves as easily in Western genres as he does Chinese . . . Lee's duality – this unresolved tension – is his trademark. (20)

Certainly, Lee's cross-cultural dexterity is impressive. Though Dilley's praise of Lee's *oeuvre* is a bit un-nuanced, she does something else that is very useful. Noting that Chinese film scholars do not always dedicate entire chapters to

Ang Lee, Dilley lists various omissions that occur in certain key texts. Dilley observes, for example, that Rey Chow does not discuss any of Lee's films in the whole of her 1995 volume on passion and sexuality in contemporary Chinese cinema.[12] Dilley observes the same omission in Tonglin Lu's 2001 volume: *Confronting Modernity in the Cinemas of Taiwan and Mainland China*. Lu does not dedicate any of the book's analysis to Lee even though the volume includes extended analyses of the films of Edward Yang, Hou Hsiao-hsien, and Tsai Ming-liang (Dilley 21).

Non-academic critics argue that Lee serves as a model for all 'Asian-American' directors because he holds true to his Taiwanese roots even in the face of a wildly successful Hollywood career (Tyam). This sort of discourse obscures the fact that Lee is, fundamentally, a Hollywood director at this stage in his career. If one were to describe him as accurately as possible, one might say that Lee is both a Taiwanese and naturalised citizen of the United States who learned the craft of film-making in the United States but whose success has allowed him to move fluidly between Taiwan and Hollywood (and now India).

Yeh and Davis argue that Lee's: 'evocation of Chinese film traditions from the past, *despite never having worked in the Chinese film industry*, is a potent sense of historical custody' (their emphasis, 215). Lee is able to define himself as an 'authentic' Chinese director because it is not in any film producer's best interest to question it. In both his professional and his personal life, Yeh and Davis comment, Lee represents an odd dualism, residing in a contradictory space between Western outspokenness and Eastern 'li' (manners, courtesies or values) (180). I would say, more accurately, that Lee locates himself in *both locations at once*, occupying a position on the side of Western outspokenness and Eastern 'li' simultaneously. If Lee's story represents an iteration of the American dream (184), Yeh and Davis rightly ask, why should it be necessary to question his status as an 'authentic' Taiwanese film-maker in the first place (184)?

Lee himself has commented on the wide gap between Hollywood and non-Hollywood (or art house) film-makers. Worrying that this divide could alienate film-makers on both sides, and in turn, discourage cross-over film-making, Lee comments: 'directors who do not produce for American markets think they are ineligible to aspire to popular genre filmmaking and are obliged to make art films for festivals' (Yeh and Davis 188). Lee's observation, while apt in many ways, also minimises the decision-making capabilities of other Taiwanese directors who may have intentionally avoided the 'Hollywood route'. His comment also neglects the idea that directors might actually prefer to make art films.

Over the course of his career, Lee's films have become increasingly grander in scale. Ti Wei, in Chris Berry's volume, *Island on the Edge*, notes that, after his first three films, Lee's overall aesthetic shifts from locally to globally oriented (101). After the 'Father Knows Best' trilogy, Wei argues, Lee moves increasingly away from nostalgia and lament for the loss of Taiwanese identity and towards a desire to integrate fully into American identity (111). In *Pushing Hands*, an older Chinese t'ai chi instructor, Mr Chu (Sihung Lung), moves from his home in Beijing to a suburb of New York City to live with his son, Alex (Bo Z. Wang), his American daughter-in-law, Martha ((Deb Snyder) and his grandson, Jeremy (Haan Lee). Over the course of the film, Mr Chu is forced to move away from his Confucian values as he learns to embrace the 'Western' emphasis on the individual. Though the plot sounds mundane, it contains elements of magic realism or, at least, moments of spiritual phenomena that cannot be explained by traditional notions of empiricism. Mr Chu, for example, is highly skilled at activities involving his hands, such as t'ai chi and calligraphy. His t'ai chi skills, in particular, seem to contain a mystical quality: in one scene, he manages to knock a heavyweight man across an entire room with one stroke of his hand. In another scene, he grabs his friend's injured hand and squeezes it until it feels better. Mr Chu's hands seem to contain a magic life force. In contrast, his stepdaughter Martha's hands deal only with trivial tasks: because she is a writer, she constantly types on a computer, but has frequent bouts of writer's block. While Mr Chu cooks, Martha uses her hands to clean up messes in the kitchen.

Eat Drink Man Woman, the second film in the loose trilogy, also contains elements of Chinese philosophy (though the magic realist aspects are less apparent). The film, set in Taipei this time, centres again on a character named Mr Chu (played by Sihung Lung again). In this film, however, Mr Chu is a widower and a master chef. Mr Chu struggles with the fact that all three of his daughters, Jia-jen (Kuei-mei Yang), Jian-Chien (Chien-lien Wu), and Jian Ning (Yu-wen Wang), have not yet married. Further, each of the three daughters represents a different 'challenge' to traditional Chinese culture: Jia-jian has converted to Christianity, Jian-chien is strongly individualistic and Jia-ning begins a questionable relationship with her friend's former boyfriend. Over the course of the film, Mr Chu must come to accept each of his daughters and their respective 'breaches' of traditional Chinese culture. Though Mr Chu continues to cook a traditional Chinese banquet for his daughters every Sunday night, the banquet represents one of the last remaining links that the family has with tradition. In this film, as in *Pushing Hands*, Mr Chu's hands are magical. In the opening scene, Mr Chu uses his hands to kill, skin and fry a fish – a scene that is shot so seamlessly that it is often described as 'pornography for food lovers'. Through the beauty of his cooking, Mr Chu is able to restore a certain level of stability and harmony to his family. As Carl J. Dull points out in his chapter in *The Philosophy of Ang Lee* entitled 'Can't Get No Satisfaction: Desires, Rituals, and the Search for Harmony in *Eat Drink Man Woman*', Mr

Chu's cooking helps his family find *tian,* or Heaven. As Dull further notes, this concept of *tian,* as it arises in Lee's film, was first set forth by the ancient Chinese philosopher Xunzi. Xunzi observed that the satisfaction of basic desires allows for elevation towards *tian.* Reaching *tian* means reaching our capacity for virtue and, for this reason, humanity should aim to form a triad with heaven and earth. The question: can humans form some sort of mystical union with the cosmos? is a long-debated idea but it seems to be an idea that both Ang Lee and Xunzi share. It is also interesting to note that Xunzi, like Lee, was secular.[13]

Though the final film in the trilogy, *The Wedding Banquet,* also deals with Chinese tradition and the loss of that tradition, Lee seems to move away from this theme in his subsequent films. In her article in Berry's volume, Ti Wei describes the final scene of Lee's *The Wedding Banquet* to demonstrate the shift that occurs at the end of the 'Father Knows Best' trilogy away from the 'loss of tradition' theme and towards broader, non-Taiwanese-centric concerns. In this final scene, Mr Gao (the father figure, played by Sihung Lung) is flying back to Taiwan with his wife after a long stay with his son, Wai-tung, in New York. Finally, by the time this final scene takes place, Mr Gao has come to the realisation that Wai-tung is gay. As the parents say their final goodbyes, Mr Gao says to his son's boyfriend, Simon (Mitchell Lichtenstein), in Mandarin: 'Thank you for taking care of our son.' Though Mr Gao and his wife are sad as they walk towards their departure gate, it appears that they are crying with tears of joy – that they are happy. The old couple walk towards the security gate.

One might think that the film would end here. In a typical Hollywood film, it most likely would. The central conflicts have been more or less resolved and the story has ended on a relatively positive note: Mr Gao may never fully approve of his son's relationship with Simon but at least he has taken the first step towards acceptance. Wai-tung and Simon have a baby on the way (carried by a surrogate, Wei-Wei) and Mrs Gao is better off in her happy illusion that her husband will never know the truth about his son. But the film does not end here. Mr and Mrs Gao approach the airport security guard who raises his palm and motions them to stop. Mr Gao raises his arms high over his head for the security guard while his wife stands to the side with a look of despondency on her face. I intentionally describe Mrs Gao's facial expression as 'despondent', as opposed to mere 'sadness', because her expression is just as chilling as Mr Gao's submissive stance.

Ti Wei, commenting on this final scene, argues that, despite Lee's effort to portray Taiwanese culture as complex and multifaceted, the director privileges Western identity and that: 'Western culture is always shown as stronger' (106). Wei, in fact, describes the shot as the cinematic equivalent of a 'surrender to the West' (106). Though I am hesitant to suggest that

Figure 5.1   Simon, Wai-tung and Wei-Wei saying 'goodbye', Hollywood style.

Figure 5.2   Mr and Mrs Gao: 'I'm happy too'.

this final shot can be interpreted *only* as a symbol of 'surrender', it is, nevertheless, a creepy and unnerving way to end the film. Does Taiwan figuratively 'lose' Lee to the United States here, as Wei implies? While it would be odd to assume that the film text could somehow signal a director's shift towards a new self-identity, one might well suggest that the film subtext portrays the inevitability of surrender and the loss of identity. The 'true'

Figure 5.3   Final shot, final humiliation.

bleak message of the film is, in fact, hidden behind a superficial Hollywood ending.

This reading of the final scene of *The Wedding Banquet* makes an earlier scene – in which Mr Gao offers Simon a red envelope (a traditional *hongbao*) – open to a slightly darker interpretation as well. Wai-tung never finds out that his father knows that he is gay but Simon does, late in the film. Though Simon is appreciative and polite, he is confused by Mr Gao's response. In this scene, the two men sit on a pier with their backs to the camera. Mr Gao hands Simon the envelope. 'Happy birthday,' he says, in English.

'Mr Gao!' Simon exclaims, 'I didn't know that you spoke English!'

'I watch, I hear, I learn,' he replies, again in English. Switching to Mandarin, Mr Gao adds: 'If I didn't let them lie, I would never have gotten my grand-child.' Simon, who speaks little or no Mandarin, is confused again: 'I don't understand!' Mr Gao, not bothering to translate, responds in English: 'No, I don't understand.' This scene can be interpreted in two ways. From Simon's perspective and, perhaps, from the perspective of a 'Western' audience, the exchange between the two men is a moderate success: Mr Gao expresses acceptance of his son's homosexual identity by way of the *hongbao*. Simon is surprised, yet delighted, to find out that Mr Gao accepts their relationship (more or less) and that he wants to help support their partnership.

On the other hand, the scene can be interpreted in a far more negative light. From the perspective of someone familiar with the conventions of the red enve-lope tradition, Simon's actions could appear uncouth, if not rude. Simon opens the envelope immediately, unaware that this eagerness to open it in front of the gift giver is considered rude. Though Mr Gao assures Simon that he now considers him a son, he is clearly uneasy, sighing throughout the entire conversation. Mr Gao further demands that Simon never tell anyone about 'their secret' (the fact that Simon knows that Mr Gao knows that his son is gay) for 'the sake of the family'. Then, muttering to himself in Mandarin (because he knows that Simon will not understand), Mr Gao admits that he has been allowing his family to lie to him so that his original plan, to get a grandson, will not be thwarted. 'I don't understand!' Simon responds, unable to catch a word of this utterance. Simon's 'I don't understand' can be interpreted in a variety of ways: (1) Simon literally does not understand what Mr Gao is saying; (2) more figuratively, Simon does not understand why Mr Gao has suddenly become such an accepting person; and (3) a combination of both misunderstandings at the same time. Unfortunately, it seems unlikely that Mr Gao has accepted the entire situation as readily as Simon would like to believe. In fact, there is a distinct tinge of resentment in Mr Gao's voice when he replies: 'No, *I* don't understand'. These are the final angry words of a confused man, unsure about his son's future, spoken at the end of an already awkward conversation.

CRITIQUING LEE: *LUST CAUTION* AS EXOTIC PORNOGRAPHY

Rey Chow writes about *The Wedding Banquet* in the sixth chapter of her book on Chinese cinema, *Sentimental Fabulations: Contemporary Chinese Cinema in the Age of Global Visibility*. In that chapter, entitled, 'All Chinese Families Are Alike: Biopolitics in *Eat a Bowl of Tea* and *The Wedding Banquet*' (2007), Chow argues that *The Wedding Banquet* [along with another film: *Eat a Bowl of Tea*, directed by Wayne Wang (1989)] is set against the diasporic backdrop of North America as a means of showing the imminent need for ethnic minorities to reproduce. The Chinese 'Other', in other words, fears becoming extinct in the modern Western world. She writes:

> Apart from the actual sexual issues faced by the characters in the stories . . . it is now ethnicity itself, in the form of Chinese culture (together with its values), that is imagined in the 'repressed' manner human sexuality was presented by Freud – as a figure that is primitive, besieged, minoritized, and/or threatened with scarcity and extinction. (127)

To accept Chow's reading of *The Wedding Banquet*, however, one would also have to accept the idea that the film's ending is unquestioning of the security guard's actions towards Mr Gao. If we are to read Mr Gao's surrender to the security guard in the airport as a creepy, ambivalent ending, then we might not agree with Chow's statement that the film 'ends on a relatively happy note' (127). The 'biopolitical'[14] imperative to reproduce, the idea that pushes the action of the film forward, Chow says, is a guise for the real thesis of the film: to show how an ethnic culture struggles to survive in a world dominated by Western culture and values. As I have argued, however, this film deserves a slightly more nuanced reading. *The Wedding Banquet* ends ambiguously; in the final scene, the film spectator may feel ambivalent about Mr Gao's return to Taiwan and about his son's decision to raise his unborn child with both his boyfriend and his surrogate. If Chinese culture has become 'repressed' in a dominating Western sphere of control, then this film certainly does not celebrate that fact. In the end, one must either read the film as a statement about the acceptability of renouncing control or as a statement about the ambivalence of the act of renouncing control. These readings are not equivalent. Certainly, Mr Gao renounces control of his body to the US security guard – in diegetic terms. How the spectator decides to read this act of renunciation is another question altogether. It is not at all clear that Lee endorses the themes he chooses to represent.

While scholars, such as Chow, are generally critical of Lee's films, other Chinese film scholars have found more praiseworthy aspects of his work. This praise can be misguided as well. Shih Shu-mei, for example, in her introduction to *Visuality and Identity: Sinophone Articulations Across the Pacific* (2007), praises Lee's *Crouching Tiger, Hidden Dragon*, arguing that the heteroglossic nature of the film reflects the heterogeneity of the Sinophone world. At the same time, Shih argues, the film manages to resist China-centrism. Perhaps this is because audiences on the mainland did not care for this film. As one writer points out, when the film was released, Americans embraced it with open arms. Meanwhile: 'Mainland Chinese audiences ... reacted like they were at the butt of some sick cosmic joke.' The journalist continues: 'How else to explain the sheer implausibility and inauthenticity crammed into every frame? Where Americans saw Eastern élan, the Chinese saw fortune-cookie cutter mumbo-jumbo dressed up in crummy Mandarin Chinese accents.' According to the reporter, mainland audiences were displeased with Lee's implicit endorsement of the Chinese diaspora and the idea of 'One China'. The reporter seems to be referring to the language issue within the film, that is, using actors who were not of Han Chinese descent. It is not clear, however, if Lee meant to endorse the heteroglossic nature of the Sinophone world or if he simply wanted to employ big name actors whose first language was not necessarily *putongua* (mainland-style Mandarin).

In his review of *Visuality and Identity*, Sheldon Lu counters Shih's praise of the film for another reason. He argues that Shih is misguided insofar as her analysis rests solely on Lee's diasporic identity and not on the transnational composition of the film itself.[15] Further, Lu argues, one cannot argue that Lee's film 'resists China' while representing Sinophone communities because the production of the film involved co-operation with a variety of Chinese sources. 'It is difficult to say', Lu remarks, 'when and where China begins and ends in the frequent cultural co-productions in the pan-Chinese area of the mainland, Taiwan, and Hong Kong.' If we are to affirm that Lee's films reflect the Sinophone and resist China-centrism, Lu rightly asks, then how are we to classify films by Wong Kar-wai and John Woo, for example?

By looking within the films themselves – that is, by performing close readings of scenes – we should be able to avoid this issue. The question of authenticity need not arise in the first place because *Crouching Tiger* is, overall, meant to entertain. In this, the film succeeds. Lee's dual identity as a Taiwanese American has, perhaps, given him the edge that he needs to reach a large, international audience. *Crouching Tiger* problematises the East–West dichotomy but it does not 'resist China' as Shih claims. This is an important distinction. Overall, Lee aims to please, not alienate, audiences. In fact, Lee's infinite desire to please his audiences and placate his actors is itself critique-worthy. Some of Lee's responses to interview questions indicate his willingness to 'bend over backwards' in an effort to impress his fan base by hiring film stars and shooting in exotic locations.

In a filmed interview at Lincoln Center (in the 'Conversations in World Cinema' series) New York, for example, Richard Peña asks Lee to reflect on the differences between American, British and Chinese actors. Lee's response to this question is slightly unexpected. Though one might expect a director to reply with something along the lines of: 'all actors are the same, and all actors are treated the same by me, no matter how famous they may be', Lee responds in almost the opposite manner. Lee explains to Peña that he has learned that film stars must be treated differently from ordinary actors: 'It's not fair to treat them as *just actors*,' he remarks, 'they're movie stars . . . you have to coddle them a little more. You build your movie not against, but around them.' Peña, encouraging Lee to situate himself within the vast landscape of Chinese-language cinema, asks the director how he views his work in comparison with other Taiwanese directors (though they are not mentioned, Peña is clearly referring to Hou and Yang, et al.). Perhaps unsurprisingly, Lee dances around the question, explaining that he has learned to make films that will entertain contemporary world audiences. 'Why go to the movies in the first place?' He asks. 'To see something exciting,' he replies. To attract a certain core audience, says Lee, you must be submissive to that audience. You must learn what they want to see, what will be important to them (but not you, the director). You must also be submissive to the actors, Lee suggests. Coddle them; don't give them orders. Once you gain the actor's trust, then you have the power to 'ratchet' up the bossiness, but only on an as-needed basis.

Lee's so-called submissive persona – and the theme of submissiveness more generally – has carried over into Lee's film-making. The 'submissive/dominant' dichotomy plays a major role in Lee's sexually explicit films especially, and has been condemned by feminist film scholars. Rey Chow, for instance, critiques Lee's 2007 film *Lust Caution*, arguing that the film revels in brutal, masochistic sexuality. In her latest book[16] in the final chapter, 'Framing the Original: Toward a New Visibility of the Orient', Chow asks the reader to consider the following:

> ... are Ang Lee's fastidious efforts as director also masochistic, in that although he believes he is carrying out a mission to restore the bygone China of his parents' generation, the mission can never be accomplished no matter how hard he tries ... and the film *Lust Caution* ... is therefore at best a knockoff? (177)

I am inclined to defend *Lust Caution* against critiques such as Chow's, not because I disagree that the film carries a troubling misogynist message but because it is not the detail of the sex scenes that make it so. Rather than view the film through the more narrow theoretical lenses of feminism, cultural imperialism or psychoanalysis, I would argue that we must be careful not to discount Lee's cinema because of its level of detail and explicit representations of sex. One must also be careful not to discount Lee's cinema because it is 'too conventional' or 'too mainstream'. Though I do not flesh out this argument here, one could argue that Lee's films share themes that are similar to those of Tsai: repressed homosexuality, isolation, alienation and a revolt against patriarchy. Many of Lee's films – *The Wedding Banquet, Eat, Drink, Man, Woman, Brokeback Mountain* – are meant to create dichotomous feelings in his audience. The Chinese media censored Lee's speech when he won the Oscar for Best Director for *Brokeback Mountain* in 2005. The Chinese authorities felt that the film's blatant portrayal of homosexual love between two male cowboys in mid-twentieth-century Wyoming was far too explicit. After the 2005 controversy, Lee claimed that the film was not about 'gay cowboys', but rather about two men who come to love each other. The Chinese authorities, however, were unable to see the difference. As we saw in *The Wedding Banquet*, scenes that seem to have an obvious interpretation are often hiding a less obvious, darker one. In other words, Lee's films often contain a multitude of possible interpretations and layered meanings.

Chow refuses to look beyond the misogyny and – from a feminist critical standpoint – she should not have to. In her chapter on *Lust Caution*, Chow argues that the sex scenes in the film are far too detailed and that what might seem like *'ethnic ars erotica'* (artistic sex scenes) are, in actuality, what she calls, *'scientia sexualis'* (gratuitously pornographic sex scenes) (177). Chow is correct in this regard; the sex scenes are not subtle. The film, rated NC-17 in the United States, depicts a young woman's sexual relationship with an older man in World War II-era Shanghai. The protagonist of the film is a young woman named Wong Chia Chi (Tang Wei), hired to go undercover to lure Mr Yee (Tony Leung) – a special agent and recruiter for the Japanese puppet government – into an assassination trap. Though the mission requires Chia Chi to pretend to be in love with Mr Yee, the reality is not far from the fiction. As actors, Tang Wei and Tony Leung's chemistry is powerful and, although the sex scenes between the two characters are characterised by violence, Chia Chi (the character) appears to enjoy her submissive role.

But Chow's critique extends further. Arguing that the film's aim at historical accuracy functions as a 'strip search' of the past, she comments:

> [The film's] lurid images have outdone the most fanciful orientalist depictions of a debauched Orient, it is because the Orient is no longer a veiled mystery but an infinitely visualizable surface, one that embodies the potency – and promise – of being stripped naked, of being opened up in the most unmentionable perspectives. (178)

Here Chow uses Michel Foucault's well-known theoretical works, *History of Sexuality* and *Discipline Punish*, to argue her point. In *History of Sexuality*, Chow explains, Foucault describes the sexuality of modern times as 'more visible' but also more taboo. Because sex is treated like a secret, we always want to talk about it. In ancient times, according to Foucault, sex was less of a secret though it was heavily enmeshed with social customs and societal practices. In *Discipline Punish*, Chow explains, Foucault notes that Bentham's Panopticon prison was designed so that a lighted area would allow the prisoners to be watched at all times. The light also disallows prisoners from disappearing into darkness. Here Chow equates the lighted area of the Panopticon with what she describes as 'the infinitely visualizable surface' of 'the Orient'. Chow intertwines these ideas: sexuality, visibility and an increasing lack of privacy to critique *Lust Caution*. As those in power have the increasing ability to survey the sexual behaviour of others, shedding light on all the 'gory' details, light itself becomes a trap. If light 'is a trap', meaning that light allows us to see the behaviour of others at all times, then viewing detailed sex scenes is also part of the 'trap' (Chow 177).

Chow's arguments, though highly thought-provoking and rich with metaphor, lead only to further questions that Chow is content with leaving unanswered. If *Lust Caution* presents the 'Orient' as 'a highly visualizable surface', then is the opposite of this an 'Orient' that is 'veiled in mystery'? The argument appears to prize a nebulous past over the world with which we are familiar, the subtle over the explicit. One would not be wrong, I think, to ask the simple question: why should depictions of sex remain couched in metaphor? Indirect language, or visuality for that matter, is not *ipso facto* something to be prized. We may not want to learn from the past, especially when it comes to sex.

Could it *ever* be preferable to show ugly details rather than remain locked in the past?

Walter Benjamin, for one, would certainly not have felt that the aura of the past should be preserved. Under a certain interpretation of Benjamin, the act of showing sex, in all of its lurid details, might actually be seen as democratising. Regardless, the argument that *Lust Caution* is distastefully explicit can be reduced to a question of personal preference; it is a choice between what someone might or might not wish to view. Certainly, we must be aware of the idea that cinema can function as 'visual entrapment', and we should not censor our discussions of this issue, but surely the suggested alternative cannot be to avoid showing details altogether. Nor can the suggested alternative be to film sex unrealistically or to represent sex only metaphorically – or even to represent sex as always non-hierarchical and non-violent. Though the director can choose whether to respect the dignity of the viewer or not, no one is being forced to watch this film (like Alex with his eyes hooked open in a *Clockwork Orange*).

James Schamus, Lee's long-time partner and screenwriter, defends the explicit nature of *Lust Caution* by pointing to the complicity of the film viewer:

> The performer always, by definition, performs *for* someone. And that audience, no matter how entranced, is always complicit: it knows deep down that the performance isn't real, but it also knows the cathartic truth the performer strives for is attainable only when that truth is, indeed, *performed*. (Schamus 64)

In another interview, Schamus elaborates on the reasons behind Lee's choices in the film. To 'translate' the emotions of Eileen Zhang's original novel, Schamus explains, Lee felt the need to 'create a space for . . . graphic representations of sexuality'. The sex scenes are not placed gratuitously throughout the film nor do they represent sex according to pornographic 'standards'. In the context of the story of the film itself, Schamus explains, the first sex scene is 'an assault' and the second is 'an interrogation'. In the third scene, Chia Chi controls the action, and in the final scene, there is no sex at all. This scene progression is meant to mirror the psychological twists of the plot; power relations shift as Chia Chi lures Mr Yee into her trap (Schamus n.p.).

Setting aside the controversial sex scenes, *Lust Caution* is a film about acting and playing roles. Chia Chi is an actress on several narrative levels: she is an actress in patriotic theatre as a college student; she is an actress as an undercover agent; and she is an actress in real life, pretending that she has not fallen in love with Mr Yee for the sake of her mission. One sequence in the film consists of a juxtaposition of scenes, emphasising the differences between Chia Chi when she is acting and when she is not. In the first of the two juxtaposed scenes, Chia Chi plays the role of a young revolutionary who has lost her brother in the fight. As she and Kuang are performing the scene in front of a full house, Chia Chi looks at Kuang with tears rolling down her face. Kuang is moved to real tears by his co-star's crocodile tears and, as a result, becomes even more entrenched within the emotion of the scene. The audience, reacting to the performance, becomes emotional as well, giving a standing ovation and repeating the final line from the play: 'China will not fall!'

In the juxtaposed scene, Chia Chi sits alone in a dark cinema, crying uncontrollably as she watches an Ingrid Bergman film. These are her real tears. One of Chia Chi's favourite pastimes is going to the cinema; we see her returning later in the film to watch 'Penny Serenade' starring Cary Grant and Irene Dunne. This time, however, the film is interrupted by Chinese propaganda. As a high-pitched voice declares: 'the Asian people have finally broken free of the Westerner's grasp', someone in the film audience shouts 'Not again!' and most of the other audience members, visibly angry, get up to leave.

In the context of Lee's film, the interruption sets up a dichotomy between Chinese films (whiny, stiff and didactic melodramas and propaganda-filled newsreels) and Western films (entertaining, dramatic, emotional and emotion-inducing). Chia Chi is touched by the raw emotions of the Western films but chilled by the didacticism of the Eastern fare. This preference for films carries over into her love life, as well. She prefers men who will hurt her and bring forth her 'emotional rawness'. Kuang's promise to her: 'I won't let you get hurt. I won't,' is the exact opposite of what she wants. Chia Chi is not in love with China nor is she in love with Kuang. In this sense, Lee again privileges Western textuality.

When Chia Chi is seducing Mr Yee, she reveals to him that she likes to go to the cinema during her spare time. Mr Yee replies that he never goes to the cinema, not because he lacks the time but because he does not like to sit in the dark. Mr Yee's statement functions as a sort of foreshadowing for the final scene of the film in which Chia Chi is captured and killed while Mr Yee sits alone in his bedroom, in the dark, facing a mirror image of himself. His wife comes to the door and asks him why he is upset. He tells her to go back to her mah-jong game: 'Keep playing,' he says. In the final shot of the film, we see the shadow of Mr Yee's head cast on to the bed, as he turns back and looks one last time at that bed – the symbol of his relationship with Chia Chi. This is the incarnation of his nightmare; Mr Yee did not aspire to be the last living 'actor' in the deadly role-playing game. Sitting alone in the dark signifies the reality that his romantic partner – the other actor in the game – has been eliminated. Facing only himself, Mr Yee is left alone in the darkness of Lee's film narrative.

CONCLUSIONS

Lee's film-making style is more conventional than 'art house', using smooth, natural editing to create an uninterrupted flow in the storyline, a musical score to create structural rhythm, and tight dialogue.[17] The viewer is engaged within the diegesis, such that Lee's directorial hand remains invisible throughout. In his volume, *The Classical Hollywood Cinema*, David Bordwell describes this invisible aspect of Hollywood storytelling: the idea that the telling of the story should be the most basic concern of the film-maker and that artifice should be concealed. Hollywood likes to believe, Bordwell adds, '. . . that it possesses a fundamental emotional appeal that transcends class and nation' (Bordwell 3).

Bordwell is not arguing that Hollywood film-makers always manage to achieve their goals, namely, to conceal their mode of storytelling, to create emotional response in an audience, or to transcend class and national boundaries. He argues, rather, that Hollywood wants the viewer to believe that there is such a thing as 'classical filmmaking' in the first place. If the audience believes in the 'fairy tale' of a classical cinema, then they will keep buying tickets, if only to escape into that promised fantasy world for a couple of hours. At the other extreme, art house purists will continue to argue that Hollywood film-making lacks originality and that the artistry of the film-maker trumps the storytelling process.

In this same chapter, Bordwell cites *Cahiers du Cinéma* critic, André Bazin, who admonished his fellow *Cahiers* critics not to minimise the importance of Hollywood cinema in the pursuit of auteurism: 'What makes Hollywood so much better than anything else in the world is not only the quality of certain directors', says Bazin, but the idea of the Hollywood myth itself. He continues: '. . . why not then admire in it what is most admirable, i.e., not only this or that filmmaker, but the genius of the system, the richness of its ever-vigorous tradition, and its fertility when it comes into contact with new elements' (Bazin in Bordwell 4).

Indeed, it makes little sense to ignore an admirable film-maker such as Ang Lee. Over the course of his career, he has managed to gain an immense following, and his fan base continues to grow. In the early years of his career, Lee's films tended to focus on characters whose identities were in transition. Characters such as Mr Gao in *The Wedding Banquet* and Mr Chu (Sihung Lung) in *Pushing Hands* are forced to relinquish their traditional values in favour of modern life in America. Taiwanese characters must learn to adapt to another way of life – to a country and culture that are foreign to them. As Lee's career progressed, the director experimented with themes and storylines that were not related to Taiwanese identity in any way. Nonetheless, the characters in films, such as *The Ice Storm* and *Brokeback Mountain*, contend with different sorts of identity transformations (coming of age and homosexuality, respectively). Lee returned to his 'Chinese roots' with *Crouching Tiger, Hidden Dragon* and *Lust Caution*, though only in a superficial sense, because the films generated interest and acclaim in countries beyond Taiwan and China. Today, Lee remains a globally minded, imaginative director with the willingness and ambition to integrate advanced special effects into his films.

In the beginning of this chapter on Ang Lee, I asked whether or not the criticisms which have been levelled against Lee are 'fair'. In line with both Bordwell's and Bazin's comments, I would argue that to omit Lee's *oeuvre* entirely from the Taiwanese cinematic 'tradition' would be a mistake. Failing to mention Lee alongside other Taiwanese film-makers, simply because his films have found success with a mainstream international audience, would be a pity as well. Ang Lee's films possess an inherent duality; caught between cultures, his stories are simultaneously borderless and universal. I am not saying that all his films deserve praise, either. A couple of them were real duds.

Lee's films are also entertaining because they incorporate magic realism. As Calvino's narrator states at the end of *The Cloven Viscount*, a different novella but one that is similar in many ways to *The Baron in the Trees*: 'I . . . amid all this fervor of wholeness, felt myself growing sadder and more lacking. Sometimes one who thinks himself incomplete is merely young' (245). At the ending of this story, the narrator's illusion of never-ending childhood shatters and the penumbra fades when he realises that he is gradually shifting into adulthood. The narrator has come to understand that the rest of the world will not necessarily live happily ever after, even after his own story ends. This is a child narrator who has come to conclusions about life after literally living through a fairy tale and, because of his experiences, he has become wiser. Similarly, in Lee's *Life of Pi*, the narrator (Pi) looks back on an earlier point in his life. Through these reminiscences, he has learned something valuable; he has come to a greater understanding of himself and the world, and he offers that new sense of understanding to the viewer. For many of the characters in Lee's films, memories are like penumbras; shadow and light intersect to form regions that are difficult to separate. In the penumbra, things appear uncertain and vague, and so they must seek out memories by wandering through familiar places. Like a photographer trying to take a good picture, Lee's camera work is steady, deliberate and filled with rich, vibrant detail.

In the introduction to their edited volume, *The Philosophy of Ang Lee*, Arp, Barkman and McRae comment: 'If there is any unifying philosophical theme for Lee's films, it is the struggle for authentic self-identity' (2013, 5). Though I agree with this assessment, I would add that this theme – the existential struggle for authentic self-identity – stems from Ang Lee's tendency towards a magical realist aesthetic. He is at his best when this aesthetic is apparent. When critics, Chow included, scrutinise and critique his depictions of sex, they presume that Lee is dedicated to realism. But Lee is not a realist film-maker.

What does Lee gain from reconstructing history and telling stories so realistically? In Italian, the word *storia* can mean both 'story' which implies a private experience *and* 'history' which implies a collective experience. Perhaps it is within this space that Lee is able to gain insight into the essence of humanity. Within this more general concept of *storia,* time can be cyclical and experiences can be either real or imagined. Perhaps, by indulging in the details of the past and the realism of the present, we gain a better grasp on the future. Continuously reliving the past can often be a form of grieving but for Lee it is catharsis. Through his details, Ang Lee moves closer to universalism and harmony with both himself and with his audience. Ang Lee does not relive the past – rather, he recreates reality according to his own vision. For Lee, in fact, past, present and future are not so dissimilar from one another; they constantly intermingle and interact.

NOTES

1. See 'Ang Lee's "Life of Pi" Oscar Win Thrills Taiwanese', *Christian Science Monitor*, 26 February 2013 <http://www.csmonitor.com/The-Culture/Latest-News-Wires/2013/0226/Ang-Lee-s-Life-of-Pi-Oscar-win-thrills-Taiwanese>
2. An English translation of the original Chinese, which was (beginning with 'did you hear . . .': '但您有听到 China 吗？别太往自己脸上贴金'
3. In the original Chinese: '李安导演获最佳导演，有人狂欢，说这是中国人的骄傲。我很是奇怪。人家李安获奖是人家个人的事儿，即使值得骄傲，那也是台湾教育，美式教育的成功，跟某些人有鸟关系' ?' and: '他用他的方式让各国的人多一个了解中国文化的渠道，作为中国人很为他高兴。'
4. On the website: 'ChinaSmak'. The article is entitled: 'Ang Lee Wins Best Director Oscar for Life of Pi, Chinese Reactions', and was written by Cecilia Miao on Thursday, 28 February 2013 <http://www.chinasmack.com/2013/stories/ang-lee-wins-best-director-oscar-for-life-of-pi-chinese-reactions.html>
5. See 'Magic Realism' <http://english.columbia.edu/magic-realism> for more.
6. He was moving with his family from Puducherry in India to Winnipeg, Canada to live and to sell his family's zoo animals.
7. See <http://www.slate.com/articles/arts/movies /2012/11/life_of_pi_ directed_by_ang_lee_reviewed.html>
8. The title, *Pushing Hands*, refers to a two-person training routine in t'ai chi (*tuishou*) that teaches students how to absorb and redirect force.
9. Lee was so affected personally by the negative reviews of *Hulk* that he nearly gave up directing altogether. His father encouraged him to continue (Diller).
10. See <http://www.time.com/time/arts/article/0,8599,1899088,00.html>
11. Other Taiwanese Hollywood-style films were not nearly as successful internationally (such as Chen-Kuo-fu's *Double Vision*, 2002).
12. In Chow's *Primitive Passions: Visuality, Sexuality and Ethnography in Contemporary Chinese Cinema* (though, as Dilley concedes, Chow did not include a discussion of any films outside the mainland in that particular volume).
13. See the *Stanford Encyclopedia of Philosophy*, the entry on Xunzi, for more on the idea of *tian*.
14. The *biopolitical* is a Foucaultian word, meaning (in simple terms) the variety of ways in which the government attempts to control the bodies of the general population.

15. From 'Sheldon Lu Review of Visuality and Identity', *MCLC Resource Center*, January 2008 <http://mclc.osu.edu/rc/pubs/reviews/lu.htm>
16. See Chow 2012.
17. See Boggs and Petrie (373–81) for an in-depth, yet clear, explanation of the elements of directorial style.

6. FILMING DISAPPEARANCE OR RENEWAL? THE EVER-CHANGING REPRESENTATIONS OF TAIPEI IN CONTEMPORARY TAIWANESE CINEMA[1]

In the late summer of 2011, Taiwan's National Cultural Association awarded Presidential Culture Awards to two members of the film industry: 'veteran' director Hou Hsiao-hsien and Lee Lieh, an actress turned producer. It was the first time that anyone from the film industry had been chosen for the culture award. Though Lee Lieh was relatively new to producing in 2011, she had already produced two major blockbuster hits for Taiwan: *Orz Boys/Jiong nan hai* (directed by Yang Yache, 2008) and *Monga/Bang-kah* (directed by Doze Niu, 2010). *Monga*, released during the Chinese New Year period, grossed NT $270 million ($8.4 million) and became the third most successful Taiwanese film of all time after Wei Tu-sheng's *Cape No. 7/Haijiao qi hao* (2008) and Ang Lee's *Lust Caution* (2007). In reaction to her major success as a producer, a reporter from *Screen Daily* described Lee 'as one of the most efficient and profitable producers by the Taiwanese film industry'.[2] Another reporter commented on the Taiwanese media's prediction that the film industry was in the process of a strong revival. After the success of *Cape No. 7* and *Monga*, the Taiwanese media began to report that the industry was likely to recoup over NT$1.5 billion in box office gross receipts.[3]

In an interview with *Screen Daily*, Lee was asked to comment on the so-called 'renaissance' in Taiwanese cinema. She responded optimistically, noting that, though reviving the industry was one of her goals, she was more interested in creating films that would reach a large domestic audience. She comments, furthermore, that one of her goals is to reverse the 'art-house trend' that has become a negative stereotype of Taiwanese cinema: 'I've known many young directors who grew up watching genre films and they don't carry the burden or mission to make art house films. They are creative, passionate about films but also easy to work with.' Of course, Lee's remark itself reinforces the art house cinema stereotype. Not everyone would agree with her contention that art house directors do not realise the importance of stars and that they are passionate about film-making but contentious and difficult. Lee claims, however, that she is not only interested in creating films for Taiwanese viewers. Nevertheless, to revive the industry, she has found that it has been necessary to create films that Taiwanese audiences will pay money to watch. Producers in markets outside Taiwan, even those on the mainland, are faced with an entirely separate set of concerns (109). Lee is attempting to find the formula that will work best with Taiwanese audiences.

Fundamentally, says Lee, the role of the producer must change for the industry to progress. Her thinking is as follows: when the director has all the power and authority, the producers are left to 'scurry to secure funding' and to take care of minor administrative details. The role of the producer, in other words, is too passive. To lure audiences into cinemas – domestic rather than international ones – producers and directors have little choice but to work together to make films that people will pay to see. The recipe for a box office hit should not be shrouded in mystery. The films that turn out to be 'cash cows' are formulated in this way, using the so-called 'Midas formula'.

According to the formula, for a film to be successful, it must contain the following elements: a child and/or young adult protagonist, a fairy-tale-like quality, a plot that involves weak people overcoming adversity and maturing, several scenes containing intense conflict, a happy ending, and a cast of rising (but not yet big) stars (107). The timing of the release is also vital to the success or failure of the film. Lee, for instance, was able to secure the coveted Chinese New Year opening slot for *Monga*. She also advertised using new media, and offered only one advanced screening. The combination of these factors created an enormous buzz around the film.

In many ways, Lee may have the right idea. According to the narrative of the media (both domestic and international), the Taiwanese film industry was in a dire situation – on the point of collapse – throughout the entire period bound by *City of Sadness* in 1989 and *Cape No. 7* in 2008. One reporter notes: 'until August 2008, the prospects for Taiwanese cinema were obscure at best'. The reporter explains that, after Hou's *City of Sadness* won the Golden Lion Award at the Venice Film Festival, Taiwanese directors turned mostly to making art house films which 'alienated mainstream tastes' (102–3). At the other end of the spectrum, film-makers made cheap and easy screwball comedies. Supposedly, everything between these two extremes – genre films or mainstream commercial films, for example – were simply not being produced.

When *Cape No. 7* was released in 2008 and garnered NT $530 million at the box office, critics were quick to dismiss the success as an anomaly. Film critic Wen Tien-hsiang wrote that the possibility of duplicating the success of *Cape No. 7* was 'about as likely . . . as dinosaurs are to reemerge from the ooze' (103). The film begins in the 1940s, towards the end of the Japanese colonial empire in Taiwan. A teacher (Kousuke Atari) is sent to Hengchun, a small town in southern Taiwan, and falls in love with a young girl with a Japanese name, Kojima Tomoko (Rachel Liang). When the Japanese surrender, however, the teacher is forced to leave Hengchun and the woman he loves. He writes seven love letters to Kojima on his journey home. The film then shifts to present-day Taiwan, as struggling rock star, Aga (Van Fan) decides to leave Taipei and return to his native town which happens to be Hengchun. In his home town, his stepfather, the town council representative or *yihui daibiao* (Ju-lung Ma), arranges for him to work as a postman. He comes across an old package of letters that are addressed in the old Japanese style: Cape No. 7, Hengchun, and are therefore undeliverable. Meanwhile, Japanese model Tomoko, sour because she is 'marooned' in Taiwan, is working as the co-ordinator for a rock concert on the beach. Aga's stepfather, who is partially in charge of the acts, insists on hiring local musicians for the show, as opposed to the Japanese rock star who is supposed to perform. This is Aga's chance to regain his former status as a 'rock star' so he joins a band (reluctantly at first) and performs a successful concert. Meanwhile, Aga and the Japanese model/ co-ordinator Tomoko fall in love and begin a relationship. As the band is performing at the concert, Tomoko finds the old letters and reads them.[4]

While *Cape No. 7* became Taiwan's top-grossing film of all time, critics in other parts of the world seemed puzzled by its success. Film critic Laura Gatewood, for instance, who writes for Emanuel Levy's movie review website, writes that the film lacks coherency and that each of the intertwining stories is underdeveloped, the characters unsympathetic, and their actions illogical. She adds that, though it was a major hit with Taiwanese audiences, the film 'failed to impress critics outside of the country and rightly so'.[5] The critic suggests that the film does not necessarily translate well for Western audiences. Nevertheless, critics of the film outside Taiwan failed to ask *why* the film was successful in Taiwan but not elsewhere. What was it about *Cape No. 7* that was, supposedly, so decidedly 'Taiwanese' in nature?

Interestingly, the mainland Chinese media also released an official 'review' of the film. Released by the Xinhua News Agency, the review describes the film as an 'exotic' experience for film-goers in Beijing who would normally never be exposed to Taiwanese culture. The new agency's review continues, noting that mainland audiences were probably struck and baffled by the mixture of languages in the opening monologue of the film which contains elements of Japanese, Min Nan (or Hokkien) dialect, and Mandarin. The reviewer critiques the inhabitants of Hengchun as they are portrayed in the film, describing them as 'inward-looking' and 'smiling but irreverent'. The reviewer, in a clear attempt to justify the extraordinary success of the film, remarks: 'Its box office success on the island shows it has struck a chord with the enthusiasm of islanders to realize a common identity and a profound concern that they may be losing their heritage as their culture is challenged by outside fashions and influences.'[6] Clearly, the film deals with themes that are sensitive for mainland China – Japan's occupation and Taiwan's secession, in particular. At first, mainland censors banned the import of the film. By the end of December 2008, however, the censors had backed down. *Cape No. 7* was the first Taiwanese film to be released on the mainland in seventeen years, and only the second in sixty years.[7]

In addition, by 2008, the film *Island Etude* (*Lian xi qu*, 2006, directed by Huai-en Chen) and *Eternal Summer* (*Shengxia guang nian*, 2006, directed by Leste Chen) had already made 10 million, while *Spider Lilies* (*Ci qing*, 2007, directed by Zero Chou) had made 50 million (105). *Island Etude* documents the life of Ming, a deaf college student (Ming-hsiang Tung), as he cycles around the entire island of Taiwan before graduation. *Eternal Summer*, meanwhile, documents the sexual experimentation of three senior school students and, in particular, the burgeoning love between two male best friends, Jonathan (Bryant Chang) and Shane (Hsiao-chuan Chang). *Spider Lilies*, finally, is a lesbian drama about a seemingly curse-plagued relationship between webcam girl Jade (Rainie Yang) and tattoo artist Takeko (Isabella Leong). Though these films earned only modest amounts in comparison with *Cape No. 7*'s $530 million, they were significant in other ways. The fact is that genre films were, in fact, being produced, winning awards and gaining followings. Nevertheless, they were aimed at a niche market, not the mainstream.

What was happening, then, throughout the entire period that began in 1989 and ended in 2008? Was this really a period of devastation for the Taiwanese film industry, as the media claim? As it turns out, international critics have been singing the praises of Taiwanese cinema since the early 1980s. Critics continued to revere Taiwanese cinema throughout the remainder of the 1980s, throughout the 1990s, into and past the new millennium. In short, the industry was being recognised by a handful of international critics even as local audiences were all but abandoning it. This is not to say that all international critics saw Taiwan's potential, only that certain critics were pointing out that *other critics* should follow suit and take heed.

In a 1999 article for the *Santa Fe New Mexican*, reporter Jon Bowman remarks: 'Taiwan's isolation in the global community has served as a blessing and a curse for its filmmakers.' The context of the comment requires some explaining: in 1999, hardly any Taiwanese films had ever been shown in Europe or in North America. Though Ang Lee was considered the most famous of the Taiwanese directors (in Hollywood, at least), other Taiwanese directors, such as Hou Hsiao-hsien and Edward Yang, would have been relatively unknown in the West at this time. At the end of the century, themes of alienation and 'rootlessness' in a new era of globalisation were prevalent but the international film community had not yet recognised that these themes were being reflected in Taiwanese cinema. This was a phenomenon that was occurring right before their eyes in Taiwan but most critics could not see it. 'That's a shame', Bowman comments. He continues, noting that although we (in the West) tend to recognise the 'Made in Taiwan' stamp on many of our goods, we do not think to consider the Taiwanese film industry. Taiwan's society, on the other hand, though '[it] is awash in American, European and Japanese influences . . . they have stayed outside the fold'. Bowman's remark, though nearly fifteen years old, remains valid. Bowman is, in essence, expressing the idea that transnationalism does not always flow bilaterally. In fact, it is precisely *because of* this uneven flow that Taiwanese cinema functions as an interesting case study: the Taiwanese film industry is transnational, intertextually diverse and hybrid and yet it remains isolated or, to put it in another way, preserved. 'I submit that's a compelling reason to seek out and study Taiwanese films,' Bowman concludes, 'how better to gain insights into our own culture than from a people who know us intimately but remain detached and independent?'

THE STATE OF THE INDUSTRY IN 2013

No amount of scholarly writing will have the capacity to save the industry. Over the past decade, in fact, even film scholars have begun to describe the industry in pessimistic terms. In his recent essay, 'Taipei at the Turn of the Century in Taiwan Cinema', for example, Lin Wenchi observes: '. . . Taiwan cinema . . . is still dominated by representations of Taipei as a city associated with illness, death, and ghosts' (227). As if this characterisation weren't depressing enough, the director of the Spot Taiwan Film House, Wang Pai-Zhang, notes that Taiwan Second Wave cinema is perceived by mainstream Taiwanese audiences as depressing, slow-moving and impenetrable. Because of this stigma, continues Pai-Zhang, the great directors of Taiwanese cinema are: 'reconnus plutôt a l'étranger qu'ici', or, 'more recognizable in foreign countries than here [in Taiwan]'. With the exception of the recent hit, *Cape No. 7,* he concludes, Taiwanese audiences are mainly interested only in American and, to a lesser extent, French films.

Many of Taiwan's recent box office successes, *Cape No. 7* (directed by Wei Te-sheng, 2009), *Monga* (dir. Doze Niu, 2010), and *Night Market Hero* (dir. Tien Lun-yeh, 2011), do not tend to reflect the aesthetic and thematic elements of the 1980s New Wave and, as a consequence, tend to be ignored by film scholars. Though it is understandable that not-so-great films would tend to be ignored for lack of visual interest, the overall effect of this general disinterest could prove counterproductive to the industry itself. If audiences in Taiwan are willing to pay to see Taiwanese-funded films, the government is more likely to provide funding to up-and-coming film-makers. Films such as *Cape No. 7*, even if they cannot be categorised as 'art house', in most senses of the term, do meet an important need domestically. The story of *Cape No. 7*, moreover, is not as different from films such as Hou's *Three Times* as we might wish to believe. Though Hou's film is more interesting visually, both films are fundamentally sweet love stories set against the historical backdrop of Japanese colonialism. Though the elite audiences of art cinema may be loath to pay to see such films, this prejudice may be just as unjustified as the refusal to pay for a ticket to an Ang Lee film.

Though I would certainly not argue that all these contemporary films should be classified as 'high art', I would also not want to ignore such films simply because they have been deemed 'too conventional'. Many of the films that have been produced in Taiwan in the past few years recall themes of the 'New Wave'. *Monga* (2010), for instance, like Edward Yang's *Mahjong* (1995) and Hou's *Goodbye South Goodbye* (1996), is a coming-of-age story about gang life, 'brotherhood', corruption and youth culture. *Night Market Hero* (2011), like Yang's *Taipei Story* (1985) and *Confucian Confusion* (1994), deals with the present-day concerns of ordinary people questioning the dominance of corporations in the traditional sphere. The film is about a young union leader named A-hua (Cheng Lung-lan) who lives with his grandmother and sells food with her at a local night market. Government politicians seek to shut down A-hua's food stall to build a shopping complex, despite the fact that one of the politicians used to be a market stall owner himself.

Though film audiences would certainly not need an intimate knowledge of Taiwanese culture to appreciate *Night Market Hero,* many of the references and jokes within the film do rely on at least some cultural knowledge. A citizen of Taipei would probably know, for instance, that the Taipei New Year Market opens every spring in anticipation of the Lunar New Year (*chun jie*) on Di Hua Street. Mandarin-speaking audiences (in both Taiwan and on the mainland) would be familiar with the phrase '*gong xi*' or 'Happy New Year' and would recognise the alternative version of the phrase –'*kung xi fa tsai*' – when it appears on a main character's shirt in the opening scene. Taiwanese audiences are likely to recognise traditional food items and special New Year dishes, such as turnip cake (*luobuo gao*) and glutinous rice cake (*nien gao*). Much of *Night Market Hero* functions as an ode to Taiwanese food, especially chicken fillet (*jipai*).[8] A majority of the film's humour relies on broad humour and parody but some of that parody depends on familiarity with the quirks of night market stall owners.

Interestingly, the original version of Tien's film was deemed untranslatable even for mainland audiences. When *Night Market Hero* was released on the mainland (a fact that is itself surprising) the dialogue was changed from its original mixture of Mandarin, Hokkien, Hakka to Mandarin only. Film-goers would immediately have missed out on the linguistic diversity that characterises Taiwan. As with *Cape No. 7*, *Night Market Hero* was not so well loved by critics and audiences outside Taiwan. Though many critics felt that the film was interesting in that it showcases local Taiwanese 'flavour', they felt that the film itself was overly long, the plot was too complex and the main actor lacked charisma. One reviewer, in particular, felt that the local flavour of the film served as both a positive and a negative, commenting: '[*Night Market Hero* is] as Taiwanese as a bowl of beef soup noodle – and therein lies both its strengths and weaknesses' (Elley).[9] Another reviewer notes that, though the film deserves credit for its attention to cultural detail and its emphasis on 'Taiwanese charm', it also manages to make Taiwanese culture universal by implanting themes related to family, honesty and loyalty. The reviewer then adds: 'It's the focus on family and local culture that makes *Night Market Hero* more than just a Taiwanese story, as similar films could easily appear in Korea, Hong Kong, Japan, etc . . .' (Kozo).[10] The problem with this comment, of course, is that one would have a difficult time finding films with themes that are *not related* to family, honesty or loyalty in some way – especially because the concepts themselves are almost too broad to define. The reviewer's statement is even more odd when one realises that he lists only other East Asian countries. If a film about the local culture of South Korea were to 'appear', as the reviewer puts it, wouldn't that simply be a film about South Korea? Does the reviewer mean to say that films with local flavour can be made in East Asian countries but not in Western countries?

If this is the suggestion, then I would counter this claim with a clear example of an American film that is funny not only because it assumes a certain base knowledge of American cultural norms but, moreover, because it assumes a certain base knowledge of the history of American music. The film, Stephen Frear's *High Fidelity* (2000), is hilariously funny but it is especially funny to Generation X and Y nerds with an unhealthy obsession with rock and roll music. Anyone who has ever walked inside a pretentious record store inhabited by sharply critical fashion followers (usually near a college campus) will recognise characters like Rob (John Cusack), the aging, compulsive store owner and Barry (Jack Black), the slightly overweight, snobby but lovable nerd (a sort of 'Comic Book Guy' of record stores). But to get a more complete essence of the film's humour, one would do well to have a working knowledge of the maxims of rock music snobbery. One such maxim, for example, is that song covers are almost always inferior to the original, even if the cover was a bigger hit.

One particularly amusing scene in *High Fidelity* alludes directly to this maxim: Barry walks proudly into the store brandishing a mixed tape that he has recently made in honour of 'Mondays'. Though Barry is quite obviously proud of his creation, Rob, his boss, is in a foul mood and does not want to hear the tape. Barry continues to whine. He is especially proud of one song on the tape: 'Little Latin Lupe Lu'. When one of the other store workers, a gawky, nervous man named Dick (Todd Louiso), suggests that the song was performed by Mitch Ryder and the Detroit Wheels, Barry is furious – his tape contains the Righteous Brothers version. 'Do you have a problem with the Righteous Brothers?' Barry screams at Dick. 'That's bullshit!' Rob is quick to defend Dick. 'How can it be bullshit to state a preference?' Barry is quick to snap back: 'Since when did this store become a fascist regime?'

To understand this joke fully, one would have to know that 'Little Latin Lupe Lu' was written by the Righteous Brothers but that their recording of the song was only a modest hit while the cover version, by Mitch Ryder and the Detroit Wheels, did better in the charts and became the 'well-known' version of the song. Of course, it is also possible to get the joke if one is familiar, at the very least, with the aforementioned music snob maxim.[11]

Thus, when postcolonial scholar, Homi Bhabha, in his book *The Location of Culture* (1994), observes that culture always appears in 'the beyond' (1), I am not sure that he is correct – at least not when applied to cases like *High Fidelity* and *Night Market Hero*. Bhabha argues that the most innovative theories of culture should trace moments of difference between cultures rather than the origination, or roots, of culture. Bhabha explains: 'these in-between spaces provide terrain for elaborating strategies of selfhood – singular or communal – that initiate new signs of identity, and innovative sites of collaboration, and contestation, in the act of defining the idea of society itself' (2). In response to Bhabha, I would argue that film scholars should be concerned, at least to some extent, with the origination of film texts. Examples of successful contemporary Taiwanese films such as *Cape No. 7* and *Night Market Hero*, cannot simply be understood in terms of postmodernism or transnationalism.

One of the broader themes of *Night Market Hero* – that local culture should be protected from corporate takeovers – would not seem unusual to anyone familiar with Tsai's nostalgia for the Taipei Skywalk and the Fuhe Theatre, Hou's obsession with mid-century-era Fengshan, or Yang's preoccupation with alienation in corporatised 1980s Taipei. The label 'New Wave', therefore, in reference to a single Taiwanese cinema movement, can be misleading. Ho Yi, staff reporter for the *Taipei Times*, recently summarised the Taiwanese film industry in 2012 as follows: 'As Taiwanese cinema rises from its art-house roots and learns to love its audience, it has become increasingly attractive to investors and grown in number over the past few years. Regrettably, quantity does not equal quality.'

Yi's statement summarises the ambivalent state of the industry as it exists in 2013. Though a larger number of films received government subsidies than in years past, most average people did not pay to see those films. Even the most successful films by box office standards (Yi mentions the feature-length version of the popular television series, *The Fierce Wife Final Episode* (2012), as an example) were panned critically.[12]

AU REVOIR SADNESS

Fortunately, some emerging film-makers seem to be questioning the 'aesthetics of death' that are still associated with Taiwanese cinema. Arvin Chen, who directed the 2010 film *Au revoir Taipei*, is one example. Though Chen is not a self-proclaimed 'Taiwanese filmmaker' (he is perhaps better described as 'Taiwanese American' or simply 'American') his successful entrance into the international film festival circuit certainly raises important questions about how Taiwanese cinema might redefine itself in the coming years.

Unlike certain theorists who might say that the move away from the art house aesthetic in Taiwanese cinema is a bad thing, I do not necessarily view this shift in a negative light. In fact, this increased ability for collaboration, travel and shared funding could work to a film-maker's advantage, allowing for more interesting films to be produced. Using Arvin Chen as an example, though he was born in California, his film *Au revoir Taipei* was fully funded by the Taiwanese government and was shot in Taipei. So, we might ask: is this a Taiwanese film or a Taiwanese American French film? The answer to the question almost does not matter because the film is interesting in its own right and because it does contain elements from the French New Wave, Hollywood and Taiwanese New Wave all wrapped into the story. Chen's brand of cinema is itself new – not quite national, not quite international.

Au revoir Taipei follows a standard Hollywood romantic comedy formula: Kai (Jack Yao) must deliver a package for a comical and relatively kind-hearted mobster, Brother Bao, to get the money to travel to Paris and to win back his girlfriend, Faye. As he sits on the floor of a local bookshop, Susie, a pretty girl who works at the shop asks him why he is studying French. She is, of course, crestfallen when she finds out that Kai is studying French to impress his girlfriend. A bit later, thugs kidnap Kai's friend Ji-yong so that they can blackmail Kai into handing over Brother Bao's package. Susie, who is confused and concerned by the situation, accompanies Kai through the streets of Taipei as he attempts to rescue Ji-yong. The film ends more or less predictably: Kai rescues Ji-yong, Susie and Kai fall in love, and the package turns out to contain nothing more than a photograph of Brother Bao's long lost love.

While the story of *Au revoir Taipei* itself is not unique, the film contains four major qualities that emphasise *renewal* over disappearance in the context of Taiwanese cinematic practice: (1) Chen's ability, as a film-maker, to utilise his feelings of displacement and foreignness to his advantage; (2) the relatively traditional stylistic elements of the film *in relation to* other contemporary cinematic representations of Taipei (that is, 'what's old is new again'); (3) Chen's use of intertextual references to European cinematic movements (such as the French New Wave) and to other Taiwanese film-makers such as Tsai Ming-liang; and finally (4) the use of language in the film which I will return to later on in the chapter.

Addressing my first point, Chen claims in a recent interview that filming in Taiwan is much easier than filming in America because Taiwan's Government Information Office (GIO) provides a large part of the funds. He argues that such generous financial support allows for, rather than inhibits, his artistic creativity. Chen has said that he would not label his film 'authentically Taiwanese' because he considers himself a foreigner to Taiwan. I would argue, to the contrary, that the film *is* 'authentic' insofar as it functions as a comment on the work of Yang and Tsai in particular. Rather than turn away from, or ignore, the past, the film continues 'the conversation', so to speak, as it raises a number of important questions: how does one define a film as either authentic or inauthentic to a culture? Even though the primary language of *Au revoir Taipei* is Mandarin, it is shot entirely in Taipei, and it seems to capture the unique spatiality of the city, the film-maker himself does not perceive the film as 'authentically Taiwanese'. Perhaps the question of authenticity becomes less and less relevant as the increasing use of intertextual practices by transnational film-makers 'levels the cinematic playing field'.

Furthermore, it is interesting to note the aesthetic portrayal of Taipei in Chen's film in relation to other contemporary cinematic portrayals of the city. As we have seen, Taipei is often linked, in a cinematic context, with the superficiality and ephemeral nature of modernity. Again, we may recall Jameson's description of Taipei in the context of Taiwanese New Cinema: 'as a superimposed set of boxed dwelling spaces in which the characters are all in one way or another confined' (154). For Jameson, therefore, the 'non-national nation-state' that is Taiwan functions as a type of analogy for our global society. Taiwan is to the world as the citizens of Taipei are to Taiwan. In the period of late capitalism, the existential angst of everyday citizens is aggravated not by an identifiable class of people but by faceless corporations.

In an early scene of Edward Yang's 1984 film, *Taipei Story*, the protagonist, Su-Chen (Tsai Chin) and a male co-worker, wander through the architectural firm where they both work. The man gazes out of an office building window, commenting to Su-Chen: 'Look at these buildings. It's getting harder and harder for me to distinguish which ones I designed, and which ones I did not. They all look the same; as if it doesn't make much difference whether I exist or not.'[13]

The Taipei that Yang's camera shows is a city filled with glass revolving doors, crowded streets, cars, buses and nondescript skyscrapers that are erected overnight. The floor-to-ceiling windows that are meant to frame Taipei's vast skyline function instead as large, eerie reminders that human progress is often tied to stifling homogeneity. In the style of an Antonioni film, the background edges into the foreground as human subjects become increasingly extraneous to the modern world. In the context of Taiwan New Cinema, Frederic Jameson describes a similar phenomenon as a cinematic spatiality that establishes an 'insistent relationship . . . between the individual space and the city as a whole' (153).

Because the skyline of Taipei is constantly under construction, it is no wonder that many Taiwanese directors, such as Edward Yang and Tsai Ming-liang, have been fixated on documenting disappearance within the city. These film-makers do not celebrate disposability. Rather, they seem to regard Taipei's never-ending 'destruction and reconstruction' cycle with faint sadness. In Hong Kong, this destructive cycle, and subsequent sadness, are magnified and have been popularized into mainstream culture, as exemplified by the animated McDull series (the central protagonist is one part angst-ridden existentialist, one part cute cartoon pig). In Taipei, film-makers like Tsai Ming-liang are preoccupied with the buildings and structures that no longer exist, such as the Fuhe Theatre and the Taipei railway station skywalk. In Tsai's *What Time?* the skywalk is the protagonist's place of livelihood; this is where he sells his watches. The eradication of the skywalk means that he will lose his place of business as well as his only source of income. Scenes shot on the skywalk expose construction cranes, looming in the background, and the sound of hammering building workers punctuates the conversations of the characters. These characters, as imagined by Tsai, are powerless in the face of urban environments that transform in the blink of an eye.

In the context of Chen's film, on the other hand, the relationship between individual space and Taipei as a whole is no longer symptomatic of postmodern existential angst. The protagonists of Chen's film are, in many ways, bound by the spaces that they inhabit. But, instead of lamenting the confinement of his characters, Chen revels in the fact that Kai cannot say 'au revoir' to Taipei. Suddenly, the local is prized and the mundane romanticised. One might imagine a Tsai Ming-liang film by the same name but with an entirely different, more negative, reading of spatiality. In the context of Chen's film, however, Taipei is beautiful, alive and vibrant. There is not even a glimmer of hopelessness to be found. Even the bad guys turn out to be soft-hearted good guys in the end. Perhaps Chen romanticises Taipei because he has, in a sense, fallen in love with the city. But, even if we were to read nothing more into this film, we really should not ignore the overall shift in tone – away from death and towards life – that a film such as *Au revoir Taipei* represents.

Chen has said that he was originally inspired to make movies after seeing French New Wave films, and these influences do manifest themselves in a number of ways in *Au revoir Taipei*. In some respects, the film's pacing is fashioned after Agnes Varda's *Cléo de 5 à 7*, a French New Wave film that takes place in real time over the course of two hours on the streets of Paris. In Chen's film, meanwhile, the majority of the action takes place over the course of one night on the streets of Taipei. As in Jean-Luc Godard's *Breathless*, the romance between Kai and Susie is stalled because of shoot-outs, close calls with the police and chase scenes involving mobsters. Like Patricia, the female protagonist in *Breathless*, Susie is carefree, independent and quirky.

But Chen does not cite the French New Wave for purely nostalgic reasons. His use of language highlights the critical tone inherent to the film. The opening scene of *Au revoir Taipei*, in fact, problematises the notion of France and the French language as romantic ideals. The very first shot of the film is an establishing shot of Taipei's skyline at night. The lilting, jazz-infused soundtrack (which includes vocals by Amber Kuo) accompanies this initial shot of Taipei's skyscrapers which glow pleasantly and colourfully against the night sky. The sequence of shots that follows confirms our initial impression of Taipei as a city bustling with life and warmth: dancers practise their routines in the park and the night markets are overflowing with locals as well as tourists. Though the streets are crowded, everyone shares the limited space in a sort of organised cheerful chaos. The camera lingers on buses, trains, cars, motorcycles and walking bodies as if to demonstrate the endless modes of conveyance and open possibilities that the city has to offer. The citizens of Taipei are not trapped or confined by the spaces they inhabit; on the contrary, they move about freely at all hours of the night. The city thrives with life. The food looks delicious.

As he sadly watches Faye wordlessly depart for Paris in a taxi, Kai's voice-over (in imperfect French) begins:

> Bonjour, Faye. Vous êtes bonne? Paris est-ce bon? Sans vous Taipei est très triste. Très très triste . . . je pense toujours à toi, imaginer nous sur les rues de Paris . . . danshi, wo meitian dou lianxi xihuan ke yi you ji hui gen ni shuo fayu. Na . . . jiu ni you kong da dianhua gei wo hao le. Jian jian![14]

This sudden shift from French to Mandarin coincides with the shift from the voiceover monologue, set against the background of Taipei, to Kai speaking into the telephone in his room. French is a part of Kai's daydreams whereas Mandarin is a part of his everyday existence. The language shift is also somewhat analogous to the structure of the film as a whole. When the film begins, Kai imagines himself and Faye on the streets of Paris – this is what he associates with the ultimate romantic dream. Taipei, on the other hand, is a neutral space for Kai, a city that exists only as a point of departure. But the camera tells a different story, distinguishing the visual from the audio. Though Kai, in his voiceover, states that he imagines himself in Paris, the camera, meanwhile, shows him riding his motorcycle on the streets of Taipei. The shift back to Mandarin, therefore, is synonymous with a shift back to the 'real time' of the film. Taipei represents cinematic 'real time' just as Cléo's Paris represents real time in the context of Varda's film. Of course, unlike Varda's Paris, there is nothing particularly depressing about Chen's Taipei.

Despite Chen's (or anyone else's) claims that *Au revoir Taipei* is nothing more than a cute romantic comedy set in Taipei, I would argue that the film carries an important, underlying message. The catchphrase from the trailer seems to sum it up the best: 'If Paris is the city of love, what is Taipei the city of?' Unlike Tsai, Chen is not interested in Paris as a cinematic setting. The French language is used only as a plot device to begin the love story between Kai and Susie. Chen establishes Taipei as the 'new city of romance' while he uses Paris as a foil or red herring. The title, *Au revoir Taipei*, is intentionally misleading because Kai never leaves. Yet the plot's sense of urgency derives from the very fact that Kai is always on the verge of leaving – *mingtian zaoshang* – a 'tomorrow morning' that never comes.

CONCLUSIONS

Though Chen's message could be interpreted as reactionary and, in many ways, anti-French, I would argue that Chen's self-proclaimed identity as an Asian American film-maker problematises such a simple interpretation. His status as a displaced American film-maker in Taipei endows him, somewhat paradoxically, with a sense of freedom that he did not have while filming in Los Angeles. Like his contemporary Tsai Ming-liang, Chen is a cinephile. He mixes an impressive variety of intertextual cinematic references into his films with carefree precision, citing retro and contemporary film-makers with equal dexterity. *Au revoir Taipei* functions not only as an ode to the French New Wave but, moreover, as a comment on Tsai's *What Time is it There?* Kai's character is, in many ways, a very sane version of *What Time*'s Hsiao-kang. While Hsiao-kang expresses his urges and desires in an immediate and physical way, Kai's physicality – though awkward – is imbued with life. The title, *Au revoir Taipei*, therefore, is not a 'goodbye to Taiwan' but, more aptly, a reactive 'goodbye' to prevailing cinematic representations of Taipei as sickly and haunted.

The Taiwanese film industry is in a constant state of transformation. The films that are successful with audiences are not always successful overseas. Even Taiwanese film industry insiders have observed that, for a film to be successful, it must follow a certain formula and contain specific elements: young protagonists, a fairy-tale-like quality, a character who overcomes adversity, scenes of intense conflict, and a happy ending. The film's cast should be composed of rising stars, and the film's release should be timed perfectly (just before the Chinese New Year is ideal). Finally, the film should be advertised with new media and shown in advanced screenings. This combination of factors should be enough to create a buzz among potential Taiwanese film-goers.

Contrary to scholars like Homi Bhabha, who have argued that culture is not necessarily 'originatory', I would argue that successful (profitable) Taiwanese cinema depends on speaking to – and communicating with – a specific core audience. But what is it about this combination of factors that is specific to Taiwan in particular? For one, many of the films which I have discussed in this chapter contain a mixture of languages and dialects. For this reason, among others, the films do not necessarily appeal to Western, or even mainland Chinese, audiences. Secondly, Taiwan New Cinema often deals with issues that are sensitive for the People's Republic of China, such as Japan's occupation and Taiwan's secession. These issues, of course, were initially exposed and dealt with by the directors of New Wave cinema in Taiwan. In this sense, then, the films of contemporary Taiwanese cinema represent progress within the industry.

I shall return, finally to Jameson, who compares Taiwanese cinema with a recipe composed of equal parts empty space and equal parts modernity. He writes:

> . . . the urban seems propitious to [this form of cinema], infinitely assembling the empty spaces of such meetings or missed encounters; while the modern (or the romantic) seems to supply the other vital ingredient; namely, the sense of authorial function or of the omniscient social witness. (114)

Jameson's description allows for the possibility of both missed encounters *and* fortunate chance meetings within the context of modern cinematic representation. Rather than pronouncing the death of death in Taiwanese film-making, therefore, I propose that Chen's film creates an alternative, double-edged, ultimately paradoxical space in which disappearance and renewal can exist simultaneously.

<h2>NOTES</h2>

1. A shortened version of this chapter first appeared in *Senses of Cinema* in June 2011.
2. See 'Monga Producer Lee Lieh' interview. From *Screen Daily*, 8 April 2010.
3. See 'Lee', pp. 102–9.
4. See 'NYAFF 09 Review: Cape No. 7' by Dustin Chang (21 June 2009) <http://twitchfilm.com/2009/06/nyaff-09-review-cape-no-7.html> (last accessed 15 June 2013).
5. See <http://www.emanuellevy.com/review/cape-no-7-2008-9/>
6. See 'Mainland Taste Subtle Favor of Taiwan through Film' (19 February 2009) by

the Xinhua News Agency for the *Beijing Review* <http://www.bjreview.com.cn/movies/txt/2009-02/19/content_179430.htm> (last accessed 15 June 2013).

7. See <http://www.screendaily.com/taiwanese-hit-cape-no7-tops-hong-kong-box-office/4042109.article>

8. See 'My Kafkaesque Life' blog at <http://mykafkaesquelife.blogspot.com/2013/02/culture-of-taiwan-lunar-new-year.html>

9. See the review by Derek Elley: 'Night Market Hero' for *Film Business Asia*, 22 July 2011 <http://www.filmbiz.asia/reviews/night-market-hero> (last accessed 15 June 2013).

10. See the review by 'Kozo': 'Night Market Hero Review', for the *Love HK Film* website <http://www.lovehkfilm.com/panasia/night_market_hero.html> (last accessed 15 June 2013).

11. Television shows, in fact, tend to rely more heavily on cultural references for humour, perhaps because television episodes are deemed to have a more current and ephemeral quality than films. The shows that I have in mind are often satires or parodies. *The Simpsons* and *Saturday Night Live*, for instance, tend to rely on the audience's knowledge of certain recent events and/or cultural norms.

12. *Will You Still Love Me Tomorrow?* directed by Arvin Chen is scheduled to be screened at the Berlin International Film Festival (6 February 2013).

13. Translated into characters from the Pinyin: 你看这些房子。我越来越分不出它们了。是我设计，不是我设计。看起来都一样。有我，没有我，好像越来越不重要.

14. [French] Hello Faye. You are good? Paris is good? Without you Taipei is sad. Very, very sad. I always think of you and imagine us on the streets of Paris . . . [Mandarin] Anyway, everyday I try to learn so that I can speak French with you. Call me as soon as you can. Bye!

CONCLUSION

... New Taiwan Cinema's representation of modernity places the New in its historical past and eludes the present of what the New has become. The multiple identificatory positions, with their entangled histories and intricate negotiation between the personal and the collective in filmic narrative and narration, mark a defining feature of New Taiwan Cinema in its efforts to come to terms with those temporal conflicts and historical problems. (Guo-juin Hong, in *Island of No Return*, 71)

New Taiwan Cinema represents modernity by turning the present into history, all the while without becoming stale. In short, New Taiwan Cinema is timeless but, at the same time, speaks to the present; the best of this type of cinema is specific to the Taiwanese experience but retains a certain element of universality. If the defining feature of New Wave Cinema is its effort to break the silence of the past by aestheticising a collective experience, then the defining feature of Taiwan New Cinema, more generally, is its ability to reinvigorate a dying industry. Taiwan New Cinema is not defined by success or failure at the box office although it is constrained somewhat by time period. Before the 1980s, the rebellious discourse which was to define New Cinema existed in literary form only.

It is certainly not necessary to divide New Cinema films by auteur as I have done here. At the same time, this decision was not arbitrary on my part. This volume was organised and centred on a core group of New Wave auteurs – an incomplete group to be sure. After choosing to write on a select group of auteurs composing the Taiwanese New Cinema movement, this volume was organised according to the aesthetic and thematic concerns of each film-maker. These decisions were not made lightly. On the contrary, each chapter has been carefully formulated to tease out the individual elements of style that are (or will come to be) associated with the work of each of these directors. These elements, of course, are not static. Rather, they constantly and consistently overlap and coincide. The Taiwanese film industry distinguishes itself from other film industries by way of transnational and cross-cultural connections. Many Taiwanese film-makers are well known (in an international context) because they are required to seek international funding for their projects. The resulting films are often highly sophisticated and rich with intertextual references. Without this unique, obstacle-laden situation, Taiwanese cinema would probably – and somewhat paradoxically – not be as 'transnationally minded' as it is in its current form.

Each chapter of this volume is devoted to the analysis of films that are, in effect, sites of cultural translation, adaptation, and exchange between Taiwan, Hollywood and Western European cinematic traditions (French and Italian, in particular). Each of the auteurs in this volume was chosen because of their insistence on active viewership – that is, each film-maker encourages the spectator not to be passive and to be aware of the cultural exchange that is taking place within the diegesis or narrative of the film itself. Often, within the diegeses of the films, the characters speak multiple languages. In this sense, the films are 'translingual' as well. Rather than argue that they somehow reflect a uniform notion of Taiwanese cinema, I argue that these films should be thought of as a model for detecting possibilities for viewing, reading and interpreting transnational and intertextual currents in contemporary world cinema movements more generally. My discussion of the Taiwanese cinematic 'tradition', in other words, relies heavily on the notion of intertextuality, citation and translation rather than on the notion of unwavering bodies of textuality.

I do not claim to define or to set the boundaries of the Taiwanese cinematic 'tradition' nor would I expect (or want) my reader to be able to do so. Any project that seeks to categorise a particular body of films will, initially, 'feel' inadequate. My choice of films might very well be called into question as representative of a certain particular film-maker's *oeuvre*. Nevertheless, despite the difficulties that may arise as a result of making choices, the need to do so outweighs the costs, in my view. If we can agree, at the outset, that the Taiwanese cinematic 'tradition' describes relationships, possibilities and fluid interchangeability, then my decision to discuss particular films rather than others, or to separate chapters by film-maker, does not reflect an assumption on my part that Taiwanese cinema is composed of rigid or inflexible bodies of textuality. There are, of course, similarities between the cross-cultural cinematic exchanges that occur within and between the films of Edward Yang, Hou

Hsiao-hsien, Tsai Ming-liang, Ang Lee, and the other film-makers mentioned in this book. Most of the films in this volume, for example, involved some sort of financial and artistic collaboration between production companies as well as an agreement for international distribution in the hopes of reaching a transnational audience. Because each film-maker has his own unique set of considerations, each mode of collaboration is significant.

Rather than focus predominantly on the particulars of terminology, which can be a tedious task, I have sought to dedicate this book to the close study of films. These are all films that I see as exemplary in some way of the Taiwanese cinematic 'tradition', though each of the films therein represents a different incarnation of cross-cultural conjugation. This study is not meant to be all-encompassing or 'complete' but, rather, it is meant as a starting point that will lead to more research, refinement and thought.

The phenomenon that I describe, in my introduction, as 'hybrid cinema' is the theoretical concept on which I base my discussion of contemporary Taiwanese cinema. As stated in the introduction to this book, contemporary Taiwanese cinema contains elements that help to form and inspire the creation of new genres. Taiwan New Cinema exhibits 'hybridity' or adaptation in some form, though my definition of 'adaptation' rests on the notion of intertextuality, citation and translation. A new genre of film-making has been created in Taiwan as the result of this combination of innovative cinematic language with recognisable visual, aural and diegetic elements. The films that comprise Taiwanese New Cinema 'reincarnate' and cite the cinema of other world traditions by carving out a new niche for themselves altogether. Within this notion of reincarnation, the most important aspect is the idea of transforming or innovating the recognisable or the familiar (something that already exists). This so-called reincarnation involves using the cinematic 'spectres' of the past to bring new life to contemporary cinema.[1] In Tsai's film, for example, scenes from Truffaut's *The 400 Blows* are shown and inserted directly into the narrative – they intrude into the character's space, in a sense. At one point, Hsiao-Kang lies in bed and watches the zoetrope scene from *The 400 Blows*. Later, Antoine's milk-stealing scene in *The 400 Blows* is inserted directly into the film 'without quotation marks' (there is no explanation or framing before or after).

As the introduction to this book makes clear, I do not endorse the notion of national cinemas as coherent bodies of textuality. At the same time, I do not call for an outright rejection of 'the national' either, for fear of losing an important mode of analysis. This is why I have proposed a revised framework (in part as a response to the non-specificity of the term 'transnationalism') that I have defined as 'East–West hybrid cinema'.

Why have I chosen to write about Taiwanese cinema? The concept of 'transnationalism' was initially proposed by Chinese cinema scholars as a model for discussing the effects of globalisation and internationalisation of Chinese cinemas, beginning in the late 1990s with Sheldon Lu. After reading Lu et al., I became interested in continuing that work and refining the theoretical work that had already been done. This is why I have argued that, though the East–West binary is misleading, looking at cinema through this lens also, almost paradoxically, proves that the internationalisation of world cinema has already occurred. Films such as *Au revoir Taipei* demonstrate the importance of finding new ways to describe cinema that is not quite national, not quite 'inter-' or 'trans-' national. Because of the elements of the national that can be recognised and discussed in films such as *Au revoir Taipei*, I would insist that it is too early to declare the study of national cinema – as the notion relates to East–West hybrid cinema – entirely dead. As Jinhee Choi suggests in his essay 'National Cinema: The Very Idea', we must not assume that non-Hollywood films reflect the 'essence' of their national origins; we can only presuppose a flexible, probabilistic relationship between the two (Choi 319). Adopting a 'relational approach' (319) to the study of national cinemas allows us the freedom to investigate the relationship between nation and text because it accounts for fluidity.

This research is far from over. As Shu mei-Shih states, one of the Sinophone's favourite modes is intertextuality, an intertextuality that constructs new identities and cultures. This is how I view the many conjugations and cross-cultural exchanges within Taiwanese cinema, as I have noted and discussed in this volume. But I have also argued that Shih's thesis can be generalised to encompass more cinematic traditions (such as mainland Chinese), and that the various cinematic conjugations therein can also be specified more precisely. The aim of this book has been, essentially, to describe the Taiwanese cinematic tradition by highlighting particular films that contain cross-overs between East Asian and Western European cinematic traditions while focusing on the important work of film-makers such as Edward Yang, Hou Hsiao-hsien, Tsai Ming-liang and Ang Lee. The hybridity of these films and their film-makers can be better understood through knowledge of Taiwanese culture and identity. Yet the Taiwanese cinematic tradition contains two seemingly contradictory themes: representations of nationhood, belonging and citizenship, on the one hand; migration, displacement and exile on the other.

Fundamentally, it is not the terminology that is particularly important or interesting but, rather, the films themselves. It is easy to forget, when writing about cinema, that one's appreciation for films as works of art can (and often should) be separated from the theoretical analysis that goes along with it. We seem to forget sometimes that film-makers are cinephiles themselves, and with a much larger fan base to please. Taiwanese New Cinema highlights convergences, cross-overs and influences, reincarnates the 'ghosts' of cinemas past, and weaves it all into something entirely new.

Resonating with this sentiment, Gilberto Perez eloquently remarks:

. . . if all that interested me about art, about film, were [*sic*] what is wrong with it, I would not be spending much time with film or with art. It is because I like film . . . that I have written this book. And I have mostly written about films that I like. (19–20)

Though these remarks may sound obvious, I believe that we are all too often distracted with the task of figuring out 'what is wrong with film', as we move further and further away from the view that artistic criticism can be an end in itself. Writing an all-encompassing volume on Taiwanese New Cinema is a daunting endeavour. The term itself can be used to refer to an enormous range of contemporary Taiwanese cinema, good cinema and bad cinema, art house films and popular films. Despite my contention that Taiwanese cinema can be used as a case study to redefine the notion of 'national' cinema altogether, I would warn against conflating criticism with theory. Avoiding this common trap first and foremost is the best way to avoid forgetting, down the line, why we chose to write about cinema in the first place.

NOTE

1. See Jacques Derrida's *Specters of Marx* (1994) for the theoretical origins of this term.

BIBLIOGRAPHY

Adams, Jonathan (2008), 'Is China's Labor Law Working?' *The Daily Beast*, 13 February 2008.

Adorno, Theodor [1970] (2005), *Aesthetic Theory*, London: Continuum International Publishing Group.

Anderson, John (2005), *Edward Yang*, Urbana-Champaign: University of Illinois Press.

anonymous (from British Naval and Military Record) (1894) 'Japan Anxious for a Fight: the Chinese are Slow and Not in Good Shape to Go to War', *New York Times*, 30 July 1894 <http://query.nytimes.com/mem/archive-free/pdf?res=950DEEDE1531E033A25 753C3A9619C94659ED7CF> (last accessed 28 February 2013).

Antonioni, Michelangelo [1982] (1996), *The Architecture of Vision: Writings and Interviews on Cinema* (American version, 1996), eds M. Cottino-Jones, C. di Carlo and G. Tinazzi, Chicago: University of Chicago Press.

Arp, Robert, Barkman, Adam and McRae, James (2003), *The Philosophy of Ang Lee*, Lexington: University Press of Kentucky.

Assayas, Olivier, 'Cinéastes de notre temps, HHH, portrait de Hou Hsiao-hsien', interview at Centre Pompidou, *Daily Motion* http://www.dailymotion.com/video/xjfv48_cineastes-de-notre-temps-hhh-portrait-de-hou-hsiao-hsien-de-olivier-assayas_creation #.UaHxL6UttFI (last accessed 15 May 2013).

Bachner, Andrea A. (2004), 'Cinema as Heterochronos: Temporal Folds in the Work of Tsai Ming-Liang', *Modern Chinese Literature and Culture* 19.1: pp. 60–90.

Badley, Linda, and Palmer, R. Barton (2006), *Traditions in World Cinema*, New Brunswick: Rutgers University Press.

Bale, Miriam (2012), 'Five Lessons from Ten Great Filmmakers: Hou Hsiao-hsien', *Fandor*, 12 October 2012 <www.fandor.com/blog/five-lessons-from-ten-great-filmmakers-hou-hsiao-hsien>(last accessed 28 February 2013).

Barthes, Roland (1977), *Image-Music-Text*, trans. Stephen Heath, New York: Hill and Wang.

Bazin, André (2004), *What is Cinema?* Volume 1, trans. H. Gray, Berkeley: University of California Press.

Benjamin, Walter (2002), *The Arcades Project (Passagenwerk)*, ed. R. Tiedemann, Cambridge, MA: Belknap Press of Harvard University.

Benjamin, Walter (1969), *Illuminations: Essays and Reflections*, trans. H. Arendt, New York: Schoken.

Berry, Chris (2009),'Futures of Chinese Cinema: Technologies and Temporalities', in *Chinese Screen Cultures*, eds O. Khoo and S. Metzger, London: Intellect.

Berry, Chris and Mary Farquhar (2006), *China on Screen: Cinema and Nation*, New York: Columbia University Press.

Berry, Chis and Lu Xinyu (2005), *Island on the Edge: Taiwan New Cinema and After*, Hong Kong: Hong Kong University Press.

Berry, Chris (2003), *Chinese Films in Focus: 25 New Take*, London: British Film Institute.

Berry, Michael (2005), *Speaking in Images: Interviews with Contemporary Chinese Filmmakers*, New York: Columbia University Press.

Bhabha, Homi K. (1994), *The Location of Culture*, New York: Routledge.

Bloom, Michelle E. (2011), 'The Intertextuality of Tsai Ming-liang's Sinofrench Film *Face*', *Journal of Chinese Cinemas* 5.2, pp. 103–21.

Bloom, Michelle E. (2005), 'Contemporary Franco-Chinese Cinema: Translation, Citation and Imitation, in Dai Sijie's *Balzac and the Little Chinese Seamstress* and Tsai Ming-liang's *What Time is it There?*', *Quarterly Review of Film and Video* 22.4: pp. 311–25.

Boggs, Joe and Petrie, Dennis (2011), *The Art of Watching Films*, New York: McGraw Hill.

Bordwell, David (2013), 'Master Shots: On the Set of Hou Hsiao-hsien's *The Assassin*', *Observations on Film Art*, 6 January 2013 <www.davidbordwell.net/blog/2013/01/06/master-shots-on-the-set-of-hou-hsiao-hsiens-the-assassin> (last accessed 28 February 2013).

Bordwell, David (2007) 'Two Chinese Men of Cinema' *Observations on Film Art* <www.davidbordwell.net/blog/2007/08/04/twochinese-men-of-cinema/> (last accessed 28 February 2013).

Bordwell, David (1985), *The Classical Hollywood Cinema: Film Style and Mode of Production*, New York: Columbia University Press.

Bowman, James (2000), '*Crouching Tiger, Hidden Dragon*', in James Bowman, *Movie Reviews* (1 November 2000) <http://www.jamesbowman.net/ reviewdetail.asp?pubid=471> (last accessed 13 June 2013).

Bowman, Jon (1999), 'Yang Masterpiece Led New Taiwanese Cinema', *Santa Fe New Mexican* in Pasatiempo (11 June 1999).

Braester, Yomi (2010), *Painting the City Red: Chinese Cinema and the Urban Contract*, Durham: Duke University Press.

Braudy, Leo and Cohen, Marshall (eds) (1999), *Film Theory and Criticism: Introductory Readings* (5th ed.), Oxford: Oxford University Press.

Brightwell, Eric (2013), 'Made in Taiwan: Taiwanese Cinema and Television', *Amoeba Blog* <www.amoeba.com> (last accessed 20 February 2013).

Burch, Noël (1981), *Theory of Film Practice*, Princeton: Princeton University Press.

Carrol, Noël and Choi, Jinhee (eds) (2006), *Philosophy of Film and Motion Pictures: An Anthology*, Malden, MA: Wiley-Blackwell.

Chang, Meg (2011), 'Night Market Hero Ushers in New Era for Taiwanese Films', *Taiwan Today* (7 July 2011).

Chen Xiaomei (1995), *Occidentalism: A Theory of Counter-Discourse in Post-Mao China*, Oxford: Oxford University Press.

Choi, Jinhee (2006), 'National Cinema: The Very Idea', in *Philosophy of Film and Motion Pictures: An Anthology*, eds N. Carroll and J. Choi. Malden, MA: Wiley-Blackwell.

Chow, Rey (2012), *Entanglements, or Transmedial Thinking about Capture*, Durham: Duke University Press.

Chow, Rey (2007), *Sentimental Fabulations: Contemporary Chinese Cinema in the Age of Global Visibility*, New York: Columbia University Press.

Cortázar, Julio [1958] (1968), 'Blow-Up and Other Stories', trans. Paul Blackburn, New York: Pantheon.

Crespi, Alberto (2005), 'Wang: cinesi, ve lo da io la Toscana', *Il Porto Ritrovato*, 21 September 2005 <http://www.ilportoritrovato.net/html/wang.html> (last accessed 1 February, 2011).

Curtin, Michael (2007), *Playing to the World's Biggest Audience: The Globalization of Chinese Film and TV*, Berkeley: University of California Press.

Davis, Darrell William, and Chen, Ru-Shou Robert (eds) (2007), *Cinema Taiwan: Politics, Popularity, and State of the Arts*, London: Routledge.

Deleuze, Gilles (1986), *Cinema 1: The Movement-Image*, trans. H. Tomlinson and B. Habberjam, Minneapolis: University of Minnesota Press.

Deslandes, Jeanne (2000) 'Dancing Shadows of Film Exhibition: Taiwan and Japanese Influence', *Screening the Past*, 1 November 2000.

De Villiers, Nicholas (2011), '"Chinese Cheers": Hou Hsiao-hsien and Transnational Homage', *Senses of Cinema* 58, 2011: n.p.

Dilley, Whitney Crothers (2007), *The Cinema of Ang Lee: The Other Side of the Screen*, New York: Columbia University Press – Wallflower.

Duncan, Derek (2008), 'Italy's Postcolonial Cinema and Its Histories of Representation', *Italian Studies* 63. 2, autumn 2008: pp. 195–211.

'Filmmaker Tsai Ming-liang on *Face*' (2009) (interview) <http://www.youtube.com/watch? v=8mxZTyCluUs> (last accessed 10 December 2010).

Frater, Patrick, 'China and Taiwan Crack Open Film Markets', *Film Business Asia*, 7 July 2010 <http://www.filmbiz.asia/news/china-and-taiwan-crack-open-film-markets> (last accessed 10 May 2013).

Furstenau, Marc (ed.) (2010), *The Film Theory Reader*, London: Routledge.

Ghermanni, Wafa (2012), 'National Identity in the History of Taiwanese Film' (YouTube video) <www.youtube.com/watch?v=WgPufMcki2M> (last accessed 28 February 2013).

Gillain, Anne (1988), *Le cinéma selon François Truffaut*, Paris: Flammarion.

'Harnessing Ang Lee's Fame to Boost Taiwan's Film Sector' (2013), *Economic Daily News*, 10 March.

Higbee, Will (2007), 'Beyond the (Trans)national: Towards a Cinema of Transvergence in Postcolonial and Diasporic Francophone Cinema(s)', *Studies in French Cinema* 7.2, May 2007: pp. 79–91.

Hong, Guo Juin (2011), *Taiwan Cinema: A Contested Nation on Screen*, Basingstoke: Palgrave Macmillan.

Huang, Chunming (2001), *The Taste of Apples*, trans. Howard Goldblatt, New York: Columbia University Press.

Huang, Jewel (2003) 'NTU to Apologize for 1974 Crackdown on Professors', *Taipei Times*, 25 December: p. 2 <http://www.taipeitimes.com/News/taiwan/archives/2003/12/25/2003084822> (last accessed 15 May 2013).

Hughes, Darren (2003), 'Tsai Ming-liang', *Senses of Cinema* 26 <http://www.sensesofcinema. com/2003/great-directors/tsai/> (last accessed 11 November 2011).

Hsu, Jen-yi (2007), 'Re-enchanting the Everyday Banal in the Age of Globalization: Alienation, Desire and Critique of Capitalist Temporality in Tsai Ming-Liang's *The*

Hole and *What Time is it There?*', *NTU Studies in Language and Literature* 17: pp. 133–58.

Jameson, Fredric (1999), 'Excerpt from *Postmodernism or, the Cultural Logic of Late Capitalism*' <http://www.marxists.org/reference/subject/philosophy/works/us/jameson.htm> (last accessed 15 February 2010).

Jameson, Frederic (1992), 'Remapping Taipei', in *The Geopolitical Aesthetic: Mapping Space and Time in the World System*, Bloomington: Indiana University Press.

Jones, Kristin Marriott (2002), '*What Time is it There?*' (review) *Film Comment* 38.

Kearney, Christine (2012), 'Ang Lee Talks About Risks, Spirituality of *Life of Pi*', *Reuters* (23 November 2012) <http://www.reuters.com/article/2012/11/23/enter-tainment-us-anglee-lifeofpi-idUSBRE8AM0Z620121123> (last accessed 15 June 2013).

Kellner, David (1998), 'New Taiwan Cinema in the 80s', *Jump Cut* 42, December: pp. 101–15.

Khoo, Olivia and Metzer, Sean (eds) (2009), *Futures of Chinese Cinema: Technologies and Temporalities in Chinese Screen Cultures*, Chicago: University of Chicago Press (Intellect).

Klein, Christina (2007), '*Kung Fu Hustle*: Transnational Production and the Global Chinese-language Film', *Journal of Chinese Cinemas* 1.3: pp. 189–208.

Kracauer, Siegfried (2004), *From Caligari to Hitler: A Psychological History of the German Film*, Princeton: Princeton University Press.

Lanzoni, Rémi Fournier (2010), *French Cinema: From its Beginnings to the Present*, New York: Continuum.

'Lee Lieh and the Rebirth of Taiwan Commercial Cinema', from *Taiwan Panorama*, Volume 36, No. 12, December 2011.

Leopold, Nanouk (2002), 'Confined Space: Interview with Tsai Ming-Liang', *Senses of Cinema* <http://archive.sensesofcinema.com/contents/02/20/tsai_interview.html> (last accessed 19 November 2010).

Levy, Emanuel (2007), 'Flight of the Red Balloon' (film review), *Cinema 24/7* <http://www.emanuellevy.com/review/flight-of-the-red-balloon-4/> (last accessed 21 February 2013).

Lim, Bliss Cua (2009), *Translating Time: Cinema, the Fantastic, and Temporal Critique*, Durham: Duke University Press.

Lim, Song Hwee, and Ward, Julian (eds) (2011), *The Chinese Cinema Book*, London: British Film Institute.

Lim, Song Hwee (2007), 'Positioning Auteur Theory in Chinese Cinemas Studies: Intertextuality, Intratextuality, and Paratextuality in the Films of Tsai Ming-liang', *Journal of Chinese Cinemas*, 1.33, September: pp. 223–45.

Lu, Sheldon and Yeh, Emilie Yueh-yu (2005), *Chinese-Language Film: Historiography, Poetics, Politics*, Honolulu: University of Hawaii Press.

Lu, Sheldon (1997), *Transnational Chinese Cinemas: Identity, Nationhood, Gender*, Honolulu: University of Hawaii Press.

Lyotard, Jean-François (1979), *The Postmodern Condition: A Report on Knowledge*, trans. Jeff Bennington and Brian Massumi, Minneapolis: University of Minnesota Press.

McGrath, Jason (2010), *Postsocialist Modernity: Chinese Cinema, Literature, and Criticism in the Market Age*, Stanford: Stanford University Press.

'Magic Realism' (2013), Department of English and Comparative Literature of Columbia University <http://english.columbia.edu/magic-realism> (last accessed 20 June 2013).

Ma, Jean (2010), *Melancholy Drift: Translating Time in Chinese Cinema*, Hong Kong: Hong Kong University Press.

Marcus, Millicent (2007), *Italian Film in the Shadow of Auschwitz*, Toronto: University of Toronto Press.

Martin, Fran (2003), 'The European Undead: Tsai Ming-liang's Temporal Dysphoria', *Senses of Cinema*, 27, July–August: pp. 1–27 <http://archive.sensesofcinema.com/contents/03/27/tsai_european_undead.html> (last accessed 19 November 2010).

Metz, Christian (1986), *The Imaginary Signifier: Psychoanalysis and the Cinema*, Bloomington: Indiana University Press.

Mills, Clifford W. (2009), *Ang Lee*, New York: Chelsea House.

Misch, Christopher (2009), 'The Skywalk is Gone But Not Forgotten', *Next Projection* <http://nextprojection.blogspot.com/2009/03/skywalk-is-gone-but-not-forgotten.html> (last accessed 15 May 2009).

Moore, Donald (2002), *Buddha's Eyes*, iUniverse Publishing.

Naficy, Hamid (2001), *An Accented Cinema: Exilic and Diasporic Filmmaking*, Princeton: Princeton University Press.

Neri, Corrado (2008), 'Tsai Ming-Liang and the Lost Emotions of the Flesh', *Positions* 16.2: pp. 389–407.

Neri, Corrado and Gormley, Kirstie (eds) (2009), *Taiwan New Cinema: Le cinema taiwanais*, Lyon: Asiexpo Edition.

'New Wave Brings New Realism' (1986), *The Economist*, Volume 298, pp. 88–90.

Peavler, Terry J. (1979), '*Blow-Up*: A Reconsideration of Antonioni's Infidelity to Cortázar', *PMLA*, 94.5, October: pp. 887–93.

Peña, Richard (2011), 'Ang Lee: Conversations in World Cinema' (You Tube video) <www.youtube.com/watch?v=gUfvKQ1qe1o> (last accessed 20 February 2013).

Perez, Gilberto (2000), *The Material Ghost: Films and Their Medium*, Baltimore: Johns Hopkins University Press.

Phelps, David (2009), 'Cannes 2009: Through the Looking Glass ("Visage", Tsai)', *Notebook*, 24 May <http://mubi.com/notebook/posts/cannes-2009-through-the-looking-glass-visage-tsai> (last accessed 11 November 2011).

Pirandello, Luigi [1926] (2006), *Shoot! The Notebooks of Serafino Gubbio, Cinematograph Operator*, Chicago: University of Chicago Press.

Rapfogel, Jared (2004), 'Taiwan's Poet of Solitude: An Interview with Tsai Ming-Liang', *Cineaste*: pp. 26–9.

Rehm, Jean-Pierre, Joyard, Olivier and Rivière, Danièle (1999), 'Tsai Ming-Liang' (interview), Paris: Editions Dis Voir.

Round, Julia (2007), 'Visual Perspective and Narrative Voice in Comics: Redefining Literary Terminology', *International Journal of Comic Art* 9.2, autumn 2007: pp. 316–29.

Ruberto, Laura E. and Wilson, Kristi M. (2007), *Italian Neorealism and Global Cinema*, Detroit: Wayne State University Press.

Rubinstein, Murray A. (ed.) (1999), *Taiwan: A New History*, London: East Gate.

See-Kam, Tan, Feng, Peter X. and Marchetti, Gina (eds) (2009), *Chinese Connections: Critical Perspectives on Film, Identity, and Diaspora*, Philadelphia: Temple University Press.

Schamus, James (2007), 'Why Did She Do It?', in *Lust Caution*, trans. J. Lowell, New York: Anchor Books.

Shih, Sandra (2007), 'Four Cities Cast Themselves on the Big Screen', *Taiwan Today* (9 November).

Shih, Sandra (2007), 'Director Aims his Lens at Taiwan's Society', *Taiwan Times* (17 August).

Shih, Shu-mei (2007), *Visuality and Identity: Sinophone Articulations Across the Pacific*, Berkeley: University of California Press.

Shohat, Ella and Stam, Robert (1994), *Unthinking Eurocentrism: Multiculturalism and the Media*, London: Routledge.

Sklar, Robert (2010), 'Engineer of Modern Perplexity: An Interview with Edward Yang', *Magasa* (original interview conducted in 2000 at the New York Film Festival for *Cineaste*) (18 October) <http://site.douban.com/106789/widget/notes/127384/note/95974619/> (last accessed 11 May 2013).

Sontag, Susan (2001), *On Photography* (first edition), New York: Picador.

Stam, Robert (2000), *Film Theory: An Introduction*, New York: Columbia University Press.

Sterk, Darryl (2009), 'The Return of the Vanishing Formosan: Disturbing the Discourse of National Domestication as the Literary Fate of the Aboriginal Maiden in Postwar Taiwanese Film and Fiction' (Dissertation) <www.academia.edu/1326002/The_Return_of_the_Vanishing_Formosan> (last accessed 28 February 2013).

Su Hui-chao (2011), 'Lee Lieh and the Rebirth of Taiwan Commercial Cinema', *Taiwan Panorama*, 36.12, December: pp.102–9.

'Taipei Subway' (2007) <http://www.wired.com/autopia/2007/10/taipei-subway-r/> (last accessed 15 May 2009).

'Taiwan Mourns Cannes-Winning Director Edward Yang's Death' (2007) (no author), *China Post* (2 June) <http://www.chinapost.com.tw/headlines/47270.htm> (last accessed 11 May 2013).

Tang, Jean (2002), 'Interview: Paradise Lost: Wang Xiaoshuai's Nostalgic *Beijing Bicycle*', *Indie Wire*, 25 January <www.indiewire.com/article/interview_paradise_lost_wang_xiaoshuais_nostalgic_beijing_bicycle> (last accessed 28 February 2013).

Trifonova, Temenuga (2007), *The Image in French Philosophy (Consciousness, Literature and the Arts)*, Amsterdam: Editions Rodophi BV.

Tu, Chao-Mei. (2010), 'Diaspora, Time and Space in Tsai Ming-Liang's *What Time is it There?*', *Space and Time in Chinese Cinema Conference*, 5–6 November, Davis, CA: UC-Davis.

Tweedie, James (2007), 'Morning in the New Metropolis: Taipei and the Globalization of the City Film', in *Cinema Taiwan: Politics, Popularity, and State of the Arts,* ed. D. W. Davis, London: Routledge.

Tu, K. C. 'Lai Ho, Wu Cho-liu, and Taiwan Literature', Foreword to 'Taiwan Literature' <http://www.eastasian.ucsb.edu/taiwancenter/sites/secure.lsit.ucsb.edu.east.cms_taiwancenter/files/sitefiles/publications/15%20-%20Foreword%20in%20English.pdf> (last accessed 15 May 2013).

Tyam, Divya (2013), 'Ang Lee: Finding His Own Voice', *Big Straw: An Asian American Interest Magazine* (Carnegie Mellon online journal) <http://hciresearch2.hcii.cs.cmu.edu/ bigstraw.org/ index.php?option=com _content&task=view&id=55 &Itemid=56> (last accessed 21 January 2013).

Udden, James (2009), *No Man an Island: The Cinema of Hou Hsiao-hsien*, Hong Kong: Hong Kong University Press.

Verdicchio, Pasquale (1997), *Bound by Distance, Rethinking Nationalism through the Italian Diaspora*, Cranbury, NJ: Associated University Presses.

Vitali and Willeman (eds) (2006), *Theorising National Cinema*, London: British Film Institute.

Wang, Vincent Wei-cheng (2011),'Cross-Taiwan Straits Relations Since the 1980s: Attitude Change and Policy', in *Cross-Taiwan Straits Relations Since the 1979: Policy Adjustment and Institutional Change Across the Straits*, Kevin G. Cai (ed.), Singapore: World Scientific Publishing.

Weaver, Jimmy (2012), 'Edward Yang's *The Terrorizers*', *The Seventh Art* (a video essay), 12 April.

Weiss, Beno (1993), *Understanding Italo Calvino*, Columbia: University of South Carolina Press.

Wenchi, Lin (2009), 'Taipei at the Turn of the Century in Taiwan Cinema', in *Taiwan Cinema/Le cinéma taiwanais*, eds C. Neri and K. Gormley, Asian Connection Series, Lyon: Asiexpo Edition.

White, Hayden (1984), *The Content of Form: Narrative Discourse and Historical Representation.* Baltimore: Johns Hopkins University Press.

Williams, Raymond (1983), *Culture and Society: 1780–1950.* New York: Columbia University Press.

Wilson, George M. (1988), *Narration in Light: Studies in Cinematic Film Theory*, Baltimore: Johns Hopkins University Press.

Wong, Edmond (1993), *Edward Yang*, Taipei: Variety Publishing Company.

Wu, Amber (2008), 'Film's Success Boosts Local Industry Outlook', *Taiwan Today* (26 September).

Yueh-yu Yeh, Davis, Darrell William (2005), *Taiwan Film Directors: A Treasure Island*, New York: Columbia University Press.

Yi, Ho (2012), 'Year in Review: Taiwanese Cinema', *Taipei Times*, 31 December <http://www.taipeitimes.com/News/feat/archives/2012/12/31/2003551389/2> (last accessed 28 February 2013).

Yip, June (1997), 'Taiwanese New Cinema', in *The Oxford History of World Cinema: The Definitive History of Cinema Worldwide*, Oxford: Oxford University Press.

Zhang, Yingjin (2002), *Screening China: Critical Interventions, Cinematic Reconfigurations, and the Transnational Imaginary in Contemporary Chinese Cinema*, Ann Arbor: Center for Chinese Studies.

Zhang, Yingjin and Zhiwei Xiao (2002), *Encyclopedia of Chinese Film*, London: Routledge.

Zhen, Zhang (ed.) (2007), *The Urban Generation: Chinese Cinema and Society at the Turn of the Twenty-First Century*, Durham: Duke University Press.

FILMOGRAPHY

Antonioni, Michelangelo (1967), *Blow-Up*, DVD, Warner Home Video, 2004.

Antonioni, Michelangelo (1972), *China/La Chine/Chung Kuo* (unavailable in the United States on DVD).

Assayas, Olivier (1997), *HHH: A Portrait of Hou Hsiao-hsien* < http://www.youtube.com /playlist?list=PL0C984CA1D48AE104> (last accessed 28 February 2013).

Bertolucci, Bernardo (1987), *The Last Emperor*, DVD, Live Artisan, 1999.

Chen, Arvin (2010), *Au revoir Taipei/Yi ye Taibei*, DVD (Taiwan only).

De Sica, Vittorio (1949), *Bicycle Thieves*, DVD, Criterion, 2007.

Fellini, Federico (1961), *La dolce vita*, DVD, Koch Lorber, 2004.

Fellini, Federico (1987), *Intervista*, DVD. Koch Lorber Films, 2005.

Godard, Jean-Luc (1960), *Breathless*, DVD, Criterion, 2001.

Godard, Jean-Luc (1966), *Masculin Féminin*, DVD, Criterion, 2005.

Hou Hsiao-hsien (1983), *The Sandwich Man/Erzi de da wan'ou*, Central Motion Pictures Corporation (unavailable).

Hou Hsiao-hsien (1985), *A Time to Live, A Time to Die/Tongnian wangshi*, Central Motion Pictures Corporation (unavailable in the United States and Europe).

Hou Hsiao-hsien (1989), *A City of Sadness/Beiqing chengshi*, 3-H Films (unavailable in the United States and Europe).

Hou Hsiao-hsien (1993), *The Puppetmaster/Xi meng rensheng*, DVD, Fox Lorber, 2001.

Hou Hsiao-hsien (2001), *Millennium Mambo/Qianxi manbo*, DVD, Palm Pictures, 2002.

Hou Hsiao-hsien (2005), *Three Times/Zuihao de shiguang*, DVD, First Distributors, 2006.

Hou Hsiao-hsien (2007), *The Flight of the Red Balloon/Le voyage du ballon rouge*, DVD, IFC, 2008.

Hu King (1969), *Dragon Gate Inn/Longmen kezhan*, DVD, Union Films, 1971.

Lamorisse, Albert (1956), *The Red Balloon/Le ballon rouge*, DVD, Janus Films, 2008.

Lee, Ang (1992), *Pushing Hands/Tui shou*, DVD, Image Entertainment, 1999.

Lee Ang (1993), *The Wedding Banquet/Xi yan*, DVD. MGM, 2004.

Lee, Ang (2000), *Crouching Tiger, Hidden Dragon/Wo hu cang long*. DVD, Sony Pictures Home Entertainment, 2001.

Lee, Ang (2007), *Lust Caution/Se, jie*, DVD, BMG Artista, 2008.

Marker, Chris (1963), *La jetée/Sans soleil*, DVD, Criterion, 2007.

Niu, Doze (2010), *Monga/Bang-kah*, Greenday Films (unavailable in the United States and Europe).

Polanski, Roman (1968), *Rosemary's Baby*, DVD, Paramount, 2000.

Truffaut, François (1959), *The 400 Blows*, DVD, Criterion, 2006.

Tsai Ming-liang (1992), *Rebels of the Neon God/Qing shaonian nuozha*, DVD, Fox Lorber, 2003.

Tsai Ming-liang (1994), *Vive l'Amour/Aiqing wansui*, DVD, Fox Lorber, 1998.

Tsai Ming-liang (1997), *The River/He Liu*, DVD, Fox Lorber, 2003.

Tsai Ming-Liang (2001), *What Time is it There?/Ni nabian jidian*, DVD, Fox Lorber, 2002.

Tsai Ming-Liang (2002), *The Skywalk is Gone/Tianqiao bujian le* (unavailable on DVD).

Tsai Ming-Liang (2003), *Goodbye Dragon Inn/Bu san*, DVD, Fox Lorber, 2005.

Varda, Agnes (1962), *Cléo from 5 to 7/Cléo de 5 à 7*, DVD, Criterion, 2000.

Wang Xiaoshuai (2001), *Beijing Bicycle/Shiqisui de danche*, DVD, Sony Classics.

Wei Te-Sheng (2008), *Cape No. 7/Haijiao qi hao*, ARS Film Production (unavailable in the United States and Europe).

Yang, Edward (1985), *Taipei Story/Qing mei zhu ma*, Central Motion Pictures (unavailable in the United States and Europe).

Yang, Edward (1986), *The Terrorizers/Kongbu fenzi*, Central Motion Pictures (unavailable).

Yang, Edward (2000), *Yi Yi*. DVD, Criterion, 2011.

Yeh, Tien-Lun (2011), *Night Market Hero/Ji pai ying xiong*, Grand Vision (unavailable in the United States and Europe).

INDEX

228 Incident, 30, 84

A Brighter Summer Day, 50–5
*A Time to Live, a Time to Di*e, 79–82
absence of wordy dialogue, 9, 80; *see also* lack of speech
accented subject, 95
Adams, Jonathan, 70
adaptation, 4, 24, 166–7
  hybridisation, 4
  intertextuality, 9, 25, 43, 89, 97, 105–7, 119, 166, 168
  translation, 4, 8, 92–4, 102, 166–7
advent of modern storytelling, 56
aesthetics of death, 12, 158
Aguirre, the Wrath of God, 49
allegoresis, 18; *see also* allegory
allegory, 18; *see also* allegoresis
Andalusian Dog, 101
Anderson, John, 121, 133
Ang Lee, 3, 4, 6, 10–11, 21–2, 30, 33, 34, 76, 92, 126–33, 142, 146–8, 150, 153, 155, 167, 168
anti-intellectual, 32, 50
Antonioni, Michelangelo, 3, 8, 47, 54, 57–8, 62–3, 70, 97, 160; *see also* *Blow-Up*
Arp, Barkman and McRae, 296

art and life, 153
  art house genre, 2
  art house aesthetic, 158
  art house cinema, 2, 31, 50, 73, 151
  art house film-makers, 12, 31, 35
  art house films, 24–5, 151, 169
  art house roots, 157
  art house trend, 150
Asian Film Commission Network, 92
Asian socialism, 2
Assayas, Olivier, 161, 171, 175, 181
Atom Films, 117
Au revoir Taipei/Yi ye Taibei, 12, 23, 21, 158–62, 168
auteurism, 6, 106, 123, 146
authentic self-identity, 147
authentic Taiwanese director, 127
autobiographical story, 50
Avatar, 17

Bailey, David, 59–60
Bazin, André, 29, 146
Beethoven, Ludwig van, 72; *see also* *Moonlight Sonata*
*Beijing Bicycle/Shiqisui de danch*e, 25–7
Benjamin, Walter, 53, 63, 144
benshi, 16–17
Bergson, Henri, 98–100

Berry, Chris, 6, 14, 24, 38, 40, 51, 57, 59, 61, 79, 83, 84, 85, 134, 136
between French and Chinese, 9, 88, 95
between French and Mandarin, 89
between reality and art, 70
betweenness, 117; *see also* in-between
Bhabha, Homi, 157, 163
biographical film, 85
Bloodstain, 19
Bloom, Michelle E., 2, 10, 30, 86, 88, 106, 114, 116, 117, 122
Blow-Up, 8, 47, 53–70; *see also* Antonioni, Michelangelo
bodies of textuality, 37, 39, 166–7
body language, 93, 117
Bordwell, David, 57, 67, 84, 85, 146–7
both locations at once, 134
Bowman, Jon, 306
Braester, Yomi, 73
Breathless, 119, 161
Brokeback Mountain, 11, 126, 132, 142, 146
Buñuel, Luis, 101–2
bureaucratic process, 91–2
butt of some sick cosmic joke, 140

Café Lumière/Kohi Jik, 80, 89
Calvino, Italo, 129–31, 147
camera eye, 99
camera movement, 8, 22 47, 54, 67, 80, 87, 100, 106
camera-as-technological-apparatus, 102
Cannes Film Festival, 53, 114, 73
Cape No. 7/Haijiao qi hao, 12, 24, 32, 150–7
censorship, 7, 20, 29, 79
Central Motion Picture Corporation, 5, 10, 20, 47, 98
Chatelain, Hélène, 65
Chen, Arvin, 12, 23, 31, 158–63
Chen, Kaige, 24–5
Chen, Kou-fu, 6, 86
Chen, Kunhuo, 30
Chen, Shui-ban, 132
Chiang Kai-shek, 1, 15, 17, 20
China Post, 73
China's army, 15
China-centrism, 44, 140–1
Chinese army, 15
Chinese blockbuster, 41
Chinese cinema, 41, 42, 43, 133
Chinese cinema production, 41

Chinese cinema studies, 42
Chinese cinema texts, 44
Chinese Civil War, 1, 15, 48, 79, 81, 82
Chinese Communists, 51
Chinese culture, 17, 93, 127, 135, 139, 140
Chinese diaspora, 31, 43, 77,140
Chinese Nationalist Party, 15
Chinese Nationalists, 17, 79
Chinese 'Other', 139
Chinese Taipei film archive, 33
Chinese/Sinophone cinema studies, 44
Chinese/transnational cinema, 42
Chinese-language cinema, 5, 21, 38
Chinese-language films, 41
Chow, Rey, 11, 134, 139–42, 147
Chu Wen-ching, 32
Chung Chao-cheng, 79
Chungking Express, 89, 91
cinema is a manifestation of the human subject, 99
cinema of transvergence, 38, 40
cinema studies, 33, 40–2, 44, 98
Cinema Taiwan, 1, 6, 34
cinematic analysis, 42, 44
cinematic reality, 36
cinematic recreation, 82
cinematic representation, 94, 162
cinematic techniques, 9, 92, 98, 100, 105
cinematic techniques of separation, 92
cinematic text, 4, 35, 107
cinematic time, 98–101
cinematic time manipulation, 101
cinematic traditions of the mainland, 43
cinematographer, 63
cinephile, 4, 122, 162
City of Sadness, 8, 22, 30, 31, 79–85, 151
Class A theatres, 16
Class B theatres, 16
Class C theatres, 16
claustrophobic shots, 119
Cléo de 5 à 7, 101–2, 161
close readings, 35, 59, 106
close textual readings, 4
coffin-like space, 118
cognate, 39
colonial Taiwan, 19
colonisation, 18
commercial film, 22, 31, 33, 35, 151
commercially viable films, 35

communication, 71, 89, 121–2
  inability to communicate, 124
Communist Party of China, 1, 15
'complètement nouvelle', 86
complex cinematic pastiche, 122
Confucian Confusion/Duli shidai, 52–3, 61, 155
contingency of time concept, 100
corpses, 65
  sleeping bodies, 65
Corriera della Sera, 60
Cortázar, Julio, 62–4, 137
cross-cultural cinematic exchanges, 166
cross-cultural conjugation, 167
cross-cultural currents, 3, 23
cross-cultural dexterity, 133
cross-cultural hybridity, 9, 88
cross-cultural relationship, 23
Crouching Tiger, Hidden Dragon, 3, 11 21, 128–9, 138, 140–1, 147
Crystal Boys, 79
cultural forces, 73
cultural narratives, 2, 22
cultural purity, 41
Cultural Revolution, 24–5
culture award, 150
culture of 'dis-appearance', 91
Cute Girl, 79–80

Daily Beast, 27
Davis, Darrel William, 1–2, 6, 22, 34, 53, 133–4
De Sica, Vittorio, 25, 28–9
dead body, 62–5
dead time, 57; see also *temps mort*
death, 4, 71–3, 103, 107, 113, 121–3, 154, 158, 160, 163
death and photography, 65, 71
death of death, 163
decolonisation, 1
Defending Diaoyutai, 77
Deleuze, Gilles, 38, 99–100, 112
democratic population, 2
Democratic Progressive Party, 2, 7, 22, 78
democratisation, 31, 50, 97
Den Kenjiro, 17
dialect films, 33
dialogue, 4, 8–9, 21, 47, 55, 80, 84–5, 106, 146, 156
diasporic cinemas, 38
didacticism of the Eastern fare, 145

Dilley, Whitney Crothers, 133
director-based films, 35
disjointed connectivity, 9–10, 95, 97–124
displaced status of the protagonists, 95
disposability, 160
Doane, Mary Ann, 99–100
Doinel, Antoine, 108, 115, 117–18, 121, 167
Doka policy, 17
domestic audiences, 7, 26, 31–3, 88, 150
domestic studios, 24
dominance/minority resistance, 43
du jour, 40
dual identity, 141
durée, 98
Dust in the Wind, 8–9, 79, 82–3

Eastern *auteur*, 122
East–West dichotomy, 4
East–West hybrid cinema, 41–2, 167–8
East–West hybridity, 3
Eat Drink Man Woman, 131, 135
Economist, 49–50
Ella Shohat and Robert Stam, 92–3
Emilie Yueh-yu Yeh, 6
empty space, 54–7, 104, 117, 163
essence of humanity, 148
Eternal Summer, 153
ethnic ars erotica, 142
Eurocentric position, 42
Eurocentrism, 42–4, 92
European cinema, 23, 31, 110, 112
European cinematic influence, 42
Eyes of the Buddha/Da Fo De Tong Kong, 17–19

Face, 116; see also Tsai Ming-Liang
fairy-tale film, 102
fairy-tale-like quality, 151, 162
'Father Knows Best' trilogy , 131, 135–6
FeiDa courier company, 25–7
Feiyi Lu, 6
fetishism, 91
  fetishism of the present, 91
fictional activity, 68
  fictional agent, 68
  fictional showing, 68
  fictional story, 67–8
Fifth Generation, 24, 30, 59, 79
Fig Tree, 78
film commission, 91–2
film history, 5, 21, 33, 39

film industry, 2, 92, 97, 134, 154–7
  Taiwan's film industry, 12, 52
  Taiwanese film industry, 22, 33–4, 50,
    97, 151, 154, 157, 162, 166
film narrative, 37, 77, 105, 145
film studies, 23, 34, 37, 40–1, 99, 122,
  133
film text, 3, 137, 157; see also cinematic
  text
First New Wave, 5–6, 22, 30, 52
fleeting ephemerality, 87
Flight of the Red Balloon/Le voyage du
  ballon rouge, 9, 76–89
Flowers of Shanghai, 80
Ford, Hamish, 57
form of translation, 93
'fortune-cookie cutter mumbo-jumbo
  dressed up in crummy Mandarin
  Chinese accents', 140
Foucault, Michel, 143
Frater, Patrick, 24
Frederic Jameson, 8, 47, 53–61, 104–5,
  122, 159, 160, 163
French film-making tradition, 89
French New Wave, 3, 10, 21, 23, 25, 27,
  31–3, 119, 121, 158–62
French tastes, 89
Freud, Sigmund, 100, 139
From Caligari to Hitler, 39
Fuhe Theatre, 104, 111, 116, 157, 160
Futures of Chinese Cinemas, 39

Gatewood, Laura, 152
German cinema, 39
German expressionism, 39
global channels, 42
global Chinese-language film, 41
global forces, 39
global/local dichotomy, 43
globalisation, 31, 41, 57, 154, 167
  consumption, 27, 41, 120
globality, 57
glocal (global + local), 42
Golden Horse International Film Festival,
  22
Golden Lion award, 31, 151
Gong Hong, 20
Goodbye Dragon Inn/Bu san, 9, 10, 98,
  106, 110, 116
Gou-Juin Hong, 33
Government Information Office, 22, 24,
  31, 131, 159

grand narrative, 8
graphic match, 58–65
grass-roots appeal, 32
Gubbio, Serafino, 63
Guo Lian-Guei, 25–6, 28–9
Guo-hui Hong, 39
Guo-juin Hong, 6, 21, 165

Han people, 78
Han Chinese descent, 140
  Han descent, 43
He Qiwu, 90
Healthy and Social Realist films, 20
healthy cinema, 20
Healthy Realism, 20
Hemmings, David, 59–60
Herzog, Werner, 49
heterogeneity, 140, 143
heteroglossia, 89
heteroglossic nature, 140
HHH:A Portrait of Hou Hsiao-hsien,
  81
Higbee, Will, 38–40
Hiroshi Shimizu, 20
Hiroshima mon amour, 101–3
'His Son's Big Doll', 85
historical drama, 80, 88
historical fiction film, 49
historical film, 79
historical narratives, 18
historiography, 18, 33, 34
Hollywood, 10, 11, 15, 15, 23, 24, 31,
  41, 50, 58–60, 126, 131, 132, 133,
  136, 138, 146, 153, 158, 168
  Chinese/Hollywood, 10, 126–48
  Hollywood career, 134
  Hollywood film-making, 146
  Hollywood formula, 58
  Hollywood insiders, 133
  Hollywood model, 31
  Hollywood notions of narrative, 58
  Hollywood romantic comedy formula,
    158
  Hollywood stereotype, 59
homogeneity, 41, 103, 160
Hong Kong cinema, 3, 37, 50
Hong Kong culture tends, 91
Hong Kong film-makers, 91
hongbao, 138
Hou Hsiao-hsien, 4–5, 8–9, 21–3, 30–2,
  34, 38, 48, 50–4
Hsiang-t'u, 78–9; see also nativist

Hsiao-kang, 2, 10, 98, 101–2, 105, 109–23, 162, 167
Huang Chien-yeh, 73
Hughes, Darren, 97–8, 114
hybridity, 3, 4, 9, 23, 43, 88, 167–8
cross-cultural hybridity, 9
  East–West hybridity, 23
  East–West hybrid cinema, 41, 167–8
  hybrid cinema, 31, 42–3
  hybrid identities, 88
  hybrid of East Asian and Western
    cinematic traditions, 35
  hybrid theory, 100
  hybridisation, 4

I Don't Want to Sleep Alone, 10, 98, 124
idea of empty, 55
identity confusion, 88
identity crisis, 1, 23, 34
  loss of identity, 137
  loss of Taiwanese identity, 135
identity-seeking nation, 1
'Il était une fois . . .', 101
imperial Japanese film culture, 14
impersonal office space, 54
In Our Time, 5, 7, 34, 47, 49–50, 84
In the Mood for Love, 37
inherent duality, 147
innovative cinematic language, 4, 167
interior locations, 111, 120
interior monologue, 102
interior shorts, 4, 54
interior space, 54, 103
international appeal, 31, 32, 133
international art house scene, 32
international audience, 4, 31, 128, 141
  mainstream international audience,
    147
international cinemas, 31, 38, 49
international export, 35
international funding, 32, 166
intertextuality, 4, 9, 23, 25, 43, 89,
    97–125, 166–8
intertextual references, 114, 159, 166
intertextual cinematic references, 162
intratextuality, 107–8, 123
Introducing Taiwan Today, 16
'in-between', 95, 157; *see also*
    between-ness
Island Etude, 153
Italian neo-realism, 31

Jameson, Frederic, 47, 53, 55–8, 61,
    104–5, 160
Japanese cinema, 16
  Japanese cinematographers, 16
  Japanese film studios, 15
  Japanese film-makers, 19
  Japanese imperial films, 20
Japanese colonialism, 12, 19, 21, 40, 155
  'heroic' Japanese occupiers, 19
  Japan's occupation, 153
  Japanese colonist, 20–1
  Japanese empire, 15, 20, 36, 83
  Japanese military, 15
  Japanese occupation, 8, 78–9
  Japanese occupiers, 19
  Japanese regime, 19, 20
Japanese media, 15
  control of media, 17
Jian family, 53, 71
Jiba Hiroki, 20
jigsaw puzzle, 61
Jinhee Choi, 334

Kellner, Douglas, 5, 20
Khoo, Olivia, 39
Kill Bill, 3–4
King, Tanaka, 17, 19
Kinski, Klaus, 49
Klein, Christina, 41
Kracauer, Siegfried, 39
Kuomintang,1, 2, 7, 15, 20, 30, 79
  KMT government, 77–8
  KMT Nationalists, 95
  KMT-ruled government, 40

L'Eclisse/The Eclipse, 54
La Jetée, 65
'Las babas del Diablo'/'The Devil's
    Drool', 62; *see also* Michel,
    Cortázar, Julio
lack of speech, 9, 80, 84; *see also* absence
    of wordy dialogue
land of the dead, 119
language of post-modernity, 36
late capitalist urbanisation, 57
late capitalism, 43, 57, 159
Lee Lieh, 150
Lian/Visage/Face, 9
Life of Pi, 11, 126, 128–32, 147
Li-kong Hsu, 131
Lim and Ward, 33, 34
Little Latin Lupe Lu, 157

local and the global, 42
local audiences, 50
    local Taiwanese audiences, 113
    local tastes, 3, 32
    local viewers, 32
local indigenous cultures, 78
'local/universal' dichotomy, 3
localisation, 32
loneliness, 9, 79, 103, 106, 118, 121
Lust Caution, 11, 139, 142–4, 147,
    150

Ma, Jean, 6, 9, 32, 88–9
magic realism, 128–9, 135, 147
    magic realist fable, 129
    magic realist genre, 128–9
    magic realist scenes, 129
    magic realist tale, 131
    magical realist aesthetic, 147
mainstream audiences, 32
mainstream commercial films, 31, 151
mainstream tastes, 31, 151
mainstream culture, 160
Mandarin-language cinema, 21, 24, 30
Mandarin-language films, 7, 21
Map of the Seven Star Cave, 20
Marey, Etienne-Jules, 100
margins, 43
Marker, Chris, 65
martial arts genre, 21
    martial arts classic film, 110
    wuxia genre, 88
Martin, Fran, 3, 23, 103, 105, 107, 112,
    114, 119, 121, 123
Marx and Coca-Cola generation, 27
Masculin Féminin, 27
mass-market feminism, 27
mass-market populism, 27
material realism, 98–9
    material reality, 36
McGrath, Jason, 24, 31
McKibbin, Tony, 80
Mei Ling Wu, 22
messy business, 39–40
meta-cinema, 107, 116
Metzger, Sean, 14, 39
Michel, 62–4; *see also* 'Las babas
    del Diablo'/'The Devil's Drool',
    Cortázar, Julio
Midas formula, 31–2, 128, 151
Millennium Mambo/Qianxi manbo, 9,
    80–9

Ming dynasty, 78
mingtian zaoshang, 162
Misch, Christopher, 116–17
Miss 19, 27
Mitch Ryder and the Detroit Wheels,
    157
Mo Yan, 24
mode of translation, 92
modern cinema, 67
Modern Man, 63
modern 'Western-style' city, 57
modern-day urban space, 29
modernisation, 15, 48
modernised Taipei, 47
modernism, 47
modernist aesthetic, 30
modernist iteration, 70
modernist narratives, 55
modernist path, 58
modernist/postmodernist aspects, 59
modernist/postmodernist contrast, 58
modernity, 17, 36, 56–7, 99–100, 103–4,
    122, 127, 159, 163, 165
Monga/Bang-kah, 23, 150, 151, 154–5
monologue, 73, 94, 102, 152, 161
Moonlight Sonata, 72; *see also*
    Beethoven, Ludwig van
Moore, Donald, 19
    movement image, 99
    movement of images in time, 99
moving image, 65
multi- or transnational space, 56

Naficy, Hamid, 76–7, 89, 95
narrative objectivity, 89, 95
nation is in crisis, 39; *see also* identity
    crisis
national, 4, 167–8
national authenticity, 127; *see also*
    national identity
national cinema, 23, 31, 34–9, 168
filmic nationalism, 23
    national cinema model, 34
    national cinema without nation, 33
    national cinematic tradition, 34–5
    national discourse, 36–9
    national identity, 41, 78, 80; *see also*
        national authenticity
    national psyche, 34, 36
    national self-definition, 1
    national/transnational cinema debate,
        133

nationality, 42, 127
nativist literature, 21, 77–9; *see also*
    Hsiang-t'u
nativist tradition, 70
New Cinema, 12, 21, 25 34, 77–9, 106
new genre, 4, 21, 167
New Taiwan Cinema, 3, 5, 22, 84, 165
New Wave auteurs, 165
    Taiwanese New Wave cinema, 25, 59,
    111
Nien-jen Wu, 60, 71, 86
Night Market Hero/Ji pai ying xiong, 12,
    154–7
non-national nation state, 56
nostalgia, 2, 4, 9, 42, 81, 88, 91, 107,
    115, 135, 157
    nostalgia for the past, 2, 9, 81
    nostalgia for the present, 87–8
Novak, Marcos, 38

objective distance, 3, 84, 95
oeuvre, 6, 9, 11, 60, 98, 106, 107, 128,
    132, 133, 147, 166
omniscient reader, 56
ontologically ambiguous space, 85
Orz Boys, 150
other critics, 153

Pai Hsien-yung, 79
*Painting the City Red: Chinese Cinema
    and the Urban Contract*, 29
Panorama Taiwan, 31
'patchwork culture', 59
Peavler, Terry J., 63
Peña, Richard, 141
People's Republic of China, 17, 83, 325
perceived unity, 88, 89
perception of images, 204
Perez, Gilberto, 36, 168
photography is like death, 65
Pierce, Charles Sanders, 10, 100
Pirandello, Luigi, 63–4
Pocahontas, 17
polylocality, 43
pornography, 116, 135, 139
    Exotic Pornography, 139
    pornographic sex scenes, 142
    pornographic 'standards', 291
post-boundaried artist, 193
postcolonial discourse, 42
postmodern condition, 107–8, 123
postmodern existential angst, 160

'postmodern' form, 58
postmodernist film, 70
postmodernist trope, 70
postmodernity, 108, 123
post-Mao, 27–9
post-millennium films, 9, 89
post-sadness, 22
pre-modern aesthetic, 56
propaganda, 51
    Chinese propaganda, 145
    Nazi propaganda, 39
    propaganda-filled newsreels, 145
    propaganda-oriented genres, 21
puppeteer, 85, 92–4
Puppetmaster/Xi meng rensheng, 53, 80,
    85
pure perception, 99
Pushing Hands/Tui shou, 131, 135, 146
putongua, 140

Quasi una fantasia, 72
question of authenticity, 141, 159

Radical Elsewhere, 112–15
Rayns, Tony, 52–3, 61
realistic film, 28
*Rebels of the Neon God/Qing shaonian
    nuozha*, 10, 98, 108, 123
recusatio, 18
Red Balloon, 9, 76–97, 139
red envelope tradition, 138
Red Sorghum, 24
rengasi, 16
representation of time, 70, 102
Republic of China, 1, 15, 34, 77
Resnais, Alain, 101
'revenge' genre, 3
rhizome, 38
rhythm of events, 70
Righteous Brothers, 157
Round, Julia, 146
Ru-Shou Robert Chen, 6

Sandwich Man/Erzi de da wan'ou, 7, 8,
    79, 80, 85
Sayun Hayun, 20
    Sayun myth, 20
    Sayun's Bell, 20
Schamus, James, 11, 114
'scientia sexualis', 142
Screening China, 42
Second New Wave, 6, 30

Second Wave, 7, 12, 22, 34, 86, 89, 106, 154
seeing is a form of technology, 99
self-orientalisation, 92
self-proclaimed identity, 162
self-reflexive film, 102, 111
separate spaces, 118
sequence of cartoon drawings, 67
sex scenes, 11, 142–4
Shanghai, 48, 80
Sheldon Lu, 39, 41, 140, 168
Shiang-chyi, 2, 10, 93, 101, 103, 109, 111, 112, 116–23
Shih, Sandra, 91
Shih, Shu-me, 31, 43, 44, 76–7, 89, 91–5, 140–1, 168
Shohat and Stam, 92–3
Sight and Sound, 52
simulacrum, 99
simultaneous time, 101, 105
Sino-French cinema, 30
'Sino-French' film studies, 122
Sino-Italian cinema, 31
Sino-Japanese War
  first, 15
  second, 15–17
Sinophone, 24, 30, 43–4, 76–7, 89, 92–4, 168
Sinophone cinema, 30
Sinophone cinema studies, 41
Sinophone film-makers, 92
Sinophone visuality, 77
Sinophone world, 140
Sixth Generation, 25–6, 29, 30–1
slow-motion/fast-motion technique, 90
'Smoke Gets in Your Eyes', 87
social panorama, 61
'Son of Taiwan', 127
Song Chuyu, 22
Song Hwee Lim, 34, 107–8
sophistication, 3, 23
space of representation, 36
spatiality, 56, 59, 105, 108, 159–60
spectator's subjective notion of cinematic time, 100
Spider Lilies, 153
State Administration of Radio, Film, and Television, 24
Sterk, Darryl, 17–18
storia, 148
Su Chui-hong, 31
subjective idealism, 98

subjective image, 9
subjective realism, 99
subjectivity, 37, 58, 61, 70, 100
submissive persona, 141
'submissive/dominant' dichotomy, 141
suburbs, 61, 135
synchronous monadic simultaneity, 56, 122

T'ien-wen Chu, 84, 86
taboo subjects, 8, 79, 83, 89
Taipei Film Commission, 24, 31
Taipei Skywalk, 2, 157
Taipei Story, 28, 50, 54, 57, 84, 155, 159
Taiwan Motion Picture Study Society, 20
Taiwan New Cinema, 6, 21, 25, 30, 51, 86, 106–7, 160, 163, 165, 167
Taiwanese art house, 23, 31, 47
Taiwanese cinematic tradition, 21, 39, 77, 132, 168
Taiwanese colonial history, 32
Taiwanese experience, 79, 83, 165
Taiwanese film industry, 7, 21–4, 33–4, 36, 50, 53, 97, 150–7, 161, 162, 166
Taiwanese media, 73, 132, 170, 7, 15
Taiwanese national cinema, 4, 35
Taiwanese New Cinema, 34, 159, 166–9
Taiwanese New Wave, 5, 22, 40, 49, 59, 84, 89, 158
Taiwanese Second Wave, 2, 5, 106
Taiyu pian, 33
Taking Woodstock, 132
Tarantino, Quentin, 3–4
temporality, 17, 99
temps mort, 57
text of the film, 3
textual studies, 35
The 400 Blows, 3, 10, 23, 101, 103, 115, 117–18, 120, 167
The Assassin, 88
The Baron in the Trees, 129–30, 147
The Boys, 98
The Cinema of Small Nations, 34
The Geopolitical Aesthetic, 55, 57
The Hole/Dong, 9
The Ice Storm, 11, 132, 146
The Material Ghost, 36
The Revival of an Old Well, 17
The River/He liu, 9–10, 98, 103, 106
The Skywalk is Gone/Tianqiao bujian le, 98, 116

The Terrorizers/Kongbu fenzi, 8, 47, 50, 57–9, 70
The Wayward Cloud, 10, 98
The Wedding Banquet/Xi yan, 11, 131, 136, 139, 142, 146
Theorising National Cinema, 37
Third World cinema, 36
Three Times, 80, 85, 86–8
Ti Wei, 134, 136
time image, 99
Tonglin Lu, 134
transcendental subject, 110, 118
transnational, 35, 38–41, 98, 140
transnational audience, 167
transnational cinema, 89, 95–8, 101, 103, 185
'transnational' circle, 42
transnational dexterity, 88
transnational production model, 10, 98
transnational/national cinema debate, 36
transnationalism, 21, 23, 40, 154, 157, 167
true narrative time, 101–3
Truffaut, François, 3, 10, 23, 97, 103, 105, 108, 111, 114, 115, 117–18, 122, 167
Tsai Ming-liang, 23, 30–4, 47, 54, 80, 93, 95, 97–124, 134, 142, 155, 157, 159, 160, 162, 167, 168
Tweedie, James, 2, 103–4, 118

Udden, James, 8, 9, 33, 84, 89
unintended effect, 100
unity of the perceiving, 36
universal appeal, 62; *see also* international appeal
universality, 57, 61, 82
universally 'human' experience, 86
untranslatable nature, 9, 81, 87
untranslatability, 8, 88
urban citizens, 30
    urban space, 10, 27, 29, 42, 56, 116–17, 122
    urbanisation, 57
    urbanites, 56

Varda, Agnes 101–2, 161–2
Venice Film Festival, 31, 80, 151
veracity of representation, 58, 70
Victorian-era storytelling, 56

Visage, 9, 10, 98
visual and linguistic differences, 93
    visual distinctions, 93
    visual separation, 93
visual themes, 65, 90
Vitali and Willeman, 37
Vive L'Amour/Aiqing wansui, 9, 10, 98, 103
voiceover, 8, 81–2, 87, 161
voyeuristic cinephile, 122

Wang Pai-Zhang, 154
Wang Xiaoshuai, 19, 25–30
Weaver, Jim, 58–9, 69–70
Wedding Banquet/Xi yan, 11, 131–42
Weiss, Bono, 130
Wenchi, Lin, 12, 154
Western cinematic theory, 42
Western film theory, 42
Western gaze, 120
Western tastes, 92
What Time is it There?, 2–3, 10, 23, 93, 98 100–22, 160, 162
White Chick, 65–9, 87
White, Hayden, 18
Williams, Raymond, 21, 35
Wong, Edmond, 48
Wong Kar-wai, 6, 37, 84, 89, 91, 141
Wu Cho-lui, 78
Wu Feng the Righteous Man, 20
Wu in Lu and Yeh, 7
wuxia genre, 88

Xiao and Zhang, 16, 20, 82
Xunzi, 136

Yang, Edward, 3–8, 21–2, 25, 30, 47–72, 95, 103, 107, 127, 134, 154–5, 159–60, 166
Yasujiro Ozu, 80, 89
Yeh and Davis, 6, 53, 133–4
Yellow Earth, 24
Yi Yi, 53–4, 71–3
Youguan Danwei, 52

Zhang, Yinjing, 33
Zhang Wang, 25
Zhang Yimou, 24–5, 83, 92
Zhang Yuhe, 19
Zhangke, Jia, 25
Zhou Yufen, 58, 69–71